D0498402

Greenhill
Books

FIGHTING WITH THE SCREAMING EAGLES

Dedication

**For my wife Christine, without whom
none of this would have been possible.**

FIGHTING WITH THE SCREAMING EAGLES

With the 101st Airborne
from Normandy to Bastogne

Robert M. Bowen

Edited by
Christopher J. Anderson

Greenhill Books, London
Stackpole Books, Pennsylvania

Fighting with the Screaming Eagles:
With the 101st Airborne From Normandy to Bastogne
first published 2001 by
Greenhill Books, Lionel Leventhal Limited,
Park House, 1 Russell Gardens, London NW11 9NN
and
Stackpole Books,
5067 Ritter Road, Mechanicsburg, PA 17055, USA

© Robert M. Bowen, 2001
The moral right of the author has been asserted.

All rights reserved. No part of this publication may be reproduced,
stored in a retrieval system or transmitted in any form
or by any means, electronic, mechanical or otherwise,
without the written permission of the Publisher.

British Library Cataloguing in Publication Data
Bowen, Robert
Fighting with the Screaming Eagles: with the 101st Airborne
Division from Normandy to Bastogne
1. United States. Army. Glider Infantry 327/401 - History
2. World War, 1939-1945 - Campaigns - Europe
3. World War, 1939-1945 - Personal narratives, American
I. Title II. Anderson, Christopher J.
940.5'412'73

ISBN 1-85367-465-6

Library of Congress Cataloging-in-Publication Data
A catalog record is available from the library

Edited and designed by Donald Sommerville
Printed and bound in Great Britain by
Creative Print and Design (Wales), Ebbw Vale

Contents

List of Illustrations

Pages 177–192

26. Men of Company B, 401st GIR at the Battle of the Bulge
27. Sgt. Richard Gill
28. Bastogne lies in ruins
29. The 101st advances from Bastogne
30. Glidermen fire on German positions
31. Glider infantryman cleaning his rifle
32. Men of 401st with abandoned German staff car
33. Captured 101st Field Hospital
34. Makeshift hospital at Bastogne
35. & 36. Stalag XIIA
37. Waddlington, O'Mara and Feldman
38. Garrett, Fortuna and Feldman
39. Robert Lott at Berchtesgaden
40. Wrecked half-track at Berchtesgaden
41. Divisional ceremony at Berchtesgaden
42. Bowen wearing a British battledress jacket
43. Bowen recovering at White Plains, NY
44. Colonel Allen with the Regimental flag
45. A post-war dinner for surviving members of the 401st
46. Bowen at home in Linthicum, MD
47. Bowen with Christopher Anderson

All photographs are from the author's collection, unless noted otherwise in the captions.

List of Maps

8

Foreword

GEORGE E. KOSKIMAKI

Sergeant Robert Bowen joined the 101st Airborne Division's 401st Glider Infantry Regiment in 1943. His wife Christine, to whom he was married in 1939, saved all the letters he wrote while in the service. He wrote every day except when combat situations did not permit that luxury. Later, while trying to recover from horrible wounds received during combat and made worse by time spent as a prisoner of the Germans, Bowen would use these letters to refresh his memory of events as he recorded his memories of his time with the 101st "Screaming Eagles" Airborne Division. Readers will be amazed at how vividly he recalls incidents from training and combat alike.

The use of airborne troops in combat was first visualized by Benjamin Franklin way back in 1784, a year after the first successful balloon ascent in France. Franklin expounded on this possibility:

"Where is the prince who can afford to so cover his country with troops for its defense, as that ten thousand men descending from the clouds might not, in many places, do an infinite deal of mischief before a force could be brought together to repel them?"

Though late in developing the concept of overhead envelopment, American military planners did note the success of the German military forces in their lightning-like strikes from the air in Crete and Holland. A test platoon was formed to study the feasibility of dropping men and equipment by parachute and glider. Thus were developed the 82d and 101st Airborne Divisions in August 1942.

In an era when flight was still considered a relatively new and exciting phenomenon, an organization that was trained to be transported to battle from the air was bound to capture popular imagination. From the very beginning, the new airborne divisions were considered elite organizations. Enticed by the jump boots, silver wings and extra jump pay awarded to each paratrooper after completion of his training, the new divisions attracted thousands of volunteers. Even so, the rapid expansion of the airborne divisions meant that the Army was hard pressed to find the necessary recruits, and recruiters, army public affairs officers and the media went out of their way to highlight the daring young airborne soldiers with their jump wings and boots.

Often lost in the telling, however, was the fact that the new airborne divisions included glider infantrymen as well. Unlike the paratroopers, the members of the glider regiments were assigned to their regiments and, at least initially, were not provided with wings, boots or any other special symbol to mark them as members of these new elite organizations, nor were they given extra pay. Despite their relative obscurity, these men were expected to travel to battle in the flimsy metal and canvas CG-4A Waco glider. As many were soon to discover, travel in the primitive gliders of the day could be extremely hazardous. Horrible crashes during training were a common occurrence. A poster frequently seen hanging in the barracks of the glider regiments featured photographs of gliders horribly wrecked during landing. Around the pictures ran the words, "Join the glider troops! No flight pay! No jump pay! But never a dull moment!"

Lacking the paraphernalia that went with being a paratrooper meant that many people thought of the glidermen as somehow not quite as elite as the rest of the division's members. Civilians were not the only ones who held that belief. In bases across the South, paratroopers and glidermen frequently fought one another, and I often remember hearing my fellow paratroopers refer to the glidermen contemptuously as "legs." Once in combat, however, the glidermen would prove on countless battlefields that they were every bit as elite as their paratrooper brethren. During the bloody battles in Normandy and Holland, and at the epic siege of Bastogne, a crucial component of the 101st's success was due to the efforts of its glider infantrymen and artillerymen. By VE-Day, as the division rested in the surroundings of Adolf Hitler's Eagle's Nest retreat, those of us in the division's paratrooper units were well aware of the contributions of the glidermen and there were none of us who did not consider them full and equal partners in the division's accomplishments.

Unfortunately, the second-class stigma that so unfairly attached itself to the glidermen during the early days of the war has, to a degree, remained with us to this day. Of the tens of thousands of pages written about the exploits of the airborne divisions during World War II, very few are dedicated to the contributions of the glidermen. In focusing on the exploits of the paratroopers, many historians have failed to tell the whole story of the airborne forces.

Fortunately, Sergeant Bowen's account of his time in the 401st Glider Infantry Regiment serves, in some small way, to redress that imbalance. Veterans who served in infantry units will become deeply engrossed in his account as it unfolds: Bowen tells his story just as if it happened yesterday. All of us who suffered through basic training with hard-hearted noncoms pushing us to the limit will enjoy reliving some of these days of long ago. Glider veterans will recall with understanding Bowen's description of his reception to the 101st. Today it has a nostalgic ring to it, but how we suffered those first days in the service of our country. Children and grandchildren of veterans will relive some of the actions their loved ones experienced in the war through the reading of this fine account.

While Bowen's description of his service with the 101st will help old soldiers remember what their own service was like, I also hope that it serves to remind the reader, be they veteran, historian, family member or student, of the vital role the glidermen played in the airborne's great success during World War II. I salute Bowen for this excellent account of what army life was like, and for the way the airborne soldier, and particularly the glider trooper, is honored through the simple telling of one man's association with his platoon members.

George E. Koskimaki
Northville,
Michigan, 2001

George E. Koskimaki was a member of the 101st Airborne Division. After earning his jump wings he became the radioman for division commander Maxwell Taylor. He is also the unofficial historian for the division association and has written three books on the 101st.

Introduction

There are many reasons why authors write books, from financial gain to the love of writing. Mine fell somewhere in between. I thought I had a story to tell which might interest readers who would never be able to experience the things I did or saw during World War II. Few readers would ever have, or want, the opportunity to participate in the greatest invasion in history, the D-Day landing in Normandy; the greatest military blunder of the war, Operation *Market Garden*; or one of the greatest land battles ever, the Battle of the Bulge. Yet, I was there and survived them all. More important, perhaps, I wrote about them while they were fresh in my mind. I began this memoir in 1945–46 while at Walter Reed Medical Center recovering from wounds. The task of writing this account of my service began as a means of coming to terms with what I had experienced during my time in the 101st Airborne Division. As the years passed and I learned more, I added to the manuscript, adding details that I did not remember when I first came home. I was aided in this by my wife, who had saved every letter I wrote to her while I was away.

Were my experiences any different than the dozens of other books written on the subject? Of course they were, because every individual experience is seen through a different set of eyes. No matter the vast numbers of people involved in the Second World War, it was different for each of us. For example, on one occasion during the Battle of the Bulge I took two squads of men to support a platoon that had been hit hard and was on the verge of collapsing. Later, I read an account from a friend who had been there with another nearby platoon and what he recorded of that day is totally different. I was amazed when I read his account. Nothing about what he wrote was familiar to me yet he was only 100 yards from where I was. The terrain features plus the fact we were fighting for our lives made the difference. In other words, only what I saw and did in the immediate area was the focus of my attention.

Secondly, how many people living ordinary lives can ever imagine being caught up in events which are now an important part of "history." Yet, I experienced such events. Before the war I had a mundane job and was earning $25 a week. Other people in the shop were making parts for planes, ships, and other war material. Only two of us went into the service, and the other became a storekeeper in Hawaii on a Navy base. Was it fate or accident that put me in the path of so many important events? I don't know. Never having had any philosophical schooling before the war—in fact, I never graduated from high school—I knew nothing about the general laws that furnish the rational explanation of anything. All I knew was that I was there and that what I experienced might interest someone else.

My experiences during the war were the most exciting of my life, times when a fraction of an inch one way or the other could have meant death. I have been in artillery barrages where the earth and buildings around me were pulverized, bombings in which buildings collapsed and burned, attacks where bullets were so close to my head that I could feel the whisper of them as they passed. Yet, I survived while many around me died. That is why I wrote this account of my time with the Screaming Eagles.

Robert Bowen

CHAPTER 1

You're in the Army Now

My road to Fort George G. Meade, Maryland, my first Army post, was a path of illusions, my head filled with all sorts of propaganda and stories that I had been told by veterans of the Great War and read in books and magazines. Most of the men in my family had served in the Navy, so going into the military seemed the natural thing to do. That is why I had gone to Citizens' Military Training Camps each summer when I was in high school, why I joined the State Guard when the National Guard was called up in 1940, and why I applied for Officer Candidate School (OCS) shortly after Pearl Harbor. It had been a big disappointment when my application for OCS was rejected in 1942. I found that the fact that I had never graduated from high school disqualified me.

Despite my experience with Citizens' Military Training and the Guard, entering the Army, which I did on February 13th, 1943, was like going to a different planet. Everything about it seemed beyond my comprehension—the Army way of doing things seemed so strange. To begin with, I often asked myself how we ever won the last war. How could anything have been accomplished in such mass confusion with so many contradictory orders? Shots, tests, examination by disinterested doctors who did not even comment upon the two missing fingers on my left hand, marching from building to building in ragged columns for more tests, and my first taste of Army food were just a few of the things that made me want to pack my bags and head for home.

Emerging from the bureaucratic maze of processing without going crazy, I joined an equally bewildered group of fellow recruits about to be shipped to a training center where we would be turned into soldiers. Once a sufficient number of recruits had been gathered we were sent off on a train headed for somewhere in the South. We were packed on board the train like sardines, our misery compounded by the smell emanating from the freshly issued clothing. Our heads were filled with vicious rumors and, despite all the lectures, we did not have the slightest idea what was in store for us. Most had never even been away from home for an extended period of time.

The train moved at a snail's pace, shaking and rattling with each uneven joint in the tracks. The clatter of its passage and the odor of the coal smoke made sleep impossible. To top it off, there didn't seem to be a siding during the entire trip that we didn't pull into, spending long hours with the engine spouting steam and blowing ear-splitting blasts of its whistle. Nerves quickly became raw, tempers flared, fights broke out and the train soon resembled an institution for the mentally deranged. If the trip hadn't ended when it did three days later I believe an insurrection would have followed.

The men waiting for us at our destination, Camp Blanding, Florida, were evidently used to such a state of affairs. They patiently got us off the train and formed into a ragged column and then marched us away in the darkness to the main camp. Our destination was a tent city where small groups of the column were gradually peeled off until all of the recruits had been assigned to a tent. The 20-odd men in my group were led down a company street and dispersed in large canvas tents, which were already partially occupied by sleeping men. Our arrival in the middle of the night ensured that our reception was not exactly warm. The men in my tent had just completed a 24-hour guard shift and were none too happy about being disturbed. Their curiosity, however, soon got the best of them and they rolled out of their bunks to see who they would have to put up with in the future.

It was there that I learned that we were now members of Company I, 104th Infantry Regiment, 26th Infantry Division. The 26th was a National Guard outfit originally from Massachusetts. My new regiment had been called up in 1940, participated in the Carolina maneuvers, and was then put to work guarding the East Coast against a feared Axis landing. Thousands of troops had been sent to surround vital defense installations, government buildings, vital bridges and communications centers along both coasts. Despite the fears of many, during its time along the coast the division had seen nothing more dangerous than hermit crabs and migrating sea turtles and it was now ready to absorb a bevy of recruits even though its own efficiency left much to be desired.

The next morning we were assigned to training platoons, being excused from all guard and fatigue details until our training had been completed. This arrangement proved to be a blessing for us. Unfortunately it also pissed off the veterans because it meant that the burden of these unpleasant duties would fall on them. I couldn't blame them, but the training was being accelerated and there was little that we could do but comply.

Our world now consisted of close order drill, manual of arms, weapons familiarization, gas mask drills, compass and map reading. Gradually, through repetition and practice, the majority of us began to get a feel for our new surroundings. Although a few men in my company became sick or died because of inadequate physicals given at reception centers, before too long most of us could complete a 25-mile hike carrying a full field pack under a broiling hot sun. We could run and flop on the ground time after time without dislodging too many teeth from contact with rifle stocks and we had dug enough slit trenches and foxholes to excavate a pit the size of the Little Grand Canyon in Vermont. We spent many nights in foxholes in cold soggy uniforms and we had eaten enough tasteless corned beef hash and baked beans to ruin our stomachs forever. Perhaps most important of all we had learned how to overcome contradictory orders from officers who seemed to be as untried as we were. Finally, after three months, we no longer resembled extras in a Laurel and Hardy routine and were returned to our companies.

With the recruits back with their companies and the regiment at full strength, our illustrious leaders decided that it was time to whip the unit into fighting shape. The best way to do this, they believed, was to embark on a series of exercises known as "problems." The problems involved us charging through brush, swamps and pine forests until we were dead on our feet. We fought make-believe enemies in good weather and bad, the violent thunderstorms we encountered being nearly as bad as artillery barrages. After the problems ended, we would rush back to our barracks to shower, dress, and clean weapons in order to fall in for inspection.

Our stay in Camp Blanding ended in late March 1943. It was time for the different regiments of the division to assemble in one place. We packed, boarded trains and headed for Camp Gordon, Georgia. The engineer seemed to drive the train as if he had a premonition that a bridge over a river was out and he needed to feel every inch of the way. The heat in the cars was terrific, with cinders and other debris flying into the open windows. We finally got to our destination, and unloaded the train with all of the precision of a street riot. It was hot as hell and we were carrying enough baggage to last forever. Eventually we were allowed to stagger to our assigned area, a compound of equally spaced old wooden barracks.

To our great disappointment we soon discovered that the food was even more deplorable than in Camp Blanding. Even the chowhounds in the company hesitated before entering the mess hall. Our battalion commanding officer had a thing about waste, even going so far as stationing a non-commissioned officer (NCO) by the garbage pail to see that nothing was wasted. Those who couldn't stomach the GI cuisine couldn't forsake it and expect to fill up at the post exchange (PX). Most of the shelves were emptied of cookies, cakes and candy bars soon after our arrival. Even the beer was in short supply. To add to our misery the other amenities at the camp were not much better. The post theaters were like ovens, and passes to Augusta and neighboring cities were issued with the same reckless abandon as raises in pay.

June brought even greater discomfort with steam-bath heat day and night and an acceleration in training. We were in the field for days on end, running seemingly mindless problems that did little other than piss us off more we already were. We got a new platoon leader, a gem with a Napoleon complex who put some unfortunates on extra duty for having the gall to roll up their sleeves in the 100-degree heat during a 25-mile hike. He was a young blond giant who looked as if he had been a linebacker on a pro football team. Fresh out of OCS, he wore his gold bar as if it were five stars and made damn sure we honored it. He drove us mercilessly, bent on proving that he could put our squad on par with the Rangers. His dedication was all right with us until he began issuing silly orders. Late one afternoon we were returning from a hard day in the field, hot, tired, clothing soaked to the skin by sweat and carrying full packs. To increase the misery, as we headed for home, we ran into a thunderstorm, which quickly drenched us. We got halfway up a long hill when our junior Napoleon gave the order to don gas masks and double time. It didn't take long before half the platoon had collapsed beside the road and the other half wasn't far from it. Fortunately, our company commander, Captain O'Neill happened to come by in a jeep, saw what was happening and quickly put a stop to it.

The platoon officer, however, was not my only headache. Another was an NCO named Anderson in the 3d Platoon. He was as mean as a pit bull to most of the recruits who might challenge his authority, and I was no exception. I got on his "list" early during an overnight problem. Two pits had been dug to take care of waste after eating, one for garbage, the other for cans from C rations. After disposing of my trash properly I was walking away when Anderson spotted a can in the garbage pit. He called me over, convinced that I had thrown the can in the pit, and ordered me to climb down into the mess to pick it up. Having no alternative I did what he ordered, but he could see that I didn't like it and after that he went out of his way to see that I toed the line. For the rest of my time in the company I hoped in vain that he would step into a slit trench and break his neck.

Later, however, I had some amusement at my tormentor's expense. On another night problem I was on guard duty when I heard a yell and had the pleasure of watching Anderson's pup tent rise in the air as if it had exploded. Then it staggered along the company street, poles, pegs, ropes and all. Finally it tripped over a rope and everything collapsed in a heap. Meanwhile, Anderson's tent mate sat up with a startled look on his face, not knowing what was going on until his hand went down on the ground and came to rest on a long fat rattlesnake that had crawled into the tent for warmth. For weeks afterwards the rest of the NCOs in the company teased Anderson about his zoo.

Although the months of training had hardened our bodies, they had done little to improve our morale. Our leaders had done little to encourage us. In addition, most of us were dreadfully homesick, especially those of us who were married. If it hadn't been for letters, parcels and the occasional phone call to our families, more men would have gone absent without leave (AWOL) than did. After four months in the Army most of us recruits were in the depths of despair, hating every day of our existence and desperately seeking a way out.

The realization of what lay ahead for us as infantrymen added to our fears. From what we were told, ten percent of us would be killed during our first campaign; another 40 percent would become casualties of another sort. Few, if any of us, could expect to remain with our companies until the end of the war. The figures were enough to scare even the most lion-hearted among us. Our daily existence did not help matters. Living like animals in holes in the ground, eating C and K rations for long periods of time and being treated not much better than galley slaves turned most of us off the infantry life all together. We prayed for any way out of our dilemma.

My salvation, I thought, came about the middle of June while we were on another long problem. One morning after breakfast, Howard Hill, Walter Halsey and myself were called to the company command post. Upon arrival we found Captain O'Neill in a magnanimous mood and he greeted us warmly. I sensed something was up when he took us aside and began talking to us like a concerned father. He praised our performance while in the company and said he had been instructed to submit names of men whom he thought were more advanced than others in their training. We had been selected from the list submitted and, therefore, were being transferred to another unit which needed qualified infantrymen. When he said our new home was going to be the 101st Airborne Division, however, I nearly fainted. Paratroopers! Glider troops! This was not exactly the escape I had hoped for.

We returned to our tents, trying to make light of our transfer but secretly very apprehensive about it. We said our goodbyes to everyone and left for our barracks in a waiting jeep. We spent several days preparing for our move while others from the 26th who were being transferred to the 101st were assembled. Then it was off to Fort Bragg, North Carolina, the home of the 101st.

CHAPTER 2

Marking Time

Our group reached Fort Bragg on June 23d, 1943, joining a mob of men from other outfits sent to the 101st as replacements. It was a typical June day in North Carolina with temperatures near the boiling point and the only breeze created by a flock of crows that watched us from nearby loblolly pines. Bragg was a Regular Army base with all of the support elements of such a place, a sprawling octopus covering thousands of acres.

Orientation to the division took place the following day in the post theater. Sharply dressed airborne personnel who looked at us all with jaundiced eyes conducted our introduction to the airborne, though most of the men of the division were away on maneuvers in Tennessee when we arrived. We were given a review of the airborne and our new division in particular. The 82d and 101st Airborne Divisions, we were told, had sprung from the old 82d Infantry Division in August 1942. The 101st consisted of two glider infantry regiments, the 327th and 401st, and a parachute regiment, the 502d, plus artillery, engineer and other units. Later that month a second parachute regiment, the 506th, was attached to the division. We came away from our briefing knowing that we were replacements for one of the two glider regiments, although some of our number would be assigned to parachute regiments in non-jumping roles.

It was made clear to me on that first day in the 101st that there were major differences between parachute and glider troops, the first volunteers and the latter assigned. Paratroops drew hazard pay, wore distinctive uniforms and had undergone rigorous jump training. Glidermen, on the other hand, drew no extra pay, wore ordinary uniforms and were given normal training. Glidermen, generally, were draftees who thought they had drawn a miserable line of duty, one where they were expected to risk their necks in the "flying coffins" because they were ordered to.

The divisional commander, Major-General William C. Lee, was known as the "father of the airborne" for his work in the pioneering days of this new branch of the Army. Lee's aim was to create a division, which, though lightly armed, could land behind enemy lines and seize and hold objectives until relieved by regular infantry. His assistants were Brigadier-General Donald F. Pratt and Brigadier-General Anthony C. McAuliffe; the former was instrumental in developing the airborne concept, the latter in developing much of the early clothing and equipment used by the airborne troops.

After orientation we were sent to 100-man "casual" companies. The commander of the company I was assigned to was a paratroop captain and he seemed to detest the very ground we replacements walked on. Every morning he would rail about how the Army had taken a turn for the worse with our inclusion. Following a few days of this abuse it dawned on me that the reason for his bellicosity was that none of us were jumpers. In all the time we were with the casual company he never uttered a single word of praise for our efforts and it was then that I received my first lesson on the difference between the paratroopers and glidermen.

Our NCOs were a mixed bag of paratroopers and glidermen. Most had been on the Tennessee maneuvers, gotten sick or gone on furloughs and, like us, were waiting for the division to return. They were firm with us but amiable and none of them exhibited the animosity of our CO.

The following few weeks were great, a complete reversal of my time in the 26th Division, with a light training schedule and plenty of spare time. There were a lot of lectures, mostly about military topics, and, of course, some on venereal disease. The VD films were graphic, making one want to be celibate for the rest of one's life. Afterward, a couple of chaplains talked to us about the moral and religious aspects of the war.

I liked everything about Bragg but the sand and the heat. The food was decent and plentiful, the PXs were well stocked and there were passes to Fayetteville, not too far distant. This delightful sojourn came to a screeching halt when the daily inspections began.

The Army has a manual for everything but the proper procedure for using the latrine and many of us believed that even that was being contemplated. A Saturday inspection of the barracks was routine. However, to have an inspection daily was not, and that is what now began. Each man in the casual company was required to have a certain amount of clothing and it all had to be accounted for. Shortages were noted and, if an item was missing, a statement of charges was filled with the cost of the item coming from the unfortunate soldier's monthly pay.

Each morning after breakfast and police call we were greeted by our sergeant bellowing, "All I want to see are asses and elbows." Hearing that invitation prompted us to throw everything we owned into barracks bags, which were then lugged to a sandy drill field. Ranks were opened and our gear spread in a prescribed manner. After waiting a couple of hours under the broiling sun, an officer would come around, noting shortages, then everything would be repacked and taken back to the barracks. Some time later the supply room replaced the missing articles. The routine was maddening.

About the same time as we were enduring these inspections, someone noted that many of us had not qualified in all phases of training. Captain Stoner, the casual company CO, somehow learned that I was an artist so he had me design a large chart with names and the prescribed courses. As the courses were completed, names were checked off. It meant repeating courses that most of us already had, but anything to keep us busy. For me, the firing range was the most enjoyable as I got to fire the M1 Rifle, M1 Carbine and Browning Automatic Rifle (BAR). Those of us who made Expert Rifleman got to instruct others. I loved it, especially when I got to train a batch of newly commissioned second lieutenants.

Halsey, Hill and I spent most of our off hours together. Howard Hill was from the Eastern Shore of Maryland. He had been married about the same time as me. Walter Halsey was younger, a year longer in the Army, and with a wild streak. We became good friends during that period but were separated when the division got back. Hill and Halsey eventually went to the 327th and I went to the 401st. We didn't see much of each other after that.

Hill was killed in action on June 7th, 1944, leaving a wife and a son who was born while he was overseas. I met Halsey while we were fighting in Holland, along the Rhine where I was leading a night patrol. I came across this slit trench in late November 1944, just south of the river. It was daybreak and two men crawled out from under frosty raincoats, cold, wet and miserable. It took me a few minutes to recognize Halsey he had changed so much. Gone was the natty dresser. Now his clothing was filthy, his face unshaven for days, and his rifle coated with rust. We spoke for a short time, both embarrassed and I left, never to see him again.

An army survives on rumors and we had our fair share.

Fortunately, one concerning furloughs came true. Howard Hill and I packed our bags and caught a bus to the station.

The furlough lasted for nine glorious days and allowed me to visit with my wife in Maryland. Back in the sweatbox at Bragg, we fell into the routine again with guard and fatigue details now thrown in for good measure. Some of these details were enough to make one consider desertion. Guarding prisoners was one of the worst. Armed with a shotgun loaded with slugs, we were given a batch of men dressed in blue fatigues with big yellow Ps painted on them. These prisoners had to perform the worst duties imaginable. When they had finished with a coal detail they looked as if they had just come from deep in a mine, when they got done with the garbage detail they smelled as if they had been cleaning cesspools. Recruits were told that they would have to serve the prisoner's time if any escaped. Although we eventually learned that this was a standard Army joke, it was not until after we had spent many nervous hours watching our charges.

The closest thing to being killed or maimed on any of the details was the one involving handling ammunition. The detail would be taken to a rail yard to unload artillery shells, 105s and 155s, for example, from boxcars onto trucks. The 155s were so heavy one had to roll them on edge. To drop one on your foot guaranteed a trip to the aid station. While we were going about this loathsome chore, some wise guy would be sure to ask us if we remembered, "the time in Galveston when a bunch of these went off and wiped out an entire city?"

Working the rifle pits below the targets was as near to hell on earth as one could get because of the abominable heat and the chance of getting a stray round through your head. There were, however, always comical things happening in the pits. On one occasion an officer who was an excellent shot but obnoxious was firing. When word of the officer's identity got to the pit detail, every time he fired "Maggie's Drawers," signifying a miss, went up. The frustrated officer finally caught on and gave the pit detail hell. Another time I was in the pits when rapid firing exercises were going on, an officer who couldn't hit the side of his head with his hand was spraying rounds like water out of a garden hose. One of my crew kept sticking his hand over the pit edge, trying for a wound, which might get him a discharge.

Once you pass the recruit stage and get to know how the Army system works, you realize that the only way to live with it is to beat it at its own game. In my company we had the undisputed champion, Ken "Rip" Ripple, from Baltimore. Tall, well-built and wearing thick glasses, Ripple had been an athlete at City College. Having learned to play the bugle in the Boy Scouts, he volunteered for the job when Captain Stoner asked for a bugler. It was a day the captain would regret. Rip soon had the frozen-faced captain climbing the walls. After flunking out of the Army Air Force because of his poor sight, Rip knew more than most about the Army way of doing things. As he had to play various calls during the day, he usually did this from his bunk, thrusting his bugle out of the window and blowing away. Then it was back for a nap until the next one. At night he prowled like a stray cat. For other duties he could disappear like a bursting bubble, especially when he heard Captain Stoner scream, "Where's that goddamned bugler?" Rip never missed a chow call but when work had to be done he was the epitome of the vanishing man.

All good things come to an end, however, and ours did when the main body of the division got back from maneuvers at the end of July. This time there was no ducking details, as a lot of work had to be done, and we near broke our backs doing it. Roll calls were made and we were marched en masse to the rail station to work as stevedores. It was mind-numbing work but we got it done. We then packed all our gear and moved from our barracks to a tent city. A couple of days later, the division marched into camp, looking like Confederate soldiers just before Appomattox, dirty, disheveled, and with clothing and equipment worn from over a month in the field. They were as unimpressive a lot as I had ever seen. But there was something about them that told me that these guys were different—and they were. A day or so later, the tents were taken down and we were sent to our companies.

More than a dozen of us went to Company C, 401st Glider Infantry Regiment. Upon arrival in the company each of us was interviewed by 1st Sergeant James Long, a stump of a man with penetrating eyes and an unsmiling face. Matt Pas, the clerk who did most of Long's administrative work because the sergeant could not, took us to our platoons.

I was sent to the 1st Platoon, the best in the company naturally, with gems for platoon leader, platoon sergeant and squad leader. Lieutenant John E. Aspinwall was tall, lanky and eager. He was married and came from Staten Island. Staff Sergeant Yeiser O'Guin came from central Tennessee, a quiet-spoken professional with a dry sense of humor. Sergeant Verland "Doc" Harrell, short, wiry, serious, a heavy equipment operator before the war, ran the squad with a firm hand. His assistant, Private First Class (PFC) Jerry Hanss, was young,

just past 20, and with the highest IQ in the battalion. However, he
was immature in some ways, a fact that bothered Doc. The company
commander was Captain John A. Kindig, a solid chunk of a man who
sported a flaming moustache. His biggest failing was getting the
company lost on several occasions while on maneuvers. The exec was
1st Lt. Preston E. Towns, a lanky six foot seven beanpole from Atlanta
who could curse like a sailor and who took no guff from anyone. The
only one in my squad whom I knew before joining was James C.
Mitchell, from Baltimore. He and I had been in casual company
together.

Naturally most of the talk in the barracks centered on the recent
maneuvers in which the 401st had performed exceptionally well.
General Lee had gotten a couple of broken ribs in a glider crash and
swore he would never ride in another glider. Lieutenant Thomas E.
Parlaman had drowned while saving another man. I heard about
glider crashes, injuries, and some deaths. The biggest beef of the men
in the company was about glider troops not receiving hazardous duty
pay like the paratroopers and not having a uniform that set them apart
from ordinary infantry.

With more than half the company on leave after the maneuvers,
most of the fatigue details continued to fall on us replacements.
Gradually, however, the furloughs ended and the company got back
to full strength. Rumors were thick as flies around the garbage cans
that we were about to go overseas. New arms, clothing, equipment
and other gear were substituted for worn items. Booster shots were
given to everyone and once again we were required to have a certain
amount of combat training on our records. To correct deficiencies we
assaulted "Nazi" villages using live ammunition, attacked obstacle
courses with pop-up targets and crawled along the ground while
machine-gun bullets snapped the air inches over our heads. The worst
was crouching in foxholes while tanks ran over us. During one of these
exercises "Pappy" Bates, our radioman, had a narrow escape when his
hole collapsed under the weight of a tank. Emerging from his hole
after the tank passed over, the irrepressible Bates shot up and said, "I
sure'n hell hope the ground over there is harder than it is here."

When the battalion began to pack and sent off an advance detail,
we were sure of a movement somewhere. Once more we began the
inspections. "Red" Adkins, a jovial West Virginian who worked in the
supply room, kept us all supplied with the latest rumors, most of which
turned out to be true. At the end of August we got instructions to pack
our two barracks bags. The A bag, containing the bulk of our gear,

was taken to the supply room, with the B bag containing just enough for a ten-day trip left with us. The camp now became a scene of frantic packing. Most everyone had sickening feelings that we were bound for overseas. As we prepared to leave, barracks were scrubbed until they shined and the area policed as if a general were inspecting. We donned clothing, equipment and on August 22d, marched to the train station, carrying our B bags. As we boarded the "Pennsy" train, the post band serenaded us. I wondered whether it was from nostalgia or because they were happy to see us go. The music slowly faded as the train left and I wondered for how many it would be a one-way trip.

The engine of our train spit smoke and black cinders into the open windows of our packed cars as we headed northward. When we reached Washington, DC, the train switched to B&O tracks that I knew would take us right through Halethorpe, Maryland, the town where I was raised. I had lived there for 23 years, since 1920 when my father built a home in a newly developed section called West Halethorpe. All I could think about as the train passed through were the familiar scenes of my former life.

Finally the train reached New York, where it ran into a siding leading to Camp Shanks, a port of embarkation. We marched through darkened streets and into a compound as secure as Fort Knox. High, double-wired fences topped with barbed wire, MPs with guard dogs, signs which said "Loose lips sink ships," the whole security bit hit us in the faces. Later, I wondered how the enemy ever knew about troops leaving for Europe. But they did, proudly announcing it over the radio with names of units, when they left and where they went.

Of course, we had to take physicals once again to weed out those unfit for foreign service. I had little to worry about; if you could walk and breathe you passed with flying colors. We were stripped, made to walk up a slight incline under the watchful eye of disinterested medics and passed for overseas duty. We even had a couple of grandfathers in the company, some mental cases and a partial cripple who had been shuffled off to the kitchen; everyone made it. Naturally, there was a battery of masochists with big needles who punctured every part of our anatomies and another bunch with the euphoria of aging undertakers who gave us lectures about the voyage and Europe.

After being poked and prodded to distraction, we practiced emergency evacuation from ships using landing nets hung from tall poles. Men at the bottom were detailed to shake the nets to simulate the action of waves. It soon became a game to see how many guys they could shake loose. They did their job so well that they nearly broke a couple of necks. And we practiced loading the train that would take us to the port and the manner in which we would load the troop ship, everything strictly by the numbers. After four days of this mayhem, we boarded a train in the dead of night, slipping out of Camp Shanks like slinky thieves.

Red Cross dollies were waiting at the docks with coffee, donuts and a goody bag. Whenever pretty women were around there were those who nearly always went bonkers, and, despite the gravity of the situation, this was no exception. One might have thought they were going on a picnic instead of being readied for some of the biggest battles ever fought. However, for me, the embarkation was no joking matter, even though I normally was never that serious about anything. When we marched to the end of the pier and I saw the transport that would take us to Europe my heart sank to the soles of my feet.

CHAPTER 3

The Reluctant Transport

Our transport, the SS *Strathnaver*, was a dingy, small, worn-out rust bucket that looked as if the waves of the Chesapeake Bay would be too much for her. She had been a liner with the British P&O company before the war, running between England and the Far East. Even by British standards, which had been relaxed significantly during wartime, she would have been overcrowded with 2,000 souls on board. The 101st had shoehorned 5,400 men into her.

Parts of the 502d Parachute Infantry Regiment, 907th Glider Field Artillery (GFA) Battalion, 326th Engineers, quartermaster and ordnance companies, 1st Battalion 401st Glider Infantry and 400 or so WACs had to go somewhere. Using the precise boarding system we had worked out previously, we filed aboard, the women and officers naturally taking the cabins, and the rest of us filling the bowels of the ship. Being the last to unload, we were the first to stumble down one narrow companionway after another until we reached F deck, and from the smell that greeted us knew that we were as close to hell as we had ever been. It was utter mayhem as men played king of the hill for the few available bunks.

I stood in silence, watching the chaos and wondering if I would have to stand for the rest of the voyage. Finally Lieutenant Aspinwall came down and directed Company C to an adjoining hall. The ceiling was low and the place was jammed with tables of different sizes. Early arrivals had grabbed hammocks from a pile and lashed them to the bulkheads over the tables, their arms and gear on the tables underneath. James Mitchell and I grabbed hammocks and after much difficulty got them strung up. The hammocks were jammed together like bananas in a bunch, just inches from one another and sagging like a fat man's stomach. When I looked at mine, I knew that there was no way I'd ever get a minute's sleep in it.

It takes acrobatic talent to mount a hammock, and a feat of balance to stay in one when a ship is rolling. The canvas swallows you like a hotdog in a roll with nothing but your feet and nose sticking out. There weren't enough hammocks for everyone, so to leave yours during the night for a trip to the latrine meant someone else taking over and a big fight. Needless to say, it was impossible to sleep properly.

I rolled out early on September 5th while the ship was under way. Dawn was straining the horizon with a purple wash as I went to a porthole. I saw the Statue of Liberty for the first time and was overcome by a wave of nostalgia for the country I was leaving. Others were crowded around portholes and I wondered what was going through their minds. Would we ever pass this way again on a return trip? I'm certain everyone thought about his or her mortality.

Lt. Aspinwall assembled the platoon in a corner of F deck later that day, explaining the system we were to follow during the crossing. Meals would be served twice daily with regular places at an assigned table. Lifejackets and helmets would be worn at all times. Strict blackout regulations would be adhered to at night. Nothing would be thrown overboard. Cold saltwater showers were available. There would be some details like guard and KP. There was a canteen that would be open for two hours each day. He was trying to negotiate for better sleeping and eating arrangements. Until then we would have to make the best out of a rotten situation.

Mitchell and I went on deck as the convoy was forming, just a few yards of open space behind the garbage disposers, which were sending out an odor like a city dump. September 6th was a bright sunny day with a mild chop as *Strathnaver* took her place in the convoy. There were all kinds of ships from tankers to freighters, all guarded by small corvettes, which ranged like well-trained sheep dogs looking after their herd.

A Limey sailor came out to watch also, telling us something about our ship's past. He ended with, "The old girl is pushing her luck with this voyage. Should've gone into drydock, you see. She's just worn herself out, especially the boilers. Could go at any moment."

"What was he saying?" I asked myself, "A couple of thousand miles to go and the ship isn't seaworthy?"

"What happens if that happens?" Mitchell asked innocently.

"It might be a long swim to land," the sailor said as he went back inside.

Our quarters had been the first disillusionment; the second was the eating set-up. Trying to serve 5,400 men with facilities designed for one fifth that number was, of course, impossible, especially the way that it was done. Tables were of different sizes, seating different numbers of men. All the food had to be drawn through the head steward who sat at a table at the front of the mess hall with an assistant. One man from each table would report to the steward's table to draw dry rations of coffee, tea, bread, jam, and so on. Each item had to be weighed for the number of men at the table. Then the wet rations were drawn and put in a large silver platter kettle as the main entrée. Kidney and oxtail stew, meat pie, boiled fish, herring, potatoes, rutabagas or some other starchy vegetable were mainstays, all thrown in the kettle in a pile. None was cooked to American tastes. After eating, plates had to be washed and stowed away. The problem was, however, that the hot water ran out before we finished cleaning up. Pretty soon most of us had diarrhea.

Nightfall brought strict blackout and a search for a place to sleep. Mitchell and I latched on to a couple of hammocks, staked out a place in a small room adjacent to the mess hall, got hold of a few British navy blankets, heavy and gray in color, and settled in. Despite the efforts of the hammock to break my spine, I managed to get a little sleep.

A boat drill was held the second day out of port and went off better than expected. Had it been the real thing, however, there is no way the troops on F deck would have been able to get out in time. There was the usual flap about the meals with the food just as bad and the service no quicker. That night we had to hunt for sleeping places again because ours were taken. Mitchell, while small in stature was big in complaints. "Jesus Christ," he said, "the least they can do is to feed and sleep us properly before they throw us to the wolves."

The third day out we went out on the miniature deck beside our quarters and got the shock of our lives. The convoy was gone. We were alone on a rolling sea with nothing but a tiny Canadian corvette guarding us. Although it was barely after dawn, and the visibility wasn't that good, we could see there wasn't another ship in sight.

We soon discovered that one of the *Strathnaver*'s boilers had burned out, just as the sailor had predicted. We were headed painfully slowly for an unknown port with a solitary corvette as our guardian. Some wag said in case of a U-boat attack it would be about as potent as the war paint the Plains Indians put on their faces to protect themselves against the bullets of the U.S. Cavalry. One thing was sure, no ship ever left an American port with more lookouts than had the *Strathie*.

Our weary ship now plowed through increasingly heavy seas, wind tossing water high over the decks and soaking anyone foolish enough to venture outside. We seemed to be going little faster than a man paddling a canoe against floodwaters. Naturally, the rocking caused much seasickness and our hold began to smell like a sick ward. To escape the odor Mitchell and I bundled up in our raincoats and went outside. On September 11th, land was sighted, much to the relief of our sick. I saw massive red cliffs guarding the entrance to a large harbor. Bobbing tugs came out to meet us, coached us tenderly through the submarine nets and into a berth at a long pier. Later we learned that we were at St. John's, Newfoundland.

Newfoundland is the easternmost point of North America and, at the time, was still a British province. I later learned that it was the home of fishermen who led a hard life trying to make a living catching cod on the Grand Banks.

For security reasons the town was put off limits to the passengers of the *Strathnaver*. Nevertheless, we learned that most of the inhabitants were of British and Irish extraction. The harbor itself was surrounded by high steep hills and looked like a travelogue photo with its brightly painted houses, flat topped and small, and the larger steep roofed buildings of trade, all connected by sidewalks. I could see the spires of churches against the horizon and roads reminiscent of San Francisco, so steep it was a wonder traffic could move on them. Naturally, the harbor was lined with piers and ships of every description with a more than normal naval presence. At night, we understood, an anti submarine net was laid at the harbor's entrance to keep out prowling U-boats.

The weather became a lazy man's delight with balmy sunny days, which we basked in while waiting for our ship to be repaired. We did little but clean weapons and have abandon-ship drills. However, we still had the British food to contend with, the fish seemed to be getting riper with every meal, and there was little left in the canteen which appealed to our tastes except the hard candy and chocolate. We lined the railing each day, whistling at the local girls who seemed to spend an inordinate amount of time hanging up their wash in the sloping backyards just a few feet from the ship. The haranguing from the girl-crazy GIs got so bad that a general order was sent out banning the whistling. It didn't do much good.

Because of the stifling smell in the hold, it was decided that Company C would rotate to A deck every 24 hours, which meant lugging all of our gear up and down the ship's narrow companionways. Mitchell and I beat the game by finding a spot on the top deck by the main stack and making a nest out of a batch of British blankets, our shelter halves and raincoats. We stayed there as long as we were aboard, getting away with it because we showed up at formations and couldn't be checked because of the overcrowding.

After a week on board without baths, everyone was getting as ripe as skunks. We tried the cold saltwater showers but came out smelling like seaweed. Eventually the Army came to our rescue. In the hills about five miles from the harbor was Fort Pepperell, a US Army post. It was arranged that we could go there in groups of 1,400 with 24 hours in which to shower, change uniforms, relax and drink some beer.

My company was in one of the first groups to go, hiking over the steep hills and winding roads in balmy September weather that seemed like an Indian summer. We reached the camp after a two-hour march and saw a Mecca in the wilderness. It seemed like a luxurious hotel after the barracks at Bragg and the primitive quarters on board *Strathnaver*. The fort's amenities included hardwood floors, tiled baths, large recreation rooms filled with all sorts of reading material, and a mess hall with the best food I'd ever eaten. After cleaning up and enjoying a good meal, I went to the theater to see a movie. Sitting beside us were some merchant seamen off tankers that had been sunk on the Grand Banks. They told terrifying tales of submarine attacks, sinkings and drifting until being saved.

When we got back to the ship, a training schedule had been drawn up, mostly daily rat races of ten or so mile hikes over the hills. It was a good way to see the country and to escape from the ship. As the main occupation of the locals was fishing, many of the hillsides were covered with low, wooden racks used to dry cod. Then there were the daily loading drills, so boring that they became nerve racking. As the month passed poorer weather blew in from the Arctic. There was a lot of rain, fog and mist, though the temperature was still mild.

Each morning the WACs came on deck for exercise. Their cabins were segregated, naturally, with guards posted to keep the men out. Despite the security, some fellows slipped past using various ruses and came back with erotic stories. I doubt if any were true, but it helped spice up the daily monotony of life aboard *Strathnaver*.

After a week of so in port, the ship began to resemble a casino, there were so many games of chance going on during free time. Jim Turner, one of our cooks, came back one day with pockets stuffed with money won in a crap game. A hulk of a man from West Virginia, he was as naïve as they come despite a brash manner. Needless to say, the money was all gone within a few days. Meanwhile, once a week we returned to Fort Pepperell for 24 hours of luxury. And the loading drills continued. Finally on the 25th, *Strathnaver* was ready to try again. She didn't get far, however, striking a rock that necessitated a return to port. A few days later another departure and return because of a leaking hull. *Strathnaver* had had it, worn out and sick of the war. Another ship was being sent to pick us up and complete the voyage. While we were waiting our routine continued, monotonous and boring except for the weekly visit to the fort. Finally, on October 2d, we packed everything and left the ship, leaving our gear on the pier while we had our daily hike. When we got back *Strathnaver* was gone and a sleek gray transport was in her place. The name on the stern read SS *John Ericsson*.

Built in Germany and named the *Kungsholm* by her original Swedish owners, she had been a passenger ship before the war. Now, with an American crew, she plied the Atlantic hauling troops. Howard Hill had taken his honeymoon aboard her in 1939; now she was taking him to his death in Europe. The bunks were three-deep and crowded, but were ample, and the food was an improvement over the British rations, but still not anything to write home about, mostly tough beef from Australia. But the ship was clean and Mitchell and I didn't have to sleep outside in the weather.

We left the next day, passing the stricken *Strathnaver*. We waved to the Limey tars as we passed. We didn't head east straight away, but back to Halifax, Nova Scotia, to take on additional provisions. Some thought we were going home. We loaded the supplies the next day, however, and left for Europe. We had spent enough time in the American Theater to qualify us for a ribbon, thanks to the old *Strathnaver*, our reluctant transport.

CHAPTER 4

Atlantic Convoy

It was a great relief to be aboard an American ship even though we were jammed in a stuffy hold with seasick men. The hold was clean, dry, and not deep in the bowels of the ship. However, some things were the same: freshwater rationing, saltwater showers with soap that would not lather, daily lifeboat drills, wearing lifejackets all the time and not being able to remove our uniforms at night. While the food was an improvement, it was far from being gourmet standard. Dehydrated potatoes, powdered eggs and milk, and shit on a shingle were produced with great regularity, but were as tasteless as air. Bully beef that seemed to come from cows old enough to have walked the Chisholm Trail was always served for the evening meal, fat and full of gristle and usually winding up in the garbage pail. But there was plenty of time for relaxation, reading, writing letters and gambling in our section of the hold.

The head of my bunk abutted that of Frankie Lombardino's. Young, short and blond with a Roman nose, which looked like a banana, he was good-natured and laughed a lot. He had been a numbers runner in the Chicago rackets, according to rumors, and was a typical GI, hating discipline and wanting nothing more than to survive and return home to his wife. He taught me a mindless card game called war and some Italian phrases, which I learned later were obscenities. Frankie didn't get his wish to go home. He bled to death in a snow-covered field in Belgium during the Battle of the Bulge, pitifully begging for help but abandoned by his platoon mates because they had been through a week of unmitigated hell and were hanging on to their own lives by their fingernails.

For many of us the most interesting parts of the nine-day voyage were the daily checker matches between Walter W. Wicks, a radioman in headquarters platoon, and Frank Trudeau. Short, wiry and with a face like the gall on a wild oak, Private Wicks didn't possess a grain of humor and told stories about his prewar life which we thought were fairy tales. He came from Austin, Minnesota, and during the winter seemed to wear every uniform he possessed all the time. Trudeau, on the other hand, was an easy going Cajun from Baton Rouge, handsome, olive skinned, dark wavy-haired with a fine sense of humor. He had been an assistant squad leader but had been busted for going AWOL after the Tennessee maneuvers.

Wicks was by far the better player but had to cope with Trudeau's gamesmanship which, in some cases, was a subtle as a thunderstorm. They began playing for the company championship, then the ship's, then the convoy's, and so on. There was always a crowd around them, enjoying Trudeau's repartee as much as his skill.

Midway in the voyage, I got the shock of my life, Doc wanted me to replace Jerry Hanss as assistant squad leader. Hanss and I had become good friends but, after talking it over with him, I took the job. He was a good soldier, dedicated and intelligent, but a little young for Doc's liking.

There was always a lot of joking about men getting "gang plank fever," and the lengths some would go to avoid leaving the States. Flunking the physical was out, anyone able to walk had been passed, so other things had to be dreamed up. It seemed to us that Private Clarence J. "Vandy" Vander Sander had hit upon the right idea. From Little Chute, Wisconsin, and over six feet tall, he was as soft as a marshmallow and had a nature too sensitive for Army life. His strange behavior began nearly a year before when Colonel Allen, the battalion CO, was making a Saturday inspection of the barracks. It was cool with a fire in the coal stove and Vandy tossed a handful of .30-caliber cartridges into the stove just before the colonel entered the barracks. After the confusion that resulted when the rounds started shooting through the barracks, Vandy was taken out of circulation for a while.

While aboard *Strathnaver* his odd behavior worsened. Once he stepped under the saltwater shower completely dressed in full combat gear to "run a test." Then he stood on the stern while we were under way, tossing his newly gotten pay away, dollar after dollar and spouting some mumbo jumbo which no one understood. Once aboard the *Ericsson*, he pulled some gaffe and Sergeant Long, who was as tough as a railroad spike and about as tolerant, called Vandy to dress him down. Vandy had a bunk nearby and ignored Long's command to report to him. He ignored a second and a third order, finally saying, "Sergeant, if you want me, please don't use that tone of voice. And, anyway, you know where I am. Come here if you want to talk to me." Mercifully for Vandy, he was sent home before we went into combat in Normandy, an honored hero according to the reports of his hometown paper.

As we sailed eastwards those of us who did not gamble busied ourselves with reading and writing letters. I wrote my wife most every day even though the letters wouldn't be mailed for weeks. My wife and I had been married in October 1939, and she had her hands full working, taking care of our home, and looking out for a yard full of beagles that she couldn't part with when I went away. Thankfully, we had no children, which I was grateful for under the circumstances.

As the voyage neared its end, lectures were given about our destination. We were going to England. We were told about the area where we were to stay, the people, the rationing, the monetary system and the effects of the war. There might be nightly bombing raids by Nazis, but the full-scale bombing campaign known as the Blitz was long over. At another meeting our artificer, Tech. Sergeant John D. Porter, talked about his visits to England before the war. Somewhat of a pill, Porter had flunked out of OCS and seemed to carry a chip on his shoulder. He was pompous and tended to take himself too seriously, so I had numerous run-ins with him about drawing equipment for my squad, nothing but cantankerousness on his part. Anyway, he was one of the few enlisted men who had traveled abroad before the war and gave a well-rounded lecture on British customs, life and countryside. Afterward, he answered all the questions tossed his way.

The voyage was too much of a good thing with all the loafing and free time. Pappy Bates said not to worry, Uncle would get his dues later. Our life of Riley ended late in the afternoon of October 18th when the *John Ericsson* pulled into Liverpool harbor, with Lord Haw Haw, the British defector who broadcast for the Germans on Berlin radio, announcing our arrival and welcoming us. German intelligence was fantastic. It had been 44 days since leaving Camp Shanks, NY, only a little less time than it took Columbus to cross the ocean on his first voyage. Like him, we faced an uncertain future, not knowing what lay ahead or whether or not we would ever get to go home.

CHAPTER 5

No Milk or Honey

After our arrival in Liverpool we were shuttled to shore in small barges with clockwork precision. Once ashore we marched along cobblestone streets through an appaling neighborhood of dirty and crowded row houses. Some of the houses were blackened by fires started as a result of Nazi bombings and others just worn with time and weather. It was a typical port, like most of the others along the coast of Great Britain at that stage of the war. People in dingy dark work clothes roamed the streets, cigarettes dangling from the corners of mouths and flashing the victory sign to us despite the poverty of their lives.

There was a train with a long string of coaches waiting for us. We tossed our gear on the overhead racks and settled back, anxious for a glimpse of a foreign country. In those days few Americans could afford to travel abroad, so everything was new to us. The train finally pulled out of the station. As we traveled through the city we passed gruesome ruins, walls of homes in heaps, blackened by fires. Thousands of civilians had been killed and wounded during the Blitz. Block after block now lay in ruins. When darkness fell blackout blinds were drawn and we all tried to get some sleep. Somewhere along the way, the train stopped and we piled out for a stretch and some coffee and donuts served by Red Cross ladies. Then we were off again, lulled to sleep by the rocking of the coach and our fatigue.

Dawn broke and the blinds rose, revealing rolling green hills, neat farms, and flocks of sheep, cattle or hogs, and cottages with thatched roofs, looking like some postcard. There were pubs in the small towns, quaint signs hanging out front, "The King's Crown," "The White Rose," and others. There were churches galore, mostly brick with ivy- and moss-covered walls, and the strangest cars and trucks that we had ever seen. Even in this idyllic setting, however, the military presence was everywhere. Olive drab vehicles and soldiers in various uniforms crowded every town and village. The country leveled off as we went east and south, still with many farms. Because of frequent stops for other railroad traffic, it was near midnight before we reached our destination, which we were told was a town called Reading.

We unloaded, formed into column and marched along empty darkened streets with little traffic, led by MPs in jeeps. A half hour's tramp brought us to the main gate of Brock Barracks. The division had been billeted along an east-west line in the Berkshire and Wiltshire counties. The other glider units were around Reading, the 327th being at Camp Ranikhet, just a mile south of the city, artillery and special troops near Newbury, and the parachute regiments around Hungerford. All were near the airfields of Uppottery, Merryfield and Aldermaston.

Brock Barracks was the home of the British Army's Royal Berkshire Regiment. There were four large brick barracks, a mess hall, latrine, gym, row house officers' quarters and some Quonset huts, the latter clustered at the eastern side of the compound. A large grassy parade field took up most of the area with guard-houses within a brick wall surrounding it all, the main post being at the main gate on the town's Oxford Road. Each two-storied barrack had a central stairway dividing the building into four large rooms, each holding more than a platoon of men. There was a small washroom latrine for each room, several toilets and washbasins in each. There was only cold water in the faucets. Each room was filled with uniformly spaced wooden double bunks and rifle racks in the central aisle. Behind the barracks was a small building with some hot water showers, the kind that were cold one moment and scalding the next, and private rooms with tubs for the NCOs.

The mess hall was as primitive as the barracks, not quite up to handling the entire 401st. Coffee was made in huge cauldrons, strong enough to remove the barnacles from a pier. Huge coal stoves with monstrous kettles for cooking spelled trouble to a crew used to something different, and for months our food was either partly raw or overdone while our cooks became familiar with the British kitchen equipment.

After unpacking and a few days of orientation, everyone was busting a gut to go into town. No way, we were quarantined for two weeks. But we did receive mail, the first in nearly two months, and I had more than 60 letters and several parcels. I learned that my brother Bill was in the Pacific with the Sea Bees and a close cousin, Joe Appelfelt, had been killed in his dive bomber over Truk Island. Butch Clark, a close friend and fellow football player, a lieutenant in the Marine Corps and a graduate of Wake Forest, had been accidentally killed in the Pacific. Several of my high school friends had been killed also. The war was getting closer all the time.

When the quarantine was lifted, passes to town were issued. Reading was an industrial city of 100,000 people, many of whom worked either in a large cookie factory or the numerous small plants making airplane parts. It was a city of row houses, parks and a lively business district with movie theaters, pubs and fish and chip shops. The Thames ran through part of the town, so there were teashops and pubs along the water with places to rent punts. The pubs drew our initial interest. Hard liquor was severely rationed but there was usually plenty of beer. It came in all sorts, bitter, mild-and-bitter, mild, stout, dark and light, and ale. There was port, too, and some rum.

Everything closed at ten, including the pubs and movies. Many of the films in the theaters were American, but there were also British ones, many of these especially loaded with propaganda about the war. There were still air raids at night, mostly by prowling Nazi bombers, and a red alert sign would flash on the screen of the movie theater when one was in progress. The British would all rush in droves to the shelters, but the Americans stayed in their seats, indifferent and unknowing to the danger.

Our first air raid came in the middle of the night shortly after our arrival, the rattling of window blackout blinds waking us up. We rushed to the windows and saw searchlight beams quartering the sky and heard the hammering of anti-aircraft guns. Of course, the Blitz was long gone, but smaller groups of Dorniers, Heinkels and Junkers still roamed the English skies at night, keeping the English on their toes while the flying rockets were being perfected. Later we were to see planes that had been shot down, on countryside fields and on trucks carrying them to junkyards. And we were to see the tin foil the Luftwaffe had dropped to jam the British radar.

Lifting the quarantine, however, also meant a return to training. "We've been goofing off long enough at government expense. Now Uncle wants something for his money," was the way Pappy Bates put it. His real Christian name was Forrest and he was one of the 1st Platoon's radiomen, an avid card player, prankster and barrack philosopher. Having none of the mien of the soldier, he seemed more like a shopkeeper I had known as a boy. Pappy was past 35, blond and a little paunchy, but he always kept up. He only dropped out of one hike that I knew of, when he had been severely injured in a glider crash during the Holland invasion. Landing within German lines, he hiked for miles with broken ribs in a harrowing escape only to collapse after reaching our lines. Sent back into the fight, he died of his injuries some days later.

Pappy was right. The weather during October and November for the most part was mild and sunny and we now trained with a vengeance. Each morning after breakfast we hiked to a nearby park, going over the basics and tackling innovations. We returned to the post for chow, then another session in the park with the last hour or so engaged in sports. Then back to Brock Barracks for a shower and a retreat formation in Class A dress uniform.

The routine was followed for weeks, with Sundays free to sleep, to attend church services, to launder uniforms, to write letters and to go into town on pass. There were several irons in our barracks, the kind that heated on a stove, so it was simple to keep our uniforms neatly pressed. There was a shortage of clothing hangers at first, until an enterprising sergeant in Company A, John Gacek, got hold of a batch. He did quite well in overcoming other shortages as well. He had been a pro wrestler from Wisconsin before the war, he was a brute of a man, all torso and no neck, but as belligerent as a Sunday school teacher. He was destined to die in Holland near the small village of Opheusden, shot down at close range by a German machine pistol. Due to the nature of the situation, it was impossible to move him for at least 24 hours, and he would have lived if he had gotten back to our lines.

After we had been in Reading for more than a month, passes to London were issued. I was in the first group to go, along with Pappy, Joe Damato, a pro ball player before the war, Abe Spector, 2d Platoon, and Herb Lawhorne, also 2d Platoon. We went by train through picturesque countryside for some 50 miles to Waterloo station, increasingly shocked by the extent of the bombing as we moved into the city. We got a cab to the Columbia Hotel, which was managed by the Red Cross with beds for the night at one shilling (less than 25¢), and meals for the same price. Contrary to what most Americans said after the war, I always found the Red Cross to be better than one could expect under the circumstances.

After checking in, we were off to see the sights. London was a depressing place during the war with block after block of ruins and many of the civilian population sent off to the country with the children away from the bombing. It was a city of uniforms of all the nations allied with us. The city looked like a gigantic movie set.

After hiring a taxi, one of those small black cars that looked like water bugs as they darted through city streets, we listened rapturously to our driver, who had a silken tongue, as he took us from one historic place to another. Hyde Park with its soapbox orators spouting like Yellowstone geysers, Wellington Barracks with its stiff-necked Guardsmen, Nelson's Column sticking up like a palm in the desert, 10 Downing Street the brains of the kingdom, St. Paul's Cathedral beside a bomb hole big enough to drop a freight car in, Westminster Abbey with all its tombs of the great from yesteryear. At St. Paul's the blockbuster bomb was still in the basement, defused but not removed. Fleet Street, the heart of the newspaper industry, was something I'll never forget, acres of destroyed buildings leveled to the ground, a wasteland.

Our last stop was the Tower of London where our driver went into gruesome detail about its use and the many royal characters who had met their ends there. We saw the Crown Jewels, really a facsimile as the real ones had been stored in a safe place since early in the war. We were also able to see the cells where so many of history's notables had come to spend their last days. We bought some cigars, had a bite to eat and something to drink at a pub. However, like all good things, our visit came to an end, and we went to Waterloo to catch a train the next morning.

Back at Brock Barracks we picked up the old routine. Most mornings we hiked to our training ground, which we called L Area. It was always a picturesque walk, passing the quaint country cottages with thatched roofs, flower boxes beneath windows, farmers in short rubber boots working on farms. One could hardly realize a war was on.

A hot meal was usually served at noon and, after another hour or so spent in map reading, compass work, patrolling, or any of the other things infantrymen are supposed to be efficient in, a couple of hours were spent on sports. Then, after a two-hour hike back to the barracks and a change to Class As, there followed inspection and retreat ceremonies. Even though most of us were dragging after training, we still went into town later for some sudsy refreshments.

The weather was mild until the middle of December, then got colder with heavy morning mists and fog. It gradually cleared during the day if the wind was right, but sometimes the hoar frost looked like snow on the fields and on our tents if we spent the night outside. And as time passed, we were to spend more time on overnight problems, a gradual conditioning for combat.

Christmas came with little of the gaiety we had known at home, which was to be expected with so many of the Englishmen being away. In our barracks we had a bedraggled pine tree with primitive decorations and a big turkey dinner was served in the mess hall. Afterward, B and C Companies had a football game, without pads or uniforms, Playing end, I was up against a 200-plus pound tackle who tore a three inch gash in my eyebrow and sent me to the dispensary.

December 26th, known to the English as Boxing Day, a day when presents were distributed to the poor and needy, was also a holiday and seemed to be as important as Christmas to the English. We were back in the field, but saw lots of hikers, picnickers and cyclists. Also, we witnessed a fox hunt with riders in red coats, prancing horses, baying hounds, the hunt master blowing his shiny brass horn, and jumps which left some of the riders flat on the ground. Most of us had never seen anything quite like it.

The temperature had dropped drastically as winter settled in and we were spending more time in the field at night. As we had no specialized clothing for winter, we wore wool shirts and trousers, which we called ODs because of their colour (OD is short for olive drab) under our fatigues along with long johns. Outer clothing consisted of a field jacket; overcoats were never worn. We also had gloves and a wool knit jeep cap to wear under our helmet. Biting winds seemed to go right through our clothing, especially at night when we were in a defensive position, but I was surprised by the few men who developed anything worse than a cold.

For one such problem I was a squad leader as Doc had drawn sergeant of the guard. Our squad had dug in around a farmyard with the icy blast of a north wind threatening to peel the skin off our faces. Unlike Doc, who went strictly by the book, I was willing to bend some rules if the situation called for it—and we were freezing. During our patrolling, we had found a British searchlight position nearby. I sent Bruno Primas, from Saukesville, Wisconsin, a new addition to our squad, and Mitchell to the position at night with chocolate, gum, and cigarettes. They brought back large tins of delicious hot tea.

The new year began with an accelerated schedule We were now spending days on end in the field. This meant extra work for everybody. Reveille was usually at some ungodly hour like 03.00. Bedrolls had to be in front of the barracks by 04.00 so trucks could take them to the training area. After breakfast we were on the road by 05.00, hiking the narrow winding highways in clammy darkness with our noses running and our teeth chattering. I can still recall the dull thumping of boots, the rattle of equipment and the coughing of the cigarette smokers, as we plowed along half asleep. Most of these problems followed a set pattern, like the one on January 20th.

This problem called for us to locate and attack the 327th who were playing the "enemy." They were located by our intelligence and reconnaissance platoon on a ridgeline bordering a wooded area. Our 2d Battalion formed a line of resistance while we made a sweeping envelopment around the right flank. A storm front had moved in, pelting us with freezing rain, as we slipped and slid over muddy hillsides and stream banks. An entire day had been taken up by the time the move was completed, our bodies shrouded in ice and the only food in our stomachs that which we could wrestle out of a C ration can. At daybreak the next morning the attack jumped off. The 327th were caught with their pants down. With two companies on line and one in reserve, we barged into the startled "enemy" who had no idea that we were within miles of their defensive line. Colonel Allen was delighted with our performance, especially when the umpires gave us a high mark.

Several days later the company left on a five-day exercise. Each platoon was placed miles from the next in a remote area. The idea was to find the other platoons, and then organize squad attacks, all under simulated combat conditions. My 1st Platoon loaded on a truck at 04.00 and was whisked in the darkness to a dense pine wood where a defensive line was set up. We pitched and camouflaged our tents and foxholes. Rations for each squad were doled out for the entire week. It was up to the squad to prepare its own meals, while always observing precautions about smoke and movement that might give the position away. Meanwhile, sentries were placed as security.

After getting everything in order, a small detail was left behind while the rest of the platoon was divided into patrols. Their job was to scout in every direction and locate the other platoons without being seen. It reminded me of the cowboy and Indian games I had played as a youth. Doc divided our squad in half, he taking one part and I the other. Lt. Aspinwall gave us maps with our patrol areas. However, the 3d squad found the "enemy" first. Staff Sergeant Loman Bowers, a taciturn West Virginian and one of the best NCOs in the company, who led the 3d squad in my platoon, located 2d Platoon in an isolated stand of trees several miles away. Aspinwall spent the next hour devising a plan to attack the 2d Platoon that evening.

Leaving at dusk and carefully following gullies and woodland, we moved by fields of winter wheat and ripe cabbages, with billowing clouds blocking out the moon as darkness descended. We reached 2d

Platoon without being seen, since most of their sentries were asleep on their feet. Forming a skirmish line and at a prearranged signal, we rose and charged through 2d Platoon's position, bashing in tents, knocking over sleeping inhabitants and stealing all the rations we could get our hands on. We even dragged a couple of struggling prisoners along, giving them a hefty boot now and then to add to the realism. Then we left as fast as we had come in, followed by a stream of obscenities from the mouth of Lt. Ray Karcy, the platoon commander. One of our gang had gone out of his way to rip up Karcy's tent, stepping on his face in the process. While he was no better or worse than most new OCS graduates, some of his caprices did not sit well with some of the enlisted men, and when a chance to get even presented itself, it was grabbed.

We spent a week in the field, cold, wet and hungry most of the time, before the problem ended. And just before it did, I was called to Lt. Aspinwall's tent and told my promotion to sergeant had finally come through. It had taken four months but I was not complaining because the extra money was most welcome.

CHAPTER 6

The Calm Before the Storm

Training got more intense in February with 48-hour weeks and additional requirements such as a 25-mile hike with full combat load in 12 hours. Live ammunition exercises were begun as well as glider landings and assaults from landing craft.

Having spent seven months in the glider infantry without ever flying in one, I now got my first experience. Naturally, many members of the company had been through it before. They had told me the usual horror stories about our gliders. The vets called them "flying coffins" or "puke ships," the latter a name well-earned. They regaled the untrained with stories of how the metal-tubed structures collapsed like burst balloons when hitting a tree while landing, or splintered like a balsa model airplane after piling into a ditch. Despite their dire predictions, however, I was still anxious to fly in one.

"She'll fly like a bird," Pappy, the platoon sage, told us newcomers with tongue in cheek.

"Yeah, like a penguin," John Meadows replied. Fortunately, he was wrong, as he was about many things. He even thought he would survive the war and return to Indiana. Unhappily he was mistaken about that, too. He died in the snow at Bastogne with a .50-caliber bullet through his head, the victim of a misdirected strafing attack by a P-51 Mustang.

Pappy like to tell the story of how a large flight of gliders carrying our battalion landed in a pasture in North Carolina. About 400 men, armed to the teeth, immediately charged across the field towards an exit in a barbed wire fence, only to be met head on by an irate farmer armed with a double-barreled shotgun. "Hold on," he yelled at Colonel Allen, "yer skeering hell outta my hogs. What the hell's going on?"

When I got my first close look at a CG-4A, I was appalled. Instead of a sleek bird that could ride air currents like a soaring eagle, I saw an ugly duckling, which I thought would probably have trouble getting off the ground. Because of its minuscule landing gear, as ridiculous as feet on an albatross, it looked more like a boxcar with an upper wing. I wondered if this thing could even fly?

The CG-4A could carry 13 men, a pilot and co-pilot, or a jeep and trailer, or 75mm howitzer, boxes of rations, jerrycans of gasoline or water, or cloverleaves of ammunition. The aircraft had a welded steel framework fuselage and wing, covered by fabric; the fuselage was 48 feet in length with a nose which could be raised to allow large items of cargo to be removed. It was pulled by a tug plane, usually a C-47, at 120 miles per hour.

Before taking to the air, we spent a lot of time learning how to tie knots and how to secure equipment so it wouldn't break loose on landing and smash the pilot against the windshield. We used knots which popped open like a hot Mexican jumping bean with a tug on the loose end of the rope. Fast evacuation was an important part of unloading the glider.

Finally, I was taken aloft for the first time and was pleasantly surprised when the flight went off without a hitch. In most of the half dozen or so flights I made, it was usually no more than a bumpy ride with the wind whistling through wing struts and the noise of the tug motors making talk between those of us in the glider difficult. The terrain around Reading was beautiful when viewed through the portholes in the fuselage. After being airborne for a while, the pilot would cut loose from the tow ship via a latch over his head. It would then be suddenly quiet with only the noise from the air through the struts disturbing the silence. Soon we would be on the ground and all around us other gliders would be landing, coming onto the tarmac of airfields with methodical precision and stacking like candy bars in a carton.

Although our fears were somewhat relieved after a few successful landings, some of us wondered about the suitability of the fragile glider for combat. In addition to carrying 13 heavily armed soldiers, every glider would also be carrying a variety of food, fuel or additional ammunition.

After one flight "Boarpig" Fortuna asked, "What happens if a bullet hits that shit," pointing to some ammunition canisters strapped to the floor.

"You pray like a minister at a revival," Frank Trudeau replied.

When we were not working with gliders, more time was spent on the range. We learned about German weapons and we saw a demonstration run by a platoon of "German" soldiers who were really Americans.

At this time there were changes in the company organisation as well. Captain Kindig left for division headquarters and Lieutenant Preston Towns was promoted to take over. Lieutenant Karcy went to the weapons platoon and immediately got involved in a feud with Tech. Sergeant Claude Breeding, one of the best men in the company. 1st Lt. John Landry took over 2d Platoon. A washout from the air force, we initially thought he was a dud.

In March I got a seven-day furlough and spent it in Southampton because I didn't have the money to go to Torquay or London, which were our favored destinations. There was little to do there but view bomb damage, duck nightly air raids and drink weak beer in the pubs. However, the civilians were first rate, kind and without the usual British reserve.

While I was away, there were several changes to the division. On February 5th General Lee had suffered a heart attack. We were still waiting for his replacement when the decision was made to reorganize the 101st. Based on lessons learned during the Sicily invasion in July 1943, the decision was made to increase the number of paratrooper units with the division and decrease the number of glider units. As a result, the 2d Battalion of the 401st was sent to the 82d Airborne Division where it became the 3d Battalion of the 325th Glider Infantry Regiment. My battalion was then assigned to act as the 3d Battalion of the 327th Glider Infantry Regiment. Despite our new organization, the members of the battalion always referred to themselves as the 401st. In addition, on March 14th, a new commanding officer took over the division, Maj-Gen Maxwell Taylor, a veteran of the 82d Airborne Division who had been in North Africa and Italy.

On March 23d there was a division review for British Prime Minister Winston S. Churchill and General Dwight D. Eisenhower. Afterward, there was a battalion parachute jump and a landing by a serial of gliders. During the review Eisenhower toured our ranks, asking questions and chatting. My good friend Homer Johnson was one of those he talked with.

Early in April we went to Wales on a firing problem, taking a train from Reading station and passing through some of the most picturesque country I had ever seen. All along the route we saw troops and there was little doubt in our minds what they were all there for, the only question was when.

Wales, as I knew it, was a country of treeless moors covered by high, brown grass. When we arrived it was bitterly cold and an icy wind cut through us. To add to our misery, even though the ground was high, it was as wet as a swamp. As we carried out our exercise, the water seeped through our uniforms and rain showers nearly froze us. One day was a replica of the last and we returned to the Quonset huts cold, wet and hating the fate that had put us there. On the final day of the exercise while conducting an attack against an invisible enemy, a herd of sheep bolted from the high grass to our front. Some of the men in my company began firing at them, killing 32 before the command to cease fire penetrated their thick heads. I was appalled by such wanton behavior on the part of our men. All I could do was to chalk it up to the pressure we were all under and the misery of our time in Wales.

Exercises continued. In late April the division participated in Exercise Tiger, which was intended to simulate the airborne and seaborne attack soon to be mounted on Utah Beach. Our part of the exercise involved a landing at Slapton Sands, an area that resembled the beaches in France. On April 27th, as we approached our landing area, our large convoy was attacked at night by German E-boats, which sank three tank landing ships (LSTs), killing several hundred men.

The exercise itself was easy for us; we barely got wet feet after going ashore when the bombardment stopped. We knew nothing about the tragedy of the night before. There were rumors of heavy losses, of course, but nothing we could confirm.

The days and months flew by with more and more exercises. The fact that we were doing large amounts of seaborne training told us something. There just were not enough planes and gliders for the three airborne divisions expected to make the assault into Normandy. After hearing about the seaborne assaults on Sicily and Italy and the casualties there, we did not know whether to laugh or cry.

Training was stepped up to seven days a week now. We were also completely re-equipped with weapons and clothing. The clothing included foul smelling fatigue uniforms that had been impregnated with anti-gas chemicals. The gas-proof clothing nearly gagged us. Throughout the spring months we had several alerts, cleaning the barracks, packing and moving outside for transportation that never came.

May had nearly passed when we were told to pack again and marched to Reading station with knowing civilians waving and wishing us well. We had had a wonderful relationship with them and tears were in some eyes. Of course we had our naysayers such as Robert "Bitching" Shreve. Shreve was a rifleman in the 3d squad and our chief skeptic, a neurotic vet from Akron who never could forgive the government for taking him from his good paying job at GoodYear.

"It's all bullshit," he would constantly say, "Just another way to piss us off."

"Wait until you're ass deep in Krauts and say that," Pappy Bates would reply. As usual, Pappy was right.

The battalion unloaded from the train in Plymouth on a bright sunny day with the temperature in the 70s, and marched to an encampment surrounded by a barbed wire fence and stalked by military policemen. There were so many men crammed into the compound that even a rat would have had trouble getting out of the place. As we streamed into the camp, we could see Plymouth in the distance with its bomb-blasted buildings and the port facilities on the edge of the Channel. It was easily observable because the camp was high on one of the many hills in the area.

We straggled into a large gymnasium, which had been converted to living quarters by adding double-decked bunks and a washroom. The mess hall was enormous and something rare for us because the food was good and plentiful.

The most important thing on everyone's mind was whether or not this was just another dry run. As we unpacked our gear Pappy observed, "You've been feeding at the public trough long enough boys. It's time Uncle got something for his money." He was right, because on the evening of June 2d, we were taken to a large lecture room with one wall covered by large maps and photographic overlays and a bevy of officers who were dying to display their erudition. I couldn't say my enthusiasm matched theirs.

We were then briefed on the particulars of Operation *Overlord*, the Allied invasion of Normandy. Normandy had been chosen, we were told, for a number of reasons. Among them were suitable beaches and the nearby port city of Cherbourg, which was a major port that could handle thousands of tons of supplies. Cherbourg was on the northern tip of the Cotentin Peninsula. Just to the west of it was Brest and the submarine pens that for three years the British had tried to destroy and failed.

The 82d was scheduled to drop near the town of St. Mère-Église, take the town and the nearby crossings of the Merderet River and block the Germans trying to reach the Utah and Omaha landing beaches. The 101st was scheduled to drop and seize the four causeways across the marshes inland from Utah Beach. The 101st would then take Carentan to block the Germans from moving into the landing area. Because of the shortage of planes and gliders, what we had expected was confirmed; we would not be going into battle from the sky. The regiment was scheduled to land on Utah Beach on the afternoon of D-Day. After landing we would move inland to wherever division headquarters had been established and act as a reserve regiment to be used at General Taylor's discretion.

Naturally, we were assured, the invasion would be preceded by naval bombardment, air strikes and frogmen sneaking ashore to neutralize the beach obstacles. I had no idea how the other men in the company felt, but one thing for sure, I wasn't looking forward to it at all.

After briefing by staff officers, we went to separate areas where company officers took over. Colonel Allen visited each company, answered as many questions as he could, and gave a little pep talk. He was an adroit speaker, a patriot who firmly believed Americans were equal to any soldiers in the world. He had trained us hard, and seemed disappointed that our role would not be as important as he felt it should be.

Our role would be to go ashore in the fourth wave. We would land near Causeway Number Two, push inland and wait to be called. The following day we drew ammunition and gear for the operation. As an assistant squad leader, I carried five anti-tank grenades in addition to 144 .30-caliber rifle rounds, three hand grenades, two orange smoke grenades, a life preserver and a full field pack. I wondered how I would ever get through the surf with it all. The others were equally puzzled, especially Fred Grethel, the assistant in the 2d squad who was one of the clowns in the 1st Platoon and made a joke of everything.

There was a lot more to do than listen to talks about the operation. After being briefed by Colonel Allen and others we occupied ourselves making out wills, writing letters and attending church services. Platoon leaders had to make sure each man knew his job and NCOs made aware of the mission to be carried out. During one of these discussions with Lt. Aspinwall I was called to the bunk of our platoon medic. He lay squirming in agony and groaning as if he were about to die. I knew at once it was a life-threatening emergency and had him taken immediately to the aid station. He and another medic died that evening; two others lost their sight. They had extracted wood alcohol from the heat tablets given to us and mixed it with lemon powder to make a cocktail. My platoon would now be going into combat for the first time without the benefit of a medic.

The following morning we packed and left the camp, hiking in a warm sun down a long hill to the docks. A Landing Craft, Infantry (LCI) was waiting for us, most of the crew lining the rails with ominous looks on their faces. No wonder, they had been through this sort of thing before. The ship still bore the scars of its service during landing operations in Italy. Once on board we went down narrow companionways to canvas bunks and unloaded our gear. Some of us were given jobs to do while we were on board. Mine was to help operate one of the ship's 20mm guns. We spent most of the day being instructed in loading, aiming and firing the gun, which we didn't really mind because it helped occupy our thoughts.

The following day our LCI left port to pick up a large convoy which was heading northward. It was June 4th and the invasion was scheduled to begin the next day. We steamed all day with a cold weather front moving in with rain and wind that churned the water of the Channel. Once again those in our company who had trouble with motion sickness lay like corpses on their bunks, the contents of their stomachs spewed all over the deck in sickening globs until they could be cleaned up. The weather was so bad that the invasion had to be called off. We got word it would be on June 6th, come rain or shine.

CHAPTER 7

D-Day: Operation *Overlord*

Lights went out at 23.00 on June 4th (known as "D minus 2" or D-2). Very few of us got any sleep. Even though we had never been in combat, we had gone through enough problems to see men killed and injured. Less than a month before we had gone to Tidworth for a firing problem, ran through it and sat beside our filled-in foxholes awaiting the order to assemble when a 155mm shell came screaming toward us. Doc, Jerry Hanss and I sat talking. We hugged the earth as the shell skimmed over us and hit 200 yards away beside a crew from the signal company who were picking up communication wire. Two of them were killed outright and four others were seriously wounded. The incident really shook me up and I wondered if the careless gunner ever realized or cared about what he had done.

We had been taught that fear is a normal problem of men in combat, that the difference between good troops and bad is the ability to control that fear and go about getting the job done. Could we do it? Would our pride smother our fears? Would we let our friends down? I finally fell asleep wondering.

Everyone was awakened at 04.00 the next day. Those able to conquer the stench in the hold gulped down cold C rations and drank tepid coffee that had been heated on our portable stoves. We donned our chemically treated fatigues and put on our heavy cartridge belts, bandoliers of ammunition, rifle grenades, bazooka rounds, land mines, packs and all the other odds and ends we were expected to carry into combat. Echoes of the battle already beginning ashore sifted into the hold as dawn broke. The sharp blast of cannon fire, the roar of airplane motors, the thunder of bursting shells and bombs filtered down to us as we clung to stanchions for support during the bombardment. Our LCI bobbed like a cork on water, telling us the Channel hadn't lost its bite. We had been told that we would go in about 09.00 yet we were ready two hours before. It was the old story again, hurry up and wait. Little did we know that *Overlord* wasn't going as planned.

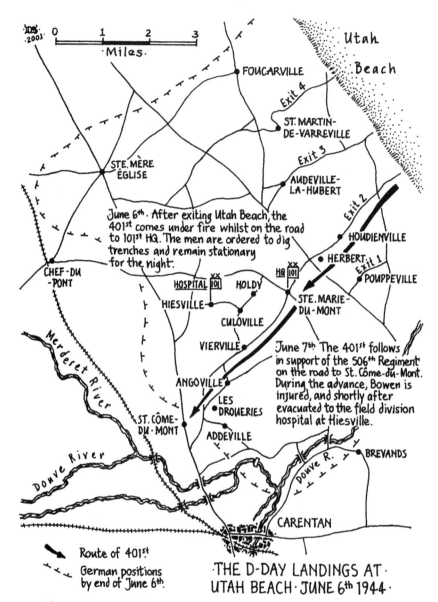

.THE D-DAY LANDINGS AT.
UTAH BEACH · JUNE 6th 1944 ·

The 101st was ordered to secure the four causeways leading inland from Utah Beach (shown as Exits 1–4). It was then to seize, hold and establish bridgeheads north-east of Carentan, to block German movement into the peninsula. The 401st battalion was to exit the beach via causeway no. 2, push inland towards the division HQ at Ste. Marie-du-Mont and await further instructions from General Taylor. The actual events of D-Day, as befell Bowen and other members of his company, are indicated on the map.

Few of the parachute and glider elements ever found their drop or landing zones. Most had landed miles from where they were supposed to due to the darkness and anti-aircraft fire. General Taylor found himself alone after the jump and it would take him until noon to round up just 115 men of the 14,000 he actually commanded. The 82d and 101st had been scattered the length and breadth of the Cotentin Peninsula. Perhaps it was just as well that we did not know this or the extent of the even worse foul-up on Omaha Beach.

As we waited my thoughts drifted to the new mattress covers that had been given to us as we came aboard. They had caused some discussion at the marshalling area. Bitching Shreve had said in his normal bellicose manner, "What the hell's this for—to piss us off more?"

Boarpig Fortuna, replied, "For Christ's sake, Shreve, haven't you learned a damn thing in the two years you've been in the Army? That's the sack they'll put your pieces in when a goddamn Jerry shell blows the shit out of you." Shreve's face blanched, not sure how to react. He was a lonesome person without a friend in the entire company. The entire time I knew him I never saw him laugh or even smile.

"This is it men, Let's go!" Lieutenant Aspinwall's voice rang out as he pushed along the crowded aisle. He had led the platoon with fervor since the day he had joined the company, a fair and compassionate man and a credit to the officer corps. We had just learned of the birth of his daughter and knew he was very happy about it. I thought he should have been company commander because he outclassed all the other officers in the company.

We filed up the companionway to the pitching deck, carrying our heavy loads like acrobats on a high wire. The Channel was covered by a mass of ships, fighting the choppy water, which made them bob like corks. Destroyers darted through the mass, firing shells at the shoreline while LSTs and LCIs disgorged troops into smaller craft. They streamed shoreward toward a string of vehicles lying disabled in a line short of the beach. Some were afire spewing black smoke skyward. Airplanes shuttled back and forth with loads of bombs that they dropped somewhere inland. Warships farther out in the Channel hurled salvoes of shells at the beach. The noise was deafening, the spectacle inspiring.

As we waited on a side ramp for a smaller landing craft (LCVP—Landing Craft, Vehicle or Personnel) to pick us up, one of the Navy crewmen said, "If I was in your shoes I'd be shitting my pants."

Grethel shot back, "What do you think's in mine?"

John Meadows, also expressed his feelings. "You got to be joking," he said to the crewman, "anything's better than this goddamn tub." He was one of the seasick ones.

An LCVP manned by two black coxswains eventually pulled alongside and we clumsily went down a scramble net to the pitching deck below. I could see other boats like ours, some with silver colored barrage balloons tied to their superstructures by cables. As we pulled away Navy crewmen shouted words of encouragement and we joked about them missing all of the fun. Our fears were disguised well. We were too proud to show them.

I was huddled in the front of the boat with Lt. Aspinwall, Tech. Sergeant O'Guin, Fred Grethel, Pappy Bates and John Meadows. Behind us were Bruno Primas and Jimmy Gilstrap, rifleman from my squad. Once we hit shore our lives would change in ways none of us could ever have imagined. Although we were not thinking it at the time, we were about to embark on an experience that would affect us forever. The gruesome nauseating sights of battlefields would haunt me for the rest of my life, shake my confidence and alter my personality.

The others in the bow of that boat with me would fare much worse. Aspinwall, Grethel and Meadows would be shot to death before it was over, Bates would die of injuries following a glider crackup, and O'Guin would lose most of one leg when he was struck by .50-caliber bullets from one of our own planes. Primas and Gilstrap would lose legs, too, after stepping on Schu-mines. No wonder someone would tell me later, "You must have had an angel on your shoulder to have survived."

I looked at the shoreline. The beach seemed like a Chinese fire drill, disorganized squads of men straggling from the water and dashing for the openings in the seawall, stalled and burning vehicles abandoned in the surf, German shells shooting up geysers of sand and water as they landed with gigantic explosions, and dozens of small LCVPs just like ours landing more men on the beach. Dozens of large LSIs rolled with the waves, their landing nets crowded with struggling men.

We were still several hundred yards from the beach when a German shell came screaming our way, everyone involuntarily drawing his head into his shoulders and clutching at the sides of the boat. It dropped between our boat and the next with a crash, shrapnel shards whining over our heads. Suddenly, one of the Navy coxswains pitched forward on the boat, his brain pierced.

We passed a half-sunken LCVP, one of those that had unloaded the 4th Infantry Division earlier that morning. As we went by we noticed bodies trapped under the water or floating nearby, their faces white and staring. I looked away. Soon the boat turned off its engine and shuddered to a stop on the beach, lurching us forward. The ramp then dropped with a great splash. Aspinwall looked sternly into my eyes, and said softly, "Let's kill some Germans, Sergeant." He then turned to the rest of the men in the boat and yelled, "Let's go, men. Keep together. No straggling."

The water seemed ice cold when I landed in it, right behind the platoon leader's heels. It was chest-deep and turbulent and the weight of my gear and the soaked uniform threatened to pull me down. I stumbled in shell holes. It was like trying to wade through a vat of glue. It seemed to take forever to reach the beach but I finally made it. A shell screamed in, exploding close by in a great geyser of sand and shrieking shrapnel shards. Involuntarily I hit the sand, much too late to do any good. A loud voice from the base of the seawall shouted, "Get moving, goddammit! Get off the beach!" It was from one of the beachmasters.

I needed no urging, surging to my feet and taking off to where others seemed to be going, a 10-foot hole in the seawall. The sand was like sticky goo. A string of bodies lay in my path, one man with nothing but a bloody glob for a face, another looking as if he were asleep. Along the base of the wall a deep ditch had been dug. It was filled with wounded and Navy men who shouted for us to come through the broken seawall. But the gap was partially blocked by a stalled tank with bodies around it. One lay in a depression in the sand as if it were of some protection. Company C streamed through, leading the battalion over the causeway that led inland. On either side of the causeway were flat stretches of salt marsh grass, wire obstacles and what looked like bayberry bushes. Tanks and trucks were stalled along the road, their occupants huddled in ditches because of the incoming shellfire. I could see high poles with Teller mines attached to the top, anti-glider defenses, and signs saying "*Achtung! Minen!*" An American lay prone in ankle-deep wire, both hands missing, the middle of his body a bloody hole and a string of entrails strung out behind him.

We continued down the road on either side of the traffic and the dead, trying to get away from the incoming shells. I could hear the dull boom of the German guns inland then follow the shrieking shells as they headed for the beach where they burst in clouds of black smoke. Now the sound of small arms fire became audible, the harsh ripping sound of fast-firing German weapons and the slower pounding of the American M1s and machine guns. We weren't too far from the action, the fighting around St. Martin-de-Varreville where a German gun battery was located. But that wasn't any concern of ours; getting to Ste. Marie-du-Mont, our assembly area, was.

Our column stopped moving when the end of the stalled traffic was reached. Someone said an uncleared minefield lay just ahead. The leading tank refused to move until this was cleared by engineers. We dropped in ditches beside the road. Just off the road in a patch of brush lay the bodies of several German soldiers. In a clearing in some brush to the right, I could see the remains of a *Nebelwerfer*, one of the enemy's six-barreled rocket launchers. The launcher's missiles lay scattered around the remains of its carriage.

We waited impatiently while the engineers cleared the road with mine detectors and marked the cleared areas with white tape. It was taking too long for Colonel Allen. He came to the head of the column to speak with the leader of the engineer company and was agitated with the answers he was getting. I was standing near Captain Towns when Colonel Allen stormed up.

"Dammit, Towns," the Colonel sputtered, "those people don't know whether there are any mines in there. They're wasting a lot of time. We've got to get to the assembly area. I'm passing the word to move out. Your company will follow me." His radioman passed along the order and Colonel Allen took off with us at his heels, right through the engineers with their mine detectors and down the vacant road ahead.

The 1st Platoon led, with the engineers cursing us as we passed and calling us "a bunch of dumb bastards." We met no resistance, however. The sun was bright and warm, with the temperature in the 70s, and we soon became drenched with sweat. Once past the flat coastal plain, we came to woodland and farm country with thick hedgerows everywhere. Captain Towns got instructions to hold up, so we moved off the road and dug in beside what appeared to be a large lake but which I later found out was an area of marshland flooded by the Germans.

The ground was soft and soggy. Before I had dug a foot deep, I hit water. I quit in disgust and lay resting beside my unfinished hole, believing the holdup would only be momentary. Even though there were sounds of fighting all around, where we were was peaceful. Birds were singing in the brush and hedges and wild flowers were in bloom. It seemed impossible to me that I was in a war.

Germans were reported to be heading in our direction. Company B went through us and spread out on both sides of the road. Patrols were sent out to try to locate the enemy. The rumor was false and once more we took to the road. We hadn't gone far when I noticed a group of men moving through brush off to our left. The helmets told me they were Germans. We opened fire, a ragged volley that sent the Germans to ground near the brush. There was no time to waste on them, however, so we took off again.

We passed a party of nine dead Germans lying in a roadside ditch. All had been shot through the back of the head, their foreheads blown out. The sight turned my stomach. It had been cold-blooded, completely unnecessary. Lieutenant Aspinwall turned to me saying, "They sure look good to me." He was one of the kindest officers I had ever met, a real gentleman, and I wondered how he could be so callous.

The march soon halted again and Aspinwall informed us that we were to occupy an area nearby. No enemy had been reported there, but we had to be on the alert. We moved out and came across an 81mm mortar crew, five paratroopers set up in a lane between two hedgerows. Their attention was focused on a small village to the left of the road, which they claimed was occupied by the enemy. Seeing us overjoyed the men. They had jumped the night before but had had no contact with any friendly troops until we came along. They had not fired at the village, a cluster of gray stone buildings and outhouses, because there were no friendly troops to support them. Lt. Aspinwall contacted Captain Towns with the newly acquired information. After a short wait Towns came up and said the village was reported to be in friendly hands and that 1st Platoon was to move out immediately and occupy it.

We started across the field in a skirmish line, safeties off our weapons. We didn't get far before small arms fire began coming from the direction of the village. Bullets zipped over our heads, ricocheted off the ground and kicked up puffs of dust. We hit the ground, hunting for cover. A ragged firefight now began. Although new to combat, I knew the field was the last place we should be and I shouted for my guys to get back to a nearby ditch. Slithering on our stomachs we got there as Captain Towns came rushing up. He passed the order to cease fire. There had been a mistake. He fastened one of the small orange identity flags we had been give to the barrel of his carbine and walked out into the field. A burst of small arms fire sent him hugging the ground. He squirmed back to us and got battalion headquarters on the radio. He was told to identify himself with an orange smoke grenade. He did, tossing it far into the field and letting it burn out. He rose again, but if he hadn't dropped quickly once more he would have been killed by the blast of fire from the village.

Captain Towns let out an oath and gave the order to prepare to attack. The rifle platoons got on line with the mortars ready to drop rounds on the village. At the last minute the attack was called off. Company B had run into the same resistance on the other side of the village and Colonel Allen did not want to involve the battalion in an action that might prevent him from reaching his rendezvous with division headquarters. We moved into a nearby field surrounded by thick hedges and dug in.

The ground was baked hard and full of stones, making the job of digging a good slit trench difficult. Small arms fire still came from the village and the bullets clipped pieces of hedge away as we dug. The battalion command post was having a hot time of it because of some snipers who were in trees a couple hundred yards away. I was told to see that everyone had dug a good deep hole and made the rounds within the platoon area as dusk began to settle. Ebon Angel, Eli Pauley and Byron "Jay" L. Gunderson, riflemen in the 3d squad had dug less than six inches deep. I told them to get on with it before it got dark and went back to my slit trench.

Guards and outposts were set and we settled in for the night. In the distance we could hear the rumble of guns as our warships blasted away at targets selected by their fire control teams on the shore. As it got darker German anti-aircraft fire lit up the sky as it searched for Allied planes. It was beautiful. Most of it was to the north around Cherbourg, the objective of the 4th Division. In our immediate vicinity we were to experience what all green troops go through at first. It would be quiet for a while then an M1 or light machine gun would bark. That would be followed by a rising crescendo of small arms fire, which would gradually peter out to quiet again. Most of it was nerves, the itchy fingers of green trigger-happy men whose inward fears were showing. Company C had a good record in that respect with good fire discipline at night. But Company A developed a well-deserved reputation for killing more imaginary Germans than any other company in the battalion. The Germans were guilty of the same uneasiness as well.

We were given orders to stay in our holes at night unless an emergency arose, and we did. But our Protestant chaplain didn't. Captain John Steele was an earnest likeable man who was able to provide a religious alternative to the natural coarseness of Army life. During that first night he went forward to visit a .50-caliber machine gun post commanded by his best friend and roommate at Brock Barracks. It was very dark and shadowy among the hedgerows as the chaplain approached the outpost. He was seen and heard coming, was challenged with the password, and either didn't know or forgot the countersign. There was an outbreak of firing and Chaplain Steele lay dying on the road, our first casualty among many due to friendly fire.

I lay in my slit trench without sleeping for most of the night despite being exhausted. My body was a mass of jangled nerves, my mind troubled by what I had seen. I'm certain the others felt much the same, even the recalcitrant who always walked a fine line between court-martial and obedience. We had several like that, men who had to be driven to do the simplest things. Yet they had done what they had been trained to do without any back talk, even though it might have meant their deaths.

D-Day was an inauspicious beginning for the 101st because of the confused drops and landings. By day's end only 2,500 paratroops had been assembled under divisional command and few of the original objectives had been attained. There had been two glider landings, one at 04.00 and the other just before darkness. The first landing, even though most of the gliders wound up smashed against hedgerows, had very few casualties among personnel, just five killed, 17 injured and seven missing. However, Brig-Gen Pratt, the division's second-in-command and a very respected officer, had been killed. We learned later that he had instructed air force personnel to reinforce his glider with steel plates on the floor. The added weight made the CG-4A difficult to handle and almost impossible to stop upon landing on the small field. As a result, it had piled into a hedge, breaking the general's neck and severely injuring the pilot.

That first day in Normandy had had a profound effect on me. I had always been taciturn by nature, and the panorama I had witnessed made me more withdrawn than ever. The death, destruction, and the might of our effort had shaken me to the core. To make matters worse, that first evening was a nightmare.

Throughout the night, bursts of small arms fire would break out. The slower pounding of our automatic weapons would follow the rapid stutter of German machine pistols and guns. In the distance heavier guns from ships in the Channel boomed. In the sky our planes ranged over the beach area and beyond, dropping bombs while enemy anti-aircraft guns lit up the heavens. False reports of enemy patrols alerted us time and again and the firing would begin once more.

Dawn came with few of us having gotten any sleep. A report circulated that an enemy patrol had been spotted. Lieutenant Aspinwall called on me to get some men together to go after it. I picked Jerry Hanss, J.C. Mitchell, John Zukosky, George Lolley and "Receipt" Shannon, and we took off with Lt. Aspinwall in the lead. We searched the fields, hedges and underbrush, finding nothing but abandoned equipment left by our paratroopers and signs that the enemy had been in the area. Impressions of hob-nailed boots left in the soft earth were a dead giveaway as few Americans wore these. After an hour we returned with nothing to show for our effort.

We returned to our positions and attempted to eat a breakfast of cold K rations. It was while eating breakfast that I heard that Captain Steele had been killed. Thankfully, I learned he had not been shot by anyone from Company C.

The German patrol had done its job. For the next hour we were under constant sniper fire from a village nearby. Some of the men randomly fired back at treetops and brush. Then we heard the roaring of nearby airplane motors, looked up and saw a serial of gliders coming our way, no more than 200 feet above the ground. The Jerries saw them too, opening up with every weapon they had. The gliders began their descent to fields just around us. They came in skidding and flopping around like awkward albatrosses, most crashing headlong into the hedges. As the emerging glidermen hit the ground, we tried to cover them, firing and shouting for them to come in our direction. That any of them made it was a small miracle. But they did, formed on the road and marched away taking some wounded with them. I believe they were from our signal company.

Hardly had we left when we got our first taste of *Nebelwerfer* fire. A horrible sound came from the village, a noise like someone pulling a giant nail from a large board with a tremendous claw hammer. Then we heard the shrieking rockets heading right for us. We buried our noses in the ground as they hit in our field with tremendous explosions that sent whining shrapnel shards and clouts of stone and dirt everywhere. There were only six but before the barrage ended, I could hear someone screaming, "Medic, medic!"

The barrage ended as quickly as it had begun, leaving us with three wounded men in our platoon. Pauley, Gunderson, and Angel, whom I had warned earlier to dig deeper holes, hadn't and had been wounded. Some artillerymen without a gun were hiding in a nearby hedge. One was wounded, another badly shaken. Their unit was the 377th Parachute Artillery; their gun had been lost in the jump. While our medic was treating the wounded, we got word to pack up and form on the road. We did it as fast as we could.

As I was checking the area to see that nothing had been left behind, I heard a terrific racket from the beach less than a mile to the east. I looked up, saw a flight of Messerschmitts strafing and bombing the men and supplies. Destroyers and other ships in the Channel threw up a thick anti-aircraft fire, some in my direction. Never giving it another thought, I stood watching the show, that is until 20mm and 40mm shells began dropping on the road where I was standing. I dove for the ditch, barely escaping the friendly fire.

The company formed on the road and waited impatiently to move. It turned out to be a false alarm and we went back to the field. After settling in again we heard a report that German tanks were moving in our direction. Doc Harrell, the squad leader, asked me to check to see that no one discarded any of the Hawkins anti-tank mines and that John Zukosky had rockets for the bazooka. While I was busy with this, he left for platoon headquarters.

Everything was in order except for the demolition kit, which Jimmie Gilstrap had left in a ditch beside the road. I was furious, but he was young and irresponsible. He didn't realize how important that kit was. I went back for it, started through the hedge, got stuck in the thick branches, and then heard the shriek of incoming rockets. The explosion sent me tumbling in the ditch. I landed on my bent right ankle with all the weight I was carrying. The ankle gave way and a severe pain shot up my leg. I waited until the rocket barrage was over and tried to rise. It was nearly impossible but I did, hobbling down the road until I located the kit in the ditch. I got it and returned to our position, throwing it at Gilstrap and telling him if he left it behind again I would have him court-martialed. I got to my hole, sat down and my leg shot through with pain. Hanss had seen it all and came up. My face had turned the color of white paper; I felt cold and clammy and began to tremble.

"You're in shock Bob. I'm going to call a medic, Hanss said.

"Our medic's dead, Jerry. Died at the marshalling area," I reminded him.

I leaned back to fight the pain. It wasn't for long. John Meadows came by, singing out in his Indiana twang, "Off your asses and on your feet. We're moving out." The ankle hurt but there wasn't much I could do about it. I helped get the squad on the road and the column moved out to join the 506th near the village of Culoville where we were to join them in their attack on St. Côme-du-Mont. It was easier said than done.

The 506th's attack had run into trouble from the beginning, harassed by small arms fire from the hedges, buildings and trees. Even though their first element had left at 04.30, it took them over two hours to move 1,000 yards. That's what had caused our late departure, the fact that these Germans had to be cleared out before the rest of the column came along. The advancing troops finally reached Vierville where a half dozen Shermans joined them.

Meanwhile we ran into the same problem. Company A led off and hadn't gotten far when infiltrating Germans stopped them dead in their tracks. I heard the loud outbreak of small arms fire and we waited. The scream of rockets sent us into the ditches. Sergeant Leo McBride, from Meridan, Idaho, mortar squad leader in the 2d Platoon, thought he knew where the launcher was located. He set up his 60mm mortar and dropped a salvo of shells into a grove of trees off to the left. We got no more fire from that enemy weapon.

Once more the column began to move, almost snail like. The same thing happened again, more small arms fire, met with an explosion of mortar fire and grenades. This time it took longer to proceed. We waited in the ditches as one of our medical jeeps with Red Cross flags on the fenders raced to the head of the column. It came back a short time later with blanket-covered bodies on its litters. Some leaked bright, red blood. The order came for Company C to take the point. It was now our turn.

The 1st Platoon took the lead. We moved through a small hamlet with row homes made of gray stone, narrow alleyways and U-shaped courtyards, with outbuildings for animals and crop harvest. We passed through Company B, its men lying dead tired beside the road. Once past the town where the houses became more infrequent, we came to some hedgerows with breaks in them to allow farm vehicles to enter. There were German dead, their uniforms stained with fresh blood that leaked into pools under their bodies. It was difficult to realize that just minutes before they had been living humans just like I was, probably with wives and children at home. We moved forward in a crouch because German machine-gun fire was coming from some houses up ahead. We leaped into a ditch and came to a house with a hole punched in the slate shingles of its roof. Someone fired a bazooka. The rocket hit with a blast and the gun stopped firing.

"Let's go!" Lieutenant Aspinwall shouted, and we surged out of the ditch. He yelled at me to take a couple of men and cover the rear. I grabbed Shannon and Primas and we broke through the front door of the home, ran through to the rear and out the back door. Several Germans were running for a hedgerow. We fired. They vanished in the hedges. We went along the back of the houses, expecting any minute to run into more Germans. We could hear excited, heavy guttural voices in one house, tossed grenades through an open door and went on because Aspinwall was waving from the road. Company B was passing through. There was no time to clear all of the homes. The primary mission was to get to the 506th.

Company B ran into a concrete pillbox at a road junction, and took a side road to the west to avoid it. We followed the dirt road until we came to more homes and an excited Frenchman who was chattering and pointing to one of the houses. Hanss had taken French in high school and understood the civilian.

"He said the Boches are in the house," Hanss told Aspinwall, who turned to Doc and said, "Clear them out."

We ran through the yard, ready to fire. Hanss kicked in the front door and tossed in a couple of hand grenades then yelled in French for the Germans to come out, but they had taken off out the back door. Only an old French woman came out, tears streaming down her face. She was lucky to be alive. We got back to the road. I was nearly numb, thinking of how close we had come to killing an innocent civilian.

Company B was taking mortar fire and had suffered some casualties. We were ordered to pass through them again. It was a road lined with trees and no ditches and the men of Company B stood or lay beside the road as we trotted by. Mortar shells were dropping along the road. Lieutenant Aspinwall kept shouting to keep moving. Just ahead of me were some bunched-up men. As I got near them there was a loud explosion right among them. Men were bowled over like ten pins. I saw 1st Lieutenant Joseph M. O'Brian, one of the best officers in the battalion, lying prostrate, his helmet blown away and his face blackened by gunpowder. Someone said later that a mortar shell hit him in the chest, but another said the pins in the hand grenades he was carrying on his musette bag harness had shaken lose. Whatever, he had been instantly killed along with three others and five more had been wounded. One was Company B's mess sergeant who had been involved in a minor scandal at Brock Barracks when the government stepped in to stop a black market in stolen meat.

I had been having a rough time keeping up because of my ankle. Perhaps it was the excitement that had made it bearable, or just that I didn't want to let the other members of the company down. Whatever the reason, I kept going regardless of the pain. I never was one to baby myself, only being on sick call once since I had been in the Army. I was determined the ankle wasn't going to keep me out of the most important thing I had ever done, so I went on, limping but able to keep up.

The 506th was having a rough time, taking many casualties as they fought down the road to St. Côme-du-Mont. We hit the main road running from Ste. Marie-du-Mont to Vierville and on to St. Côme-du-Mont, constantly harassed by sniper fire from either flank but no longer stopping to counter it. We reached a large château on the west side of the road, which was being used by Colonel Robert F. Sink, the 506th's commanding officer, as his regimental headquarters. A grinning paratrooper on guard at the entrance called to me, "Boy, are we glad to see you. Those goddamn Krauts are nastier than my mother-in-law. We sure need you up here."

I looked past him at the courtyard where a cluster of German POWs stood. All of their equipment had been discarded except mess kits and gas masks. There were more around a tent marked with red crosses.

There were large trees on either side of the road as we got farther south-west, many of them decked with camouflaged parachutes. Other 'chutes were scattered in the fields, evidently one of the drop zones. All along the roadside were abandoned American gas masks and other items of equipment our paratroopers thought were unnecessary. We passed dead paratroopers in 'chutes hanging from trees, and a jeep that had overturned on four of our men whose faces were now turning gray, then a string of dead German bicycle troops, as many as 15, their bicycles cluttering the ditches. Some had been shot through the back of the head. Off to either side in the gently rolling fields were gliders, with dead GIs around them. Some of the gliders were the big British Horsas with their tail sections removed for unloading.

The sound of heavy fighting got nearer. A platoon of tanks

rumbled up from behind us and stopped. A young, dead paratrooper lay in the middle of the road, still in his 'chute with blood and brains oozing from beneath his helmet. The tank couldn't move until someone shifted the body and those around seemed too sickened to touch it even though the tanks were badly needed up front.

We flopped in a deep ditch because of one of the incessant holdups, soaked by perspiration and just about done in. It was near dusk and the sun had lost all its heat. We felt chilled. My ankle no longer hurt; the leg was numb. Lt. Aspinwall dropped by and told me to fall out when the next medical jeep came by. He thought a doctor should look at it. I refused, telling him I would evacuate myself if I really needed to.

Moving off again, we passed small groups of Norman farmers. They had bottles of wine, calvados, cider and brandy and poured alcohol into any cup that asked for it. Some of the Normans had worried faces, not sure if we could drive the Germans out, but we pushed on. The cider I had gotten was strong enough to make my head swim. Soon there was another holdup and we collapsed in the ditches. The tanks came past. Someone evidently had sense enough to move the dead trooper.

Captain Towns came down the road, checking the company. He had always treated me well in the past, never letting the difference in rank stifle communication between us. He now looked down at me with concern on his face.

"Heard you were injured. How're you doing?" he said with a soft drawl. "Think you can make it?"

"I think I can sir," I replied.

"No use pushing it," he kindly replied. "Why don't you let the Doc check it?"

A medical jeep came up the road and the captain flagged it down, asking the doctor to check my ankle and, if it was okay, to drop me off at the head of the column. I thanked him gratefully, saying I would meet him later that evening. The jeep had some occupied litters on the side and was towing a trailer with a couple of ambulatory patients on it. The doctor told me to climb on the back of the trailer where he checked the ankle. By now it had become so swollen that he couldn't remove the boot and he said it might be best to leave the boot on until we got back to the aid station.

The jeep driver then drove cautiously toward the sound of a raging firefight, but, when mortar rounds began bracketing the road, took the doctor's advice and turned on a side road to the north.

The doctor said, "This might be close guys. The last trip we made down here we got a helluva lot of sniper fire." He looked at me, the only man on the jeep fully armed. "If we run into anything this time you have my permission to fire back." He nodded to the driver and we took off.

The driver didn't spare the horses. The jeep left a rising trail of brown dust as it shot down the road. He jammed on the brakes and we slid to a stop not too long afterward. Ahead lay a scene I had only seen before in a movie, something so horrible my stomach almost wretched. A German unit had been trapped in a road cut and blown to bits. *Kubelwagens,* half-tracks, armored cars and ambulances lay smashed with bodies sprawled out in them. Patients were on litters in the ambulances, men with red cross badges on their arms laying around the vehicles. All of this in a stretch of road no more than a few hundred yards long. I think most had been killed by artillery and mortar fire by the way the bodies were contorted.

Our driver got off the road and slowly bypassed the disaster then got back on the road and headed for Hiesville. Snipers fired at us, but never came close we were going so fast. I began to wonder about getting to our aid station—it wasn't anywhere near where the jeep was going. But then I relaxed, figuring the doctor knew more about it than I did.

We came to a small village with troops of the 4th Division moving through to the north. A battle was going on just ahead of them and I could hear the steady crump of exploding mortar shells and the sharp crack of small arms. The road ahead was blocked, someone said, by a knocked-out German tank. We waited patiently until mortar shells began dropping around us. The driver shouted for us to hit the ditches and we did, all but the guys on the litters.

A platoon of tense riflemen led by a scared young second lieutenant passed us. A shell hit in the middle of the road right among the platoon. Men were knocked over into the ditches. Some screamed, reminding me of hogs I had seen butchered when I was young. Our doctor and driver ran to help, working like mad to patch up the wounded. They brought one man back to the jeep, one of his legs hanging by a few tendons. The doctor did as much as he could, wrapped him in a blanket and slid him on the only vacant litter. He then told the driver to head back.

We drove on a side road to the east, past a group of glider pilots who were headed for the beach. Most waved and grinned, their part in the operation over. We passed a burning German tank. I could see the blackened faces of crewmen inside. The stench of burned flesh was nauseating. Toward the beach I could hear anti-aircraft fire, the boom of German field pieces and the explosion of their shells. In most any direction were the sounds of individual battles, small arms and mortar fire. I felt like a spectator at a big game riding on the medical trailer, so enthralled by it all that it became unbelievable. Far to the south, in the direction of Omaha Beach, I could see planes coming and going and hear the rumble of bombing. The jeep followed a winding road through the hedges and in the near distance I could see many men and vehicles and heard the driver say this was the division hospital. It was not where I was supposed to go.

CHAPTER 8

Evacuated as a Casualty

The division field hospital was in Hiesville, two miles west of Ste. Marie-du-Mont and located in a château with a large courtyard bordering the manor house and all the smaller buildings one would expect to find on such an estate. The château was surrounded by an ancient brick wall with openings to the fields and just outside the wall a small tent city had been set up with olive-drab hospital tents marked with large red crosses. The courtyard was organized confusion with medics and orderlies running around, a sea of patients on litters and jeeps coming and going.

Darkness was setting in as we were unloaded from our jeep and helped to one of the tents. Before I could go in I had to strip off all the gear I had been carting. After shucking off my equipment I felt 60 pounds lighter. I pushed through the blackout curtain and into a tent filled with men with orthopedic injuries.

When the doctor finally got to me after a long wait he had to split my combat boot because my ankle was so swollen. He asked me some questions then reprimanded me for walking so long and far. He wasn't sure if the ankle was badly sprained or fractured, and as there was no X-ray machine ashore yet, made a casualty ticket for me, which read "possible fracture." A medic helped me and another trooper with an ankle in a cast to one of the outbuildings, a shed with an open front, a pile of discarded parachutes, and some litters with German wounded at one end. The trooper and I wrapped ourselves in discarded 'chutes and tried to get some sleep. For me it wasn't easy because several of the Germans groaned loudly most of the night. I didn't know until the next day that for these men there was no future. They had been left where they were to die because nothing more could be done for them.

The trooper and I were awakened near dawn by the sound of fighting. We hobbled outside to investigate and were told by a medic that there were small parties of Germans that had been bypassed earlier and who were now sniping at ambulances and the hospital. In fact, just the day before, a surgeon had been badly wounded while he was attending a patient. The division MPs were now involved in clearing the Jerries out of the area.

My new buddy and I sat against the brick wall watching the wounded pour in and wishing we had something to eat. I had a chocolate bar left from a ration and we shared that. A litter was placed near us carrying a trooper who had taken a bullet through the face just over his upper teeth. He was bleeding profusely and choking on his blood. I turned him on his stomach and placed the finger of one of his hands firmly against the roof of his mouth. I hoped this would cut down on some of the bleeding while I rounded up one of the frenzied medics. He was taken into the emergency tent shortly afterward.

There was a combat photographer in a jump suit taking pictures with a movie camera. He had come in by glider on D-Day and had been badly injured in a crash. One arm was in a sling, his head was bandaged and his uniform torn and bloody. Despite his wounds, he went about his job as if everything was normal for him. He seemed particularly interested in a batch of German POWs who were helping out with the wounded. A burly paratrooper carrying a large staff and speaking German told the POWs what to do.

All the injured with minor wounds were collected and put on jeeps and taken to their regimental or battalion aid stations. I was dropped off somewhere near Ste. Marie-du-Mont. While waiting to be classified I met a friend from Company C who had just been brought in. It was PFC Tony Esparza, a mortar man from the weapons platoon who had been slightly wounded in the hand by a shell fragment that morning. He told me that the company had made an attack and there had been many casualties. Tony was a happy, easy-going Mexican-American from Los Angeles, one of four Mexican-Americans in the company. He honestly admitted that when the company started across a field and mortar and artillery shells began to drop in, he was really scared. We talked until we were called to the surgeon's tent. It turned out to be not what we had expected. Tony was sent back to the company and I was to be evacuated. He made it through Normandy and Holland, but not Belgium. During the Battle of the Bulge he was hit by an artillery round and killed.

Along with several others I approached the beach on a medical jeep across one of the raised causeways bucking a constant stream of traffic coming from the opposite direction. Beside the road lay the debris of war, bodies and abandoned equipment, all covered by a layer of dust from the ceaseless traffic. Vehicles streamed ashore as if there was no end to them, tanks, trucks, half-tracks, jeeps, every sort of vehicle the army possessed. Troops were coming too; all had anxious looks on their faces.

One of them asked, "How is it up there?"

"No sweat, you get used to it," a paratrooper yelled back untruthfully.

Even though the beach seemed a shambles with troops and material pouring ashore and across the sand while incoming shells still pounded the beach with regularity, the work continued at a feverish pitch. Offshore a destroyer lobbed shells in the direction of St. Côme-du-Mont and another scurried around taking pot shots at floating mines that had broken loose from their moorings. The jeep dropped us off at the seawall where a clearing station had been set up. A mass of small boats ran from the beach to LSTs, LCTs and LCIs, bringing in men and taking out casualties. After waiting for some time, our wound tickets were checked and we were put on an amphibious DUKW, which would take us to a waiting LST.

The Channel was still choppy and the sky was hazy. I couldn't tell if it was actually cloudy or just smoke from burning material filling the sky. At any rate, there was a sickening smell of burned wood, dead men and cattle, and gunpowder. I was happy to be rid of the place, the death and destruction, and I'm sure all the men felt the same way. We had nearly reached our LST when we heard the scream of an incoming shell and an ear-splitting explosion. An ammo depot on the beach had been hit. We looked with commiserating eyes at the fireball and the frantic men around it.

A paratrooper with a broken leg murmured, "Jesus Christ, I've never seen anything like it!"

We got aboard a landing stage that hoisted us to an upper deck. An LST is a flat-backed, canoe shaped thing with a bow that can be raised or lowered. The main deck was being filled with litter cases. We who were ambulatory were shown bunks on the upper deck.

As I walked off the landing stage, I heard a raucous voice, "For Christ's sake, if it ain't old National Guard."

It could only belong to one person, Homer Johnson from Company B with whom I had become friends at Brock. Homer was a typical West Virginia redneck, a lanky, craggy-faced, easy-going former technical sergeant who had turned in his stripes in March. He had more than six years service in the National Guard and was an excellent platoon sergeant. However, there was a personality conflict, practically a running feud, between him and Captain Robert J.

McDonald, the company CO, so Johnson became a BAR man in a rifle squad. What a pity, both men were good soldiers.

I took Homer's outstretched hand. He had a bandage on the tip of his nose and one arm in a sling. A bullet had nipped the end of his prominent proboscis and gone through his shoulder. With him were two men I knew only casually, Staff Sergeant Larry Gill and Sergeant Ralph Meyers. Gill was 35, lean and balding, and came from Fairmont, West Virginia. He had shrapnel wounds in several places, inflicted by a mortar shell burst. Meyers was younger, an easy going blond from somewhere in Ohio. A bullet had struck his forearm, passed through and out the triceps muscle in the same arm.

The four of us sat on our bunks talking about our experiences while the ship was being loaded. Johnson, Meyers and Gill had been wounded in the morning attack, the same one that Esparza was in. When Company B was held up by a machine gun position, Johnson took off on his own, killing the gunners and knocking out the position. Captain McDonald later recommended him for the Silver Star, which was presented to him in August by General Eisenhower. Offered his stripes back, Homer refused, instead choosing to remain a private.

The ship finally left, went a short way and then veered sharply as it narrowly missed a floating mine. Another LST not far away wasn't as lucky. We heard a loud explosion and learned that it had sunk within minutes, taking to the bottom with it some wounded and a batch of German POWs.

We were dead tired, nearly exhausted from little sleep and less food, so we finally fell asleep. We were eventually awakened by a crewman who took us to a mess hall for a meal. I never tasted a better one after four days of nothing but a few spoonfuls out of C ration cans. We returned to our berths and slept through the rest of the trip.

The following morning the LST pulled into a quay at Dartmouth and the unloading began, alongside other ships being loaded with men and material for Normandy. We stood at the railing talking to some of the men, an armored outfit belonging to the 2d Armored Division. Naturally they were full of questions about Normandy, but we had few answers. In a battle it is rare to know anything except what goes on in your area.

We weren't much to look at as we limped down the gangplank to waiting ambulances. None of us had shaved for days, our uniforms were dirty from sleeping in holes in the ground, and some were still wrapped in bloody bandages. Civilians lined the quay, patting us on the shoulder and shouting encouraging words. I felt anything but a hero, in fact, a little guilty that I hadn't stayed with the battalion for so minor an injury. However, my evacuation had been out of my hands.

The ambulatory wounded were put on a bus instead of the ambulances. It was driven by a young medic who should have known better when one of the troopers asked him to stop at a pub as we went through Dartmouth. But he did stop and those able hobbled into the pub and were given all the beer they could drink by grateful civilians. Then we continued our trip, some three sheets to the wind.

The hospital was only a temporary stay for us. We got a good hot meal and a better night's sleep and the next morning were taken to a hospital train that would carry us to our final destination. After checking my ankle, the doctor who examined me made me a litter patient and told me to stay off the leg as much as possible. A bone might have been fractured.

It was a typical British train with a green-colored locomotive and small coaches that had been fitted to take casualties. Most of the casualties were from the 101st, 1st or 4th Divisions. There was a major from the 101st in the bunk above mine, a very happy officer with a leg wound and a briefcase with thousands of dollars in Reichsmarks which he had taken from a dead German. To pass the time the major talked about some incidents that made my stomach turn over. He told us about paratroopers being wrapped in 'chutes by the enemy and set afire and others who had been castrated and their testicles put in their mouths. I was glad when the trip was over.

We reached the 4177th Hospital Plant in Birmingham about early afternoon and were wheeled on gurneys to our wards. I went to the orthopedic section, lucky to have a bed indoors, as large tents had been set up for the expected casualties. The hospital was an improvised affair, a series of one-story buildings connected by covered walks. There was a mess hall for the ambulatory and private rooms for officers. We took off our dirty uniforms and changed to pajamas and hospital robes. I checked out my neighbors. On my right was a sailor from the USS *Corry*, a destroyer that had been sunk near Utah Beach. Both his legs had been broken and he was in a cast to his waist. He seemed to be in extreme pain as he moaned and groaned loudly for several days until he was moved to a different hospital. The man on the other side was a trooper from the 101st, also with an injured ankle. The other patients were from the 101st, 82d, 4th and 1st Divisions, some injured and others with serious wounds. Johnson, Meyers and Gill were put in one of the tents and weren't happy about it. I kidded them about not knowing how to pick the right way of being injured.

The ward physician was a young lieutenant named Middleton, a nice person who soon became a favorite of everyone in the place. There were two day nurses and one at night. One was a vivacious blond who caught the eyes of everyone. The big problem at the hospital was the length of time it took to analyze and treat some of the wounds, something that would improve with time. I wasn't complaining. Anything was better than Normandy.

The hospital staff were new, having only recently arrived in England, and showed it. After hurrying us through all the blood tests, exams and other entrance procedures, nothing seemed to be done for days in the way of treatment. A trooper from the 82d was very vocal about it. Both his arms were in casts put on by German surgeons when he was temporarily captured. His bloody wrapping was still on after a week at the hospital.

Life threatening wounds were promptly attended to, but not always successfully. A youth of no more than 18 in the bed opposite had been shot through the lungs. He was delirious most of the time, but when rational complained about blood dropping into his chest. Nothing could be done for him except to keep him insentient until he died. On the other hand, another fellow who had both legs blown off near the hips was saved, and when out of danger sent back to the States for more advanced treatment.

When I was X-rayed and examined, the physician said, "You could have broken it. We can fix that but what you have done by foolishly walking so long on it is to twist and tear the ligaments and tendons. Now only time and nature can do anything for you."

He proceeded to wrap the leg in an Ace bandage and for a week I was in a living hell because the ankle swelled and I was unable to sleep. I asked Lt. Middleton for a second opinion. He removed the bandage for several days, which reduced the swelling and then put on a soft cast. In another week I was able to get up.

Hospital routines are much the same everywhere, except in the military where myriad regulations still govern everything one does. Aside from treatment, patients had to be fed, bathed, succored, beds made with hospital corners, the ward polished like a bald man's head, and all personal effects stored like wares on store shelves. The hospital was short handed, so the ambulatory patients were used to help, and they did without compunction. However, they drew the line at one point—the officers' ward. Gill and Meyers, being NCOs, were asked to pull KP in the officers' wards. They absolutely refused even though threatened with court-martial. They stuck to their guns, however, and no action was taken.

We followed the progress of the war closely, talking with new arrivals from France, and through radio and newspaper accounts. We learned that the Allies were stalled in the *bocage*, as the Normandy countryside was known The Germans had tunneled into the base of the hedgerows, making them almost impregnable defensive positions that cost many lives to destroy. And in the 101st's area, the widespread swamps behind the causeways, made the terrain so difficult that armor was of little use and the job had to be done the hard way. It was no wonder that most of the men coming through the hospital expressed no desire for more of the same.

With my ankle beginning to heal, Lt. Middleton gave me permission to walk some, even asking me to help with some of his paperwork. I was glad to have something to do beside lying in bed and talking to Frank, the paratrooper in the sack next to me. Using a crutch I was able to reach Lt. Middleton's small office without much trouble. I spent every morning helping him with a pile of reports that was swamping him. Most had to do with classifying wounds and injuries. Anyone who was injured or wounded in the course of the battle was entitled to a Purple Heart and it had to be entered on the man's record so that he could receive the award. After lunch I had the afternoon free to visit Gill and the others and to play hearts, a card game that was new to me.

Only one man from Company C came through my ward while I was there, a fellow named Weidemeyer from the 2d Platoon whom I barely knew. I pumped him for information about the company but all he would say was, "It was hell. I don't want to go back."

However, I did meet a fellow from my hometown of Arbutus. His name was Carl Lutmate and he was one of the "bad boys" in Arbutus Elementary School, the kind who pulled the girl's pigtails and got in fights with other boys in the schoolyard. He was still in trouble, trundling about the wards in a wheelchair with a cast from neck to waist. He had overturned a jeep in Normandy and was lucky to be alive. Each day he would come to visit and we had many long talks about the hometown and boys in the service.

After three weeks had passed my Company B friends could no longer stand the confinement of the hospital and badgered the doctor about releasing them. He absolutely refused as none of their wounds was completely healed. Finally they began working on me to get Doc Middleton to discharge them.

I told them right out, "You guys are absolutely nuts. Gill's got enough shrapnel in him to set off a mine detector and you other two are so damned crippled that you can't move your arms and you expect this doctor to send you back? What the hell's the matter with you? You've got it made here."

They began with squawking about the food, the regulations, the bed checks, the tent life and so on.

"Yeah, I agree, especially about the food. But nobody's shooting or shelling you and you're not living in a hole like a gopher. None of you know when you've got it lucky."

However, seeing how much they wanted to leave, I did talk each morning to Doc Middleton and he finally agreed to discharge us, telling me that we didn't realize the blood bath which lay ahead of us. He gave us slips to draw Class A uniforms from supply, to be used only on the day of our discharge, and put us on the list for release in several days.

The uniforms were all my friends needed. Taking Frank the paratrooper with them, they slipped out of the hospital that night for a visit to the Birmingham pubs. They came back at midnight roaring drunk and dragging Frank like he was a sack of grain. They woke the whole ward trying to get Frank into bed. It was like a Three Stooges act. Each time they got him in the bed, he slipped out the other side. The young night nurse was frantic. Although the four had been AWOL, their absence hadn't been noted on the bed check report, which meant real trouble for the staff if they were found out now. In the end, Frank was left on the floor under a pile of covers, the Company B boys went back to their tents and the men in the ward went back to sleep.

We were discharged on July 1st, all of us still in bandages and against Doc Middleton's better judgment. We were taken by truck to the train station and after a short ride arrived in Litchfield, the 10th Repo Depot, a station where troops were kept and classified until they could be shipped to units which needed replacements. After the first day there we knew we had made a mistake in leaving the hospital so soon. The place was called Feezy Farms and it was one of the dark holes of the military in Europe.

To begin with the medical officer who examined us nearly went into a tantrum when he saw the cast and bandages, threatening to put us on the train and send us back. It took some fast-talking by Gill, who had been a salesman in civilian life and had a way with words, to cool off the officer and allow us to stay. He sent us back to the string of row homes that served as quarters, some seven miles from the main depot, for four of the worst days of our military lives.

Feezy Farms was a nightmare. The place was surrounded by barbed wire and cantankerous MPs, the food was terrible, the mess hall on a hill over half a mile away, and if you were a minute late a burly sergeant by the entrance would yell, "No chow for you. You're late." And he meant it. That is until an equally tough guy, Frank, my paratrooper friend, met him as he blocked the doorway when we were a few minutes late. Frank hit him twice and the mess sergeant hit the ground. We dashed past and mingled with the hundreds of other GIs who were lining up for dinner. When we left after the usual lousy meal the mess sergeant stood at the exit with two MPs trying to find the guy who had hit him. Because of the rush of men to leave the place, Frank had little chance of being caught. However, for every meal after that the mess sergeant was missing.

My Company B buddies, Frank, and two fellows from the 29th Division, shared a room on the second floor of one of the row homes. While we awaited orders, we were supposed to attend training classes and do close order drill. One day of that was enough for us. One man was selected to attend roll call each morning and answer for the rest of us. If necessary we would go on sick call, which was never checked, and spend the rest of the day in our rooms playing cards. We got away with it the whole time until midnight on July 4th when Gill and I were awakened and told to report to the orderly room. We said nothing to the others, knowing we were going back to Brock and wanting to be there before Meyers and Johnson returned.

We were given train tickets, taken to the station and shipped off for Greenham Lodge where the division headquarters was located. A truck took us to Reading and Brock Barracks. We arrived there late at night and were put in Company A's barracks.

The next morning when we woke for reveille we were shocked to find Brock filled with recruits who had come over in May and moved in when we left for the marshalling area. They were carrying on a regular training schedule and were to fill in for the casualties in Normandy.

I got the first real news about our companies from Corporal Cleon Overbay, the company clerk, who had remained behind. It was tragic news for me. Lieutenant Aspinwall had been shot to death on June

17th while leading an attack. A sniper had killed Fred Grethel as he carelessly exposed himself. Staff Sergeant Frank DeMarco, a close friend in 2d Platoon, had been killed accidentally while being helped over a wire barrier when his machine gun inadvertently discharged. Lieutenant Ray Karcy, the weapons platoon leader, was missing. He had been wounded, evacuated to the beach and put on an LST, which hit a mine and sank with all aboard. Louis Wollford, a quiet easy-going fellow from Buffalo was on the same ship. Ray Honeycutt, a circus roustabout and one of the toughest men I ever met, had been killed by a piece of shrapnel no bigger than a pea. It had struck him under the eyebrow and pierced his brain. His body was covered with flowers by civilians in Carentan, a scene which made all the papers as an international photographer snapped it. First Lieutenant Landry and First Lieutenant Mike Settani, the executive officer, had been seriously wounded and never came back. Tech. Sergeant Richard E. "Jake" Irwin was wounded, too. The company lost about 45 percent of its personnel in the campaign, most never returning to the outfit.

We who had been injured in Normandy were excused all duty until the company got back. We made the most of it. Johnson and Meyers arrived a few days after us and were mad because we hadn't told them that we were leaving. However, at Feezy Farms we had been betting who would return first and we collected. We spent most every evening at the White Rose pub, regaling the civilians with our tales. We never had to buy a drink; everything was always on the house or one of the civilians.

The division fought its last major battle in Normandy on June 17th in the vicinity of Carentan. It moved northward to Tollevast, four miles south of Cherbourg in a defensive position, which it held for two weeks. From there it moved to Utah Beach for evacuation to England by LST. It arrived in Southampton on July 13th and the 401st was back at Brock several days later. The division lost 4,670 men in Normandy. As for Company C, it would never be the same without men with whom I had become friendly, grown to respect, and hoped to return home with. The big adventure to me had lost its allure. The rest of the war would be a nightmare.

CHAPTER 9

Windmills and Wooden Shoes

When the trucks bearing the regiment came through Reading, civilians on the streets waved and cheered. The troops waved back and gave the victory sign. But when the trucks pulled into Brock and unloaded between the brick barracks, there was less animation than on the streets. I looked at the company as it fell in, the ranks little more than half the strength that they had been before Normandy, the men dirty and dusty with French mud, equipment worn, bedrolls tattered. Only their weapons shone.

The company had lost every officer except Captain Towns, and he was ailing, and all the platoon sergeants except Yeiser O'Guin. First Sergeant Long got back, and was now even more profane as he spat out orders of the day. I often wondered how the diminutive Long could be so raucous in front of a bunch of men and so insignificant in a one-on-one conversation. He could make a parade ground ring when he gave close order drill, but his knowledge in the field was limited.

The company got back to normal within a few days. Stories were told over and over about what had happened, how this one or that had fallen. Veterans can talk about these things among themselves, but not very well with others who haven't experienced combat. There were some vicious rumors, of course, like what supposedly happened to Lt. Aspinwall. Someone claimed some trigger-happy lout from the 2d Platoon killed him. At the time of his death the 2d was advancing along a parallel hedgerow. Vision was obstructed and minimal and some men were at the point where anything that moved was fair game. I doubted the story, attributing it to the rivalry between the platoons in everything we did.

They talked about the running feud between Lieutenant Karcy and Tech. Sergeant Breeding. They had never hit it off, not in training or in combat. Karcy was cultured and urbane and liked to let the good times roll. Breeding came from Bluefield, West Virginia, rustic, dedicated and a man who thought officers and men had no business fraternizing.

After Karcy was wounded and lay waiting for litter bearers to take him back, it was told that he said to Breeding, "Well, you son of a bitch, I hope you're happy. The platoon's yours." I doubted that story, too. While Breeding was a man of principle, he wasn't one who undercut another unless it meant someone's life or death.

And they talked about how Fred Grethel bought it. He used to clown around at Brock, doing pirouettes like you see in the movies when someone is shot. He died the same way, they said, on a misty morning when visibility was bad. His body was pulled through a tunnel under the hedge, a bullet through his heart.

The training schedule was extremely light for a week or so, and then division issued an order that everyone would be given a seven-day furlough. Before we left on furlough we were told that the decision had been finally made to give the glidermen some recognition of the hazards of their particular branch of the service. To begin with, we were given a metal glider badge to be worn over our breast pockets. The new badge was a pair of glider wings, similar to the paratrooper badge, with the front view of a CG-4A glider in the center. I'm sure every one of us who got the badge was honored to wear it because we had earned it the hard way. In my company a couple of slackers, really Section 8s, weren't given the badge. In other words, it was earned, not given to everyone. Another small change that meant a lot was the issuing of jump boots. Finally, in recognition of the hazards of going to battle in gliders, we received extra flight pay. It was a good move, as it raised morale and made the glidermen proud of their outfit.

After much discussion, a group of us in the 1st Platoon decided to spend our furlough in Edinburgh, Scotland, because of all good things we had heard about the place. O'Guin, Harrell, Bowers, Bates, Damato, Spector and I took off for London from where we could get the train to Edinburgh. London was in a dither because of Germany's new weapon, the V-1 rocket. They started coming over about June 13th, a few at first, then as many as 144 in a 24-hour period. They were miniature planes trailing orange exhausts and sounding like one-lung motors putting along. The motors would cut off and the planes would dive for the ground with a ton of TNT in their bodies. We saw several of the buzz bombs while in London and were glad to be out of the city.

We got to Edinburgh after an all night train ride and it was everything we could have hoped for. The people were friendly, the weather was warm, and there was plenty of food and drink. We even had bacon and eggs for breakfast. There was a lot to see. We stayed in a hotel on Princes Street in the shadow of Edinburgh castle and had the time of our lives, forgetting about family and Normandy and the loneliness of men away from home. The week went by like a blink of an eye.

More changes were in store when we got back. The replacements had moved in and now we were to have three rifle platoons instead of two. That meant reorganization. The 1st Platoon was led by 1st Lt. Robert Wagner, San Antonio, Texas; 2d Platoon by 2d Lt. Quentin Armstrong; and the 3d by 1st Lt. Howard Kohl. Frank Trudeau, who had distinguished himself in Normandy, was named platoon sergeant in 3d Platoon. Two new men, Staff Sergeant Gerald Rafferty, Easton, Pennsylvania, and Staff Sergeant Thomas Leamon, Fort Wayne, Indiana, led the 1st and 2d squads respectively and I was promoted to lead the 3d squad. Sergeant Andrew Mitchell, Rogers, Arkansas, led the mortar squad. I picked Jerry Hanss as my assistant. However, there was a problem with the ratings. Because of all the NCOs in hospital but still on our roster the company couldn't promote more NCOs than the table of organization called for. That meant many of us would be "acting" until the ratings came through.

We were issued new uniforms and equipment. Instead of twill fatigues and field jackets, we were given the new '43 pattern combat uniforms with baggy pockets, new style entrenching tools and gas masks, trench knives, helmet nets, Thompsons and combat boots that leaked like sieves.

We didn't hike as much as we had before Normandy, which suited me fine as I still had to wear a brace on my ankle. Rarely did we walk ten miles in a day, and often buses would pick us up at the training area and bring us back to Brock. We held a memorial service for the men killed in Normandy and most of us ended up misty eyed. Then another change was made which caused quite a stink. The NCOs were moved into a large room of their own. And, more importantly, a series of "alerts" began.

Because most of the replacements had had no airborne training, a practice alert was held so that they understood the procedure. It meant a tremendous amount of work to be done in a short period of time. First, the barracks would be isolated and a tight security cordon placed around the battalion area. Combat equipment had to be drawn from the supply room including Mae West lifejackets and live ammunition. Packs and bedrolls had to be made up and a duffel bag with a change of uniform and personal things left with the supply section for later delivery. When this was done, there was a trip to an airfield for briefings and glider loading. The practice alert went okay, but it was decided that the battalion should hike back from the airfield, about a ten-mile walk, and many of the replacements had trouble making it packing all their gear and ammunition.

The second alert was slated to be real, an operation termed *Transfigure*, a drop by the British 1st Airborne Division, the Polish Parachute Brigade and the 101st in an area roughly 25 miles south-west of Paris on August 19th to block the road networks while Patton attacked to the west. It was cancelled at the last moment because of the ground forces' rapid advance. The third alert on September 3d called *Linnet 1* was a drop to seize Tournai, Belgium, just across the border from Lille, France. It was cancelled for the same reason. Another alert, *Linnet 2* fell through before we even left the barracks, but the following one didn't.

Market Garden turned out to be one of the most controversial operations of World War II. It involved the newly created First Allied Airborne Army and the invasion of Holland to make an end run around the German right flank and into the Westphalia Plains where Allied armored power would have the advantage. It was a campaign to seize a road running from Eindhoven in the south to Arnhem in the north, a more than 65-mile corridor marked by many bridges over canals, rivers, and railroads. If it worked it meant bypassing the Siegfried Line. The British were to drop in the Arnhem area, the 82d around Grave, and the 101st at Eindhoven. The plan might have worked had the Germans not got a whiff of it and moved two SS Panzer divisions into the British zone. Equipped as lightly as airborne troops are, the British paras' mission quickly became impossible.

Security regulations went into effect and we moved to Aldermaston Airdrome on September 14th. We were quartered in a hangar, which had been converted into sleeping quarters by adding hundreds of double-decked bunks. There were the usual precombat jitters, especially among the veterans who knew what lay ahead. I was nearly killed, while sitting on my lower-deck bunk and cleaning a Thompson, by Ray Harris, a mortarman from the weapons platoon. He sat opposite me on a top bunk cleaning a carbine. Suddenly the carbine fired, the bullet missing my head by inches, then flying down between my spread legs, before plowing into the concrete floor and ricocheting through the roof. The first sergeant wanted to bring charges against him, but I declined. Later, that night, while leaving for the latrine, Harris tripped over a doorstep and broke his wrist.

I don't think any of the veterans were looking forward to the mission, not even Captain Towns who had received the Silver Star in Normandy. I know that I wasn't. My ankle still gave me trouble and I had to wrap it each day in a long elastic bandage to keep it from collapsing. And I wasn't confident of the new platoon leader, Lieutenant Howard Kohl.

While we sweated out the upcoming mission, we gorged on the chow—steak three times a day and all one could eat. Naturally, there were the briefings, morning and afternoon. The 401st was to land north of Eindhoven, surround a drop zone and hold it for men and supplies, which would come in later. At the same time, we would be in division reserve, to be used to support any unit that needed help.

The mission of the 101st was to capture and hold a 16-mile stretch of road behind German lines, from Eindhoven in the south to Uden in the north. This included rail and highway bridges over the Aa River and the Willems Vaart Canal near Veghel, highway bridges over the Dommel River at St. Oedenrode, over the Wilhelmina Canal at Son, and over the Dommel River at Eindhoven. The division was to hold these places while the British XXX Corps raced up from the south and on to Arnhem.

The operation was novel and risky, a corps advancing up a single, paved road, with two Germans divisions poised to attack its left flank. The only units preventing that from happening were the lightly-armed troops of the First Allied Airborne Army. To make matters worse, the terrain in that area was as flat as a pancake and laced with canals and rivers that formed natural barriers should armor be forced off the road. The tanks therefore had little room to maneuver should they run into a strong-point.

The first C-47s took off early on September 17th and several hours later they returned and we were rushed to the field. It was pitiful to see so many shot up so badly, holes torn out of wings and fuselage, fabric flapping, and ambulances screaming across the tarmac to retrieve casualties.

Fortunately, the 101st's serials didn't run into German fighters. Our fighter planes had driven them off. And our planes had knocked out many of the flak towers, which were part of the gamble of a daylight jump. However, because the C-47 pilots had been ordered to hold formation at all costs, many of the planes were badly damaged,

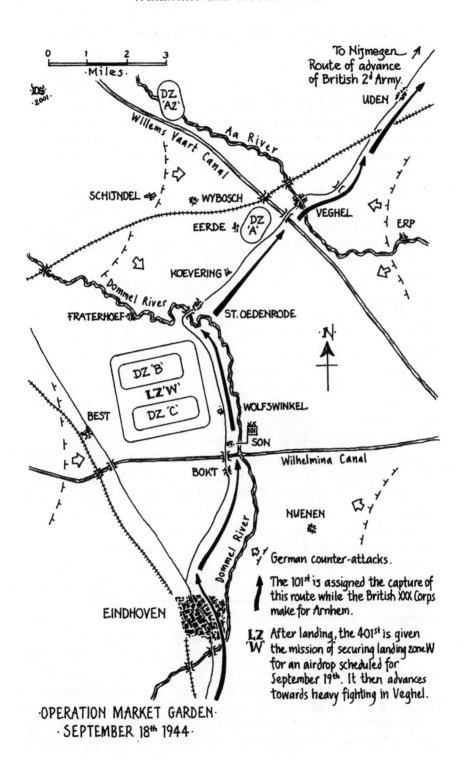

To Nijmegen
Route of advance
of British 2ᵈ Army.

·OPERATION MARKET GARDEN·
· SEPTEMBER 18ᵗʰ 1944·

German counter-attacks.

The 101ˢᵗ is assigned the capture of this route while the British XXX Corps make for Arnhem.

After landing, the 401ˢᵗ is given the mission of securing landing zone W for an airdrop scheduled for September 19ᵗʰ. It then advances towards heavy fighting in Veghel.

though only two of the 424 that took off failed to reach the drop zone (DZ).

The glider landings that took place an hour later weren't so successful. Of the 70 that took off, only 53 reached the landing zone. Some landed behind enemy lines, some in the Channel, and a few never got out of England. Nevertheless, the gliders brought in 252 officers and men, 32 jeeps and 13 trailers. It would take seven days before the entire division got into action, a handicap that affected the overall operation and did much to hurt our chances for success.

As I watched the ground crews retrieving the casualties from the planes, I had to marvel at the way they were so efficient yet compassionate. Some of the casualties had had only primary first aid, whatever the crews could render under the worst of conditions. Many were soaked with their own blood, some with limbs hanging on by a thread of skin or a tendon. And some were past all help, dead or dying.

My stomach turned over, the death scenes on the beach in Normandy and on into the interior flashing through my mind. As I walked back to the hangar, I wondered why this affected me so much. Like most people, I assume, such horror was foreign to my nature. My first brush with things of that kind happened when I was young. We lived in the suburbs near a railroad crossing. Sometimes, despite the lowered gates, cars would try to beat speeding trains. More often than not, the cars lost. There would be a terrific racket, heard blocks away, as trains going close to 90 miles per hour would plow into the cars. Sometimes, those cars would be torn to pieces. Another time I came by after a track worker had been hit by a train and on another occasion when a hobo had jumped in front of a speeding train. I was sickened by those sights, never forgetting them. I felt the same way when I saw those bodies being pulled from the planes.

We were roused before dawn on the 18th, rushed through breakfast and back to the hangar to don all the paraphernalia one needs to kill. I had discarded my MI for a BAR, hoping to add firepower to the squad but later I decided it was too heavy to carry and I had recently turned it in for a Thompson sub-machine gun.

We marched to the gliders and began loading. I had christened ours with white chalk in large letters the *Bronze Star Kid* for Frank Trudeau who would be going in with us. He had been decorated for heroism in Normandy. He wrote his wife's name under the release hook. Frank and I were good friends, having a common bond in our love of hunting and fishing. He was one of the few men in the company who had been in the peacetime Army, the same outfit in fact as Sergeant O'Guin.

We had our first accident while loading. I heard the sharp crack of a weapon and saw PFC Glen Hodge on the ground by the next glider. He had shot himself in the foot as he slipped his carbine into the canvas boot on his belt. I heard later he was court-martialed but believe it was accidental as he was a fine person who never showed any inclination of malingering.

After Hodge was taken away so his wound could be treated, we finished loading the gliders. The gliders were towed by long ropes hooked to the towplanes, and these ropes were coiled up on the tarmac like rolls of spaghetti so a lot of planes and gliders could occupy a minimum of space. As the tugs moved off the ropes uncoiled, snapping the gliders off with a mighty jerk, which is bone shaking. And so it was as we took off in a cloud of smoke from the tug's motors. We rolled down the runway, took off and rose to 1,000 feet or so where we circled until all the other gliders in our serial were airborne. We then headed for the rendezvous point near London on a bright, sunny day with the temperature close to 80. Through one of the small portholes, there were planes and gliders front and rear as far as I could see.

We reached the coast, flying at more than 100mph and prepared for the same hot reception the 501st, one of the parachute regiments in our division, had gotten the day before. The Channel was under us, glistening in the sun and nothing like D-Day when it seemed to be boiling. A glider broke loose up ahead, went down in a gentle glide then hit with a tremendous splash, it sank like a stone. There was a chain of naval rescue vessels under us. I hoped they were handy. Another glider had broken loose, a huge British Hamilcar, which carried a small tank; it didn't fare any better.

As we neared the coast, I could hear the dull rumble of gunfire. My stomach tensed. There would be Germans for the next 40 miles or so. A glider cut loose now would have little chance of reaching the landing zone. We had been in the air for more than three hours and some of the replacements were air sick, puking in their helmets. That odor and the stench from the plane's motors were sickening. I prayed for the LZ no matter what we would encounter there. In the air we were sitting ducks, like clay pigeons at a trap range.

As we continued on we hit a wall of flak, which sent deadly steel fragments hurtling through the formation. Fortunately, most exploded over us. I looked through a porthole and saw German soldiers running from homes and buildings with weapons in their hands. Looking back up at the formation I saw another glider break loose and drift downward. I found out later that Captain Towns was a passenger on that glider.

Then there was a loud crack beside my head. I flinched and looked at Frank McFadden, one of my scouts who was jammed against me. The bullet had torn through the fabric on the side of the glider, whistled between our heads and exited out the roof. It was close. We looked at each other and grinned weakly. Bullets were now ripping through the wings and through the glider's ailerons. The enemy fire also came through the glider's honeycombed wooden floorboard and glanced off the two cloverleaves of 81mm mortar ammunition that we were carrying tied down to the flooring. I'm sure everyone was worrying about our pilot. What if he were hit? PFC George Naegle, one of my riflemen who had flunked out of the air force, was acting as co-pilot, but he had no glider experience.

Off to the left was a large city, probably Eindhoven. Ahead were small fields, typical farms, flat and with many ditches and canals. Windmills and Germans in trucks and cars passed below us.

We were going about 90mph when the pilot reached up and banged the release knob, and soon we were making a long turn into a field crowded with gliders and equipment. Small arms fire rattled, mortar and artillery rounds sent up clouds of black smoke. We hit the ground with a crash, bounced a few times and streaked across the field with the brakes locked and tearing up turf. We stopped with a jerk.

"Out! Let's go!" Trudeau yelled as he kicked out a door. We needed no urging. The men on board hit the ground running, aware that other gliders were trying to find a landing place. Two gliders hit together head-on in the air and came down in a crash. Men were screaming in the ball of wreckage but that was for someone else to clean up. Overhead the air was filled with more planes and gliders. Men jumped, 'chutes marking their paths. Some hadn't fully opened when their owners hit the ground. Other men who had landed were running for the edges of the fields to get out of the paths of incoming gliders. Many lay wrecked, up on their noses or with wings drooping like broken kites.

We reached a ditch and followed it to a pine copse where the company assembled. Three gliders were missing out of the 14 carrying our company. Captain Towns' was one, Sergeant O'Guin's another and the third contained 1st Lt. Martinson. Since the CO and second-in-command were missing, 2d Lt. Armstrong, took over to lead the company to the battalion assembly area. We waited for orders. My first and last glider combat landing was over and I was glad of it. I had survived.

Lieutenant Armstrong got orders to move the company to the battalion assembly area. We found a track through a field with high grass on either side on the edge of the LZ and took off. More gliders were coming in, some landing like awkward albatrosses and we cringed as they buzzed our heads. The sky was blue and filled with fleecy clouds, the temperature near 80, and we were hot. We passed a German ambulance on the side of a trail and two young dead medics lying in the road by it. They seemed to be sleeping, sprawled spread-eagled in the track. Our fighter planes had killed them. We reached a hard-topped road and saw small groups of Dutch civilians in their native dress with wooden shoes. They all carried bits of orange cloth, the color of the Dutch royal family, the House of Orange, and waved and cheered. Some of our men gave them chocolate and cigarettes. All were deliriously happy.

We moved into an orchard and counted noses. Most had seen the missing gliders go down but knew nothing else about them. As we were about 40 miles deep in German territory, no one had much hope the missing glider loads would get back to us. We had already suffered some wounded, men hit by flak after crossing the coast. One was Ebon Angel who had been wounded in Normandy when he refused to dig his foxhole deeper. This time a bullet came through the floorboard of his glider, pierced the fleshy part of his leg and traveled on through his forearm. Two days in action, two purple hearts.

I checked my squad. Everyone seemed in good spirits and happy to have both feet on the ground. Most were worried about Lt. Armstrong leading the company because he hadn't been with us long and had never been in combat. Their anxiety turned out to be unfounded. Another worry was the enemy reaction to the landing. They were strangely quiet, just some sniping from the fringes of the LZ and an occasional mortar and artillery round.

We got orders to move. The enemy was reported to be moving across our front in an effort to cut off the 501st, which was fighting in Son. We returned the way we had come, past the wrecked ambulance and the dead medics. They were unrecognizable, mashed to bloody pulps by passing jeeps and trucks, which had come in by glider. My stomach turned over as I passed. Dutch civilians were slipping onto the LZ picking up parachutes to be made into clothing. They had a wide choice of colors: camouflage, used by the jumpers; red, signifying ammunition; blue for medical supplies; and white for air force crewmen who had bailed out.

Two glider pilots asked if they could join my squad, itching to get a crack at the Germans. Both had made landings in Normandy and Sicily but had not seen close combat. I agreed but warned them that it wouldn't be like they had pictured it.

A company was crossing a field to our left in a skirmish line while we approached a farm on our right. As the 1st Platoon got near the farmhouse, the harsh rip of a German machine gun sent everyone diving into the ditches. A hot firefight broke out. Suddenly I heard the loud shriek of a *Nebelwerfer* and I shouted to my men to get deeper into the ditch. "My God, what was that?" one of the glider pilots asked. "Something you don't want to tangle with. Screaming Meanies," I said, as the rockets shrieked over our heads and toward the field where Company A was advancing.

The six rockets burst with ear splitting cracks less than 100 yards away. Men scattered, someone screamed, the call for medics rang out. The pilot's face was grim as he watched the chaos. He was an old hand at war with two missions under his belt. But this was different to him. I felt the same way as I rode in the glider with the flak shooting up through our serial and bullets tearing through the aircraft.

A second barrage came screaming in and medics ran into the field while others tried to console the wounded. At least half a dozen men were scattered around. One was a sergeant I knew. He had been turned down for the air force because of a punctured eardrum. Now he lay in a pile of rags, killed by the rocket's explosion.

Trudeau came hustling down the ditch, saying 1st Platoon needed help and that I should take my squad for the job. We dumped our packs and ran bent double to the head of the column where 1st Platoon was in a firefight. Bullets chopped chunks of hedge away over our heads as we formed a firing line. Someone got close enough to the house to toss in some grenades. The windows bowed out and exploded. There were shouts in German from inside the house and the firing tapered off. A German cautiously stuck his head out the door and waved a white flag on the end of his rifle. We motioned them out. There were close to 30 in all; eight had been killed and more were wounded. The prisoners were sent back to the rear and we got back to the road again. When I looked for the glider pilots who had been so anxious to see combat, they were gone. I couldn't blame them, but this is what it's like in combat, small units engaged in problems of their own.

The move to help the 506th at Son was cancelled and we went back to the battalion assembly area to dig in for the night. Just after dark Captain Towns' glider load straggled in, and not long afterward the other missing two. They had all been led through the German lines by volunteers in the Dutch Resistance. The 1st Platoon lost one of its best, however. Pappy Bates had been badly injured when his glider had cracked up eight miles short of the LZ. Nevertheless, he hid his injury until reaching our assembly area where he collapsed. A broken rib had punctured his lung but wasn't found when he was taken to the aid station. He was taped up and sent back into the fight.

We had hardly settled in when we were alerted again, this time to head in the direction of Eindhoven where the 506th was in a fight for its life. A mile into the march, however, the battalion was halted, turned around and sent back to its former assembly area.

Although it had been hot all day, it was cold at night and our bedrolls were back in the glider. Most of us had used them for cushions during the flight, hoping that they might stop a bullet from hitting a most delicate part of our anatomy. I paired my men off and set up guard shifts so that a third would be awake at all times. There were no set times for meals. You simply opened a K ration whenever you were able, gulping down what you could. We had three portable stoves in the squad so whenever there was time someone would boil water for coffee. After digging our foxholes we settled in for the night, listening to the rumble of battles in Eindhoven, Best and Son.

The next morning the 401st was given the mission of securing Landing Zone W, between Son and St. Oedenrode where we had come in, to protect it for a large airdrop later that day. The battalion was formed in columns and surrounded the field. Company C held an arc on the northern side facing a large field and a copse of woodland from which German snipers had been firing from the day before. The LZ was a mess with gliders stacked randomly, the way they had come in. I wondered how the pilots could have gotten them in so precisely, almost touching one another in places. A few stood on their noses or were damaged in some other way, but generally most had come in without cracking up. There were bodies in some of those wrecked, pinned in by broken frames, and a jeep stuck out of one with men pinned under it. Several Dutchmen with horses and a wagon were crossing the field with some wooden coffins. I presumed they were for civilians who had been killed.

We had been warned that there was a danger of attack by German tanks, so our men dug with gusto. Fortunately the ground was soft and some dug so deeply that they had to install fire steps to see over the top. After seeing that everyone was properly dug in, I told the men to eat while I made a reconnaissance to our front because I had seen something suspicious in the tall grass beside the parachute bundles. I approached cautiously then saw the bodies of two paratroopers beside a light machine gun. One was a lieutenant crouched behind the gun, hands on the traversing handle. He had a bullet wound right in the middle of his forehead. The other man, a sergeant, lay with hands grasping the belt of bullets. Both were young; both looked as if they had died instantly. Later I had the gun brought in to use on our defense line.

It was noon on the 19th before the airdrop began, masses of planes and gliders bringing in the 1st and 2d Battalions of the 327th and additional supplies. They had gotten a hot reception at the coast and a hotter one as they approached the LZ when the woods to our front that had been strangely quiet suddenly came to life. Small arms and 20mm cannon began to bark, flak guns off to the right shot bursting shells right through the serials. I watched in awe, admiring the pilots of those C-47s who held their course despite the wall of flak coming at them. Some went down trailing flame and smoke. Men jumped, their parachutes marking their downward trip. Again, some were streamers, not fully opened before the men below them hit the ground.

More than 2,500 men, 140 jeeps, 100 trailers and two bulldozers were brought in on D+1. Of the 450 gliders that left England, 428 made it to LZ W. On D+2 385 gliders were scheduled to take off but due to dense fog and bad weather some did not do so. Only 209 made the LZ; 26 were missing in action, 16 crash-landed in German territory, 82 returned to England and 31 landed in friendly territory. Over 1,300 men got to the LZ but of the 136 jeeps expected only 79 made it. Of the 68 artillery pieces sent, only 40 came in. None of the 105mm cannon of the 907th Glider Field Artillery (GFA) got to the LZ on D+2.

Hunched down in our foxholes as the incoming gliders barely missed us on numerous occasions, we watched fascinated at the human drama going on before our eyes. One glider drove us deep into our holes, its wheels actually knocking down our parapets. It crash-landed almost on top of Lt. Kohl and Sergeant Trudeau, a tangled wreckage of steel frame and fabric with men trapped inside. Some of us rushed to help, a medic from a recently arrived glider among us. We pulled several badly injured men from the wreck.

The medic said, "This man's leg is broken badly. We need splints."

Lt. Kohl, who had been helping, asked, "Where do we find them?"

The medic stood up and surveyed some of the gliders. He pointed to one in the field in front of our defense line and said, "There."

I looked where he was pointing, some 200 yards in front of my foxhole. For some stupid reason, I said, "I'll go."

I dropped my weapon and gun belt and took off across the field expecting any moment for the Germans to fire. They didn't. I got to the glider and climbed in the door. The medic was right, there was a trailer inside. I ripped at the canvas cover in order to get at the contents of the trailer. I heard the scream of an incoming shell and an explosive crunch 50 yards away. I had been seen. I saw wire frames and pulled them out as another shell came screaming in. I dove in the dirt as it exploded, then took off as if the devil was at my heels. I got to the line of foxholes as another one hit near the glider. Breathless, I dropped the frames beside the medic. He looked at them and frowned.

"You brought the wrong ones," he said. "These are for arms."

I could have killed the bastard. "Why the hell didn't you say there were two kinds?' I asked angrily.

Nevertheless, I tried once again, taking off as fast as I could run and getting about halfway when another shell came in. The Germans must have been rotten shots because I was able to reach the glider and pull away a bunch of supplies before another shell hit. It was close, making the fabric on the glider reverberate because of the concussion. But I got an armful of bigger splints, jumped through the door and nearly made it back to the foxholes again before the next shell came in. I dumped the splints beside the medic and went back to my hole to recover, completely winded.

The gliders continued landing all through the afternoon. The Germans didn't put up much opposition, a few mortar and artillery shells, and later in the day, a 20mm cannon that they fired from deep in the woods. Recovery teams from our battalion were going through the gliders removing supplies and injured men. My squad helped and came across newly issued sleeping bags brought in by the 327th. We turned in everything else we salvaged that day, but we hung on to the sleeping bags.

There were a few gliders out in the field where the one with the medical supplies had landed. Trudeau came to me and said we should check them out. I thought he was crazy and told him so. But he was like that, fearless to the point of being reckless.

"You're not going to let a few goddamn shells bother you, are you?" he asked contemptuously.

"Isn't that Bronze Star enough, Frank? You bucking for a Silver?" I said. But I went anyway. Not to do so would have been a sign of trepidation, which he abhorred.

He dashed across the field to a glider without drawing any enemy fire and I was right on his heels. We rooted through the glider and a trailer hoping to find some Thompsons or perhaps a handgun a pilot might have left behind. We came away empty handed in that regard, just salvaging a couple of boxes of K rations. Trudeau told me to take off first and I did. Halfway across the field I heard the angry roar of a fighter plane engine, then the rattle of machine-gun fire. I dove for the ground as puffs of dirt erupted ahead of me. The plane flashed by—an Me109. I took off again just as another plane roared in. I hit the ground once more. The second plane was a British Hawker Typhoon, guns belching as it hung on the German's tail. Its bullets were the ones plowing into the ground near me.

The 401st spent the rest of the day recovering supplies then settled in for the night with half the men on guard at all times. At dawn a heavy mist clung to the ground, so dense it was impossible to see more than 50 feet away. I checked my squad to see that everyone had water and rations. My BAR post was in the center with John Gardner, a husky Pennsylvania mountaineer, as the gunner. He was a replacement, as was his loader, Gerald Helton, a slim, fair Tennessee boy who was the perfect adjunct because he was quiet while Gardner was talkative. Both men were hunkered down in the U-shaped pit, eyes glued to the mist.

"What's up?" I asked softly.

"He claims he heard Krauts talking. I think he's nuts," Helton quietly replied.

I squeezed in beside the men and listened. It was deadly quiet. I searched the fog, thought I saw something and grabbed the arms of the other two. I pointed. Out there we could just discern flat-topped helmets of moving men. "Let them have it," I said, and we opened fire. Gardner got off five clips, Helton a couple with his M1 and I a clip from my Thompson. I ordered them to cease-fire and waited. We woke up the whole company front. Lt. Kohl and Sergeant Trudeau came running over, and Captain Towns was on the phone. It took more than an hour for the mist to lift but when it did we saw the sprawled bodies of three Germans, part of a patrol, which got lost in the fog.

A second airdrop came that day, D+3, preceded by tow planes and gliders, and followed by flights of B-24 Liberator bombers carrying supplies. Our aircraft were protected by flights of P-47s and P-51s. The Germans threw up a curtain of flak as they neared the field. Tragically, a Messerschmitt 109 slipped through the screen and shot down three C-47s. It was a terrible sight to see them go down in flames, men jumping but at too low an altitude for their 'chutes to open fully. The B-24s had better luck but over half their loads dropped between the Germans and us and we spent several days in hair-raising patrols to recover some of the supplies. The B-24s dropped a lot of their stuff without parachutes. A box of K rations nearly beaned me, crashing on the edge of my hole. Even though it scared the hell out of me, it was a blessing. At least we had rations for a day or so. A lot of men away from the LZ weren't so lucky. They were fortunate to get one ration a day and had very little water.

My squad recovered a lot of supplies and even a couple of .30-caliber machine guns with ammo and a .50-caliber. Until they could be taken away, we used them to augment our own firepower. We scoured the immediate area behind us, places too hilly for glider landings, and found several bodies or paratroopers who had been killed on D-Day. We found rows of musette bags where the paratroopers had left them to attack Son, and we saw parts of bloody uniforms of men who had been wounded.

All the while the Germans were very quiet, only sending over the occasional mortar shell. So Captain Towns decided to test the water and sent out a patrol from the 1st Platoon led by Staff Sergeant Cecil Caraker, a lanky veteran from the early days of the battalion. He had worked in construction before the war, drifting from state to state to find work. But he knew what he was doing in the Army. I saw the patrol heading for the woods through the high grass and abandoned gliders. Suddenly, all hell broke loose. The Germans cut loose with everything they had and Caraker was lucky to get his patrol out before they were all killed. They came back through my position grim-faced but excited.

As Boarpig Fortuna passed me, he grinned and said, "Ain't this a helluva way to make a living?"

The Germans shelled my platoon area pretty heavily at dusk, setting the high grass around our positions on fire. It burned most of the night, spreading to some of the gliders to our rear. One contained cases of machine-gun ammunition, which began to go off as the fire reached them. The noise kept us awake all night. In the morning we put most of the fire out, but a pall of smoke hung over the area for days.

While we were collecting supplies and guarding the LZ the rest of the division was carrying out the individual unit missions with great success. The 506th had taken Eindhoven on the 18th, the 502d controlled Best and the 501st was in Veghel. Control of these important links was only temporary to be sure, as strong German counterattacks were in the making. But the road was open briefly so that the British ground troops could move on to Arnhem.

Farther north in the 82d's area, the same situation existed with all three of their parachute regiments in control of key points. However, because of bad flying weather, their 325th Glider Infantry Regiment was still in England, and would be for several more days. They were badly missed. The British at Arnhem were in a life or death fight because of the two SS Panzer divisions, which had moved into their sector shortly before D-Day. To make matters worse, the British radios were unable to operate properly in the hilly wooded country and one unit did not know what the other's situation was. One thing was quickly apparent: if help did not arrive quickly, the British 1st Airborne Division would be destroyed.

Quartermaster troops took over retrieving supplies from the LZ, so we had little to do except to see that the Krauts didn't slip in at night and help themselves. On their part they were very restrained and a strange stillness settled over our sector. The interlude was too good to be true.

We had just finished a breakfast of K rations when we heard a large truck rumble up to the platoon command post (CP). A young good-looking black driver got out and walked over to Lt. Kohl. I was at the CP at the time receiving instructions.

"They sent me back to pickup them bundles, suh," he said, pointing to some of those dropped by the B-24s the day before which lay scattered in the field between our main line of resistance and the woods.

Lt. Kohl looked at him with a frown. "You can't go out there, corporal. The Germans are in that wood," Lt. Kohl said. He waved at the field of gliders behind us. "Better concentrate on those. It'll be a lot safer."

"I got orders, suh. Colonel said he don't want no excuses. 'Bring them goddamn bundles back or it's your ass,' he said."

Lieutenant Kohl smiled. He smiled a lot, had a friendly face, and was reasonable with everyone. "Look corporal. Your colonel doesn't know what the situation is up here. If you want you can use my phone to tell him it can't be done right now."

"You don't know my colonel, suh. If you don't mind, I gotta do what I gotta do, suh."

In the end, Kohl saw warning was useless and told the man where he could take his truck through our lines. The driver drove slowly out into the field and stopped some hundred or so yards away. He and a helper began collecting bundles and throwing them into the back of the truck. We watched with anticipation. Suddenly an MG42 let loose a burst of fire, spraying the truck with bullets. The driver dropped like a stone, but the helper took off for our line like a scared rabbit. He dropped near my foxhole, eyes wide and breathless. Finally he said, "He's dead, man. Dead. Shot right through the head."

We waited for the firing to stop, then sent a couple of volunteers out. They brought the driver back, more scared than hurt, but he did have a big lump on his forehead. A bullet had glanced off it, breaking the skin but doing no serious damage.

The Allies conducted the largest daylight air raid of the war on September 22d. Many of the squadrons of planes crossed high in the air directly over our LZ. For over three hours there was a seemingly endless flight of B-17s headed for the heart of Germany. It gave everyone a sense of euphoria to see how powerful our air force was, but I couldn't help but feel for the men in the planes. In a short time they would be in a maelstrom of anti-aircraft guns and German fighters. The Eighth Air Force was suffering tremendous losses in raids and any feelings of animosity we ground troops had toward them vanished when we understood their situation.

We kept to our foxholes as much as possible because we did not want to draw any unnecessary mortar and artillery fire from our German counterparts. However, because the K rations we had been living on for four days didn't go very far, I took Joe Kloczkowski of Chicago and Larry Reid, Burlington, Wyoming, both good men, and tried to find some ten-in-one rations among the abandoned gliders. We searched in vain. Most everything eatable had already been cleaned up. We got back to our position in time to learn that all platoon leaders had been called to the company CP. Something was up.

Lt. Kohl returned, his normally happy face grim. The company was going into an attack just after dark, making an enveloping movement against the enemy in the woods. The 3d Platoon would lead the attack with my squad at the point. It was an honor I didn't relish because the whole thing had been done hurriedly with little planning and anything can happen at night in the way of one squad shooting into another. We pulled out of our positions just after dark, formed in a company column and hiked several miles to the line of departure. The attack was cancelled at the last minute and we went back to our positions, everyone breathing a sigh of relief.

Left: Robert Bowen enjoys a break during training at Fort Gordon, Georgia, in spring 1943.

Below: The prelude to Europe: Robert Bowen (left) photographed with Walt Halsey while the 104th Infantry Regiment trained at Fort Gordon in 1943. Like Bowen, Halsey was among those selected to join 101st Airborne Division.

Left and below: Bowen photographed during training at Fort Bragg, North Carolina, "the home of the 101st," in June 1943.

Above: Bowen pictured with his wife Christine, who kept all of his letters from Europe, and helped him piece together his experiences during the post-war years.

Top left: Bowen (left) with fellow members of Company C, 401st, William Preslar (right) and Jerry Hanss (center), while stationed at Brock Barracks.

Left: Bowen (left) and Preslar (center) pose with SSgt. Verland Harrell, April 1944.

Above: Company C of the 401st Glider Infantry Regiment during a drill at Brock Barracks, Reading, in March 1944. The 401st was stationed at Brock both immediately before and after its part in the D-Day invasion.

Above: The American Red Cross Service Club at Sens, France.

Left and below left: Red Cross girls assigned to the 401st during the Regiment's stay in Normandy. (Carmen Gisi)

Above right: Men of the 1st Platoon of Company C traveled to Edinburgh for their post-D-Day furlough in July 1944. Forrest "Pappy" Bates, looking towards camera, is pictured here in front of Edinburgh Castle; Pappy died of wounds received during the Holland operation.

Right: The 3d Platoon of Company C pictured at Zetten, near Arnhem, in October 1944. The men of 2d Squad line up for a photograph: (L–R, top row) Pvt. James Shoemaker, Sgt. George Naegle, SSgt. Gerald Rafferty, PFC Jack Sloan; (bottom row) PFC Ray Vigus, SSgt. Thomas Leamon.

Right: Division artillery commander, Brigadier General Anthony McAuliffe, briefs troop carrier crewmen prior to the Holland operation. McAuliffe would later command the division during its epic defense of Bastogne. (US Army)

Below: Members of the divisional headquarters company wait beside their glider for the start of the airborne assault into Holland. The CG-4A was constructed of painted canvas secured over a frame. (US Army)

Above: Men of Company C pose at the Mortar Squad and 3d Platoon
Headquarters, along the West Rhine in October 1944.
(L–R, top row) PFC James F. Liming, PFC Virgil L. Dousette,
PFC William W. Phillips; (bottom row) Pvt. Norman Labbe
(the radioman of the platoon), PFC Howard Thornton
and TSgt. Robert Bowen.

Above left: Men of 3d Platoon, Company C, play cards at camp
while stationed in Zetten. (L–R) PFC Morris "Pop" Zion, PFC Frank
McFadden, PFC George Damato (killed in action) and Jack Sloan.
The famous "Screaming Eagle" patch of the 101st is clearly visible on
Sloan's left shoulder.

Left: Camp facilities at Zetten. Sgt. Willis E. Adams and
Sgt. Thomas Leamon are pictured; Adams was later killed in action.

Above: (L–R, top row) PFC Frank McFadden, PFC John Gardner, Pvt. Gerald Helton; (middle) PFC Lawrence Reid; (bottom row) Sgt. Joseph "Chicago" Kloczkowski, Sgt. Jerry Hanss and PFC Harold Zimburg during a short stay in Zetten, November 1944.

Above left: Members of Company C enjoy a brief respite from "the Island." (L–R) PFC Ray Vigus, PFC William Phillips, Pvt Johnnie Diggs, Pvt. Gerald Helton and Sgt. Joseph Kloczkowski. Kloczkowski was later taken prisoner with Bowen and other members of Company C in December 1944.

Left: TSgt. Robert Bowen (seated center, with pipe) with fellow members of 3d Platoon at Zetten. Bowen had, at this stage, become leader of the platoon. During its time on "the Island" the company would return to Zetten for short breaks from the front lines.

Left: Sgt. Jack Emler (left) died from wounds received during the Battle of the Bulge.

Right: During the fighting around Nijmegen, the ambulances of the 326th Airborne Medical Company were damaged by one of the few Luftwaffe attacks the Germans were able to launch. (US Army)

Left: Two victims of "friendly fire": PFC John Meadows (left) was killed in action and TSgt. Yeiser O'Guin lost a right leg when the company's positions were mistakenly strafed by an American fighter plane.

Troopers of the 101st move up to the line outside Bastogne, Belgium, in December 1944. (US Army)

CHAPTER 10

The Fight for Veghel

The enemy had the British trapped in Arnhem on the north side of the Rhine. If they were to be saved it had to be by troops using the road between Eindhoven and Arnhem. The Germans knew this as well as the Allies and took measures to prevent it by mounting strong counterattacks all along the corridor. In the 101st's sector, the attacks hit Veghel on D+5, cutting the road and stopping the flow of troops trying to reach Arnhem. The Division took steps to counter the enemy drive by moving the 506th to the western sector of the defense line, the 502d to the southern sector, the 501st to the east and the 327th to the north.

Acting as the 3d Battalion of the 327th, we were ordered to Veghel immediately. We packed hurriedly, discarding everything not essential, like the reserve parachutes we had picked up as souvenirs and even our packs. Instead we made blanket rolls from our new sleeping bags. I had picked up a musette bag and packed all my personal articles in it. We discarded our gas masks, using the case to carry additional rations. On the morning of September 22d we pulled out to meet the trucks at a rendezvous miles to the north. The Germans in the woods did not attempt to hinder our withdrawal, or perhaps they had pulled out too. The hike was at a fast pace, and anything we had second thoughts about getting rid of was soon dumped by the wayside. On the way, PFC Frank Plasec, a radioman in company headquarters, saw a briefcase beside the road and picked it up. It was full of German occupation guilders. He gave away about $1,500 worth before he learned the money was legal tender.

The trucks were parked in a grove of trees. We climbed aboard and were off, racing for Veghel. It was a race against time, so the trucks went as fast as feasible. All along the road was the debris from battles. Wrecked British and German tanks, trucks, jeeps, and destroyed buildings filled the ditches on either side of the road. There were white crosses in the fields just off the road where the British had buried their dead where they had fallen. There were British infantry in some of the ditches, rifles pointed at woodland beside the road from which the enemy fired at the convoy. There was a great line of stalled traffic, waiting for the way to be cleared. As we neared Veghel, the sound of a major battle greeted us.

We rushed into town among screaming shell bursts which rocked the ground under us, unloading and taking cover on a street of row houses, in doorways or alleys. There were British troops there, too, from the Green Howards regiment, who said the Germans had already gotten into one edge of the town. The artillery fire was deafening, as bad or worse than in Normandy. Several houses in the town were aflame and a great pall of smoke was gathering above. The shells were falling fast and close, no more than 100 yards away. Startled, we huddled against the buildings, waiting for a shell to drop in our midst. It was one of the most terrifying moments of my life.

We waited nearly an hour as the shells tore the town apart. Finally Lt. Kohl collected the squad leaders in an alley and told us we were making an attack. His information was sketchy at best. Company C would lead off, 2d Platoon at the point, followed by 3d and 1st Platoons. Company B would be on our left with A in reserve. The plan was to hit the left flank of a German battalion advancing on Veghel. We got through the town somehow, without taking any casualties, even though the enemy barrage was continuous. With Lieutenant Armstrong in the lead we filtered into a patchwork of green fields bordered by ditches, shrubs and hedges. Not too far from the town the lieutenant bumped head on into the Germans and a fierce firefight broke out. Soon mortars began pounding our area and then the unmistakable bark of tank guns. We waited impatiently, ready to move up, then got the word. Trudeau told me to move my squad up and support 2d Platoon. We stuck to the ditches because machine-gun fire was sweeping the open fields.

Stragglers began filtering back. Frankie Lombardino, a veteran of Normandy, was grim-faced and shaking. "They're being slaughtered," he managed to gasp. "Lt. Armstrong's down and so are a lot of others." He started to leave and I pushed him into a ditch, not wishing to see him disgraced or court-martialed.

I led my squad into the oncoming mortar fire. As we advanced I came across the bodies of PFC James O'Melia and PFC Chester Mazur. O'Melia's head had been blown off, and Mazur had lost both legs near the hips.

We set up a firing line as 2d Platoon began to withdraw through us. There were cries for medics and we saw why. Some men were bringing Lt. Armstrong out on a shutter, blood-spattered and white-faced. PFC Peter Della Russo, an old friend from the casual company, was brought out too. Short, chunky and easy-going, he had come from the 26th Division with me. S/Sgt. Oakley Knapp, a machine gunner, was being helped, his head swathed in bloody compresses. T/Sgt. Larry Donoho was one of the last, telling me all his men had been accounted for one way or the other. Shortly afterward, I got orders to conduct a fighting withdrawal and we went through it just the way we had in training with half the squad covering the other from field to field. Through a screen of brush I saw British troops moving forward on our right. A mortar shell dropped right in one of their jeeps, turning it into a ball of twisted, bloody metal.

For some reason known only to the staff, Colonel Allen was told to break off the attack and withdraw to a railroad station on the edge of town. We had hardly settled when we were ordered to move again and become part of a perimeter defense around Veghel. The 3d Platoon dug in along a high ditch overlooking a field of grazing cattle. Darkness was coming fast by the time we had our defenses prepared and with it came one of the worst artillery barrages I have ever been in. Fortunately for us, most of the shells overshot our foxholes and hit the town, but it continued for more than an hour, lifted for a short time and started up again. It was overpowering, horrific.

I crouched in the foxhole watching the German shellfire tear Veghel to pieces, fascinated in a morbid way by the brilliant shell bursts, great palls of smoke, and the raging fires as houses burned. There were people in there, Dutch civilians, American and British troops, paying the price for liberation. I thought about our price so far, the deaths of O'Melia and Mazur, both young and eager, men with whom I had shared guard details at Brock but whom I never really knew too well as they were replacements. O'Melia had been reading his Catholic prayer book minutes before he had been blown apart. It made me wonder. Was it a failed answer to his prayers or a belief in nonsense? I couldn't get it out of my mind as I watched the city burning.

I was called to the CP to pick up rations and took PFC Frank McFadden with me. He was from New Jersey, a tall dark-haired, good-looking fellow around 20 who had just gotten a "Dear John" letter from his wife. He had been a good athlete in high school, a promising baseball prospect, and had turned down sergeant's stripes during the Normandy campaign because he didn't want the responsibility. We picked up a large wooden case of British rations, and, wondering, took it back to the squad area. When we pried open the lid, we nearly flipped. It was the same sort of slop that we had gotten on *Strathnaver*, kidney stew, oxtail soup, greasy pork, beans, hard tack, tea and plum pudding, great for British tastes but disgusting for Americans. Worst of all, it came in all sizes of cans, ideal to be cooked as the British did in mess sections, but terrible for us with our men spread along a line of foxholes with no means of heating it up. Nevertheless, I passed it out. Hanss and I opened a can of kidney stew with a thick layer of grease over it. We threw it away and ate the crackers and hard candy. Gardner saved the night for us because he slipped out into a field of cattle grazing nearby and brought back canteens full of fresh milk.

I had to leave the squad under Hanss' care because I was to spend the night at the platoon CP. There weren't enough men to pull guard duty and answer the 300-radio set. The CP was in a deep swale and, because none of the men had entrenching tools—they had been lost during the attack—no one had been able to dig foxholes. It began to rain, slowly at first, then a constant downpour, and by dawn everyone was cold and soaked to the skin. The only action during the night came when a machine gunner in a nearby pit dropped his carbine and shot himself in the leg.

The Germans were attacking all sectors of our defense line, probing for a weak spot. They had hit the 506th particularly hard, causing many casualties, so we were moved the next morning to take over part of the 506th's sector. I remember a great long ditch where the main line of resistance had been dug. The 506th's foxholes were wet and muddy from the rain.

Lt. Kohl called the squad leaders together and said the Germans out front were "eager beavers" with a reputation for active night combat patrols. For this reason, he was setting up an outpost line of resistance and my squad was chosen to man it. I didn't like it but someone would have to do it. It meant breaking the squad into three-man groups, moving out front 100 yards or so and digging well-camouflaged pits. It also meant that there could be no movement during daylight hours, not even for rations or water. We spent three days like that, every minute expecting the enemy to attack, but we were lucky; they had been badly mauled by the 506th and decided to pick on some other sector. I could see how bad it had been by the shell-torn ground and field gray and olive drab bodies scattered along the edges of the field.

We were pulled out on the 26th and moved to an empty field in

Veghel. Our trucks had brought our bedrolls, which had been dropped the day of the attack, so we were able to set up pup tents. After digging slit trenches and a latrine, we were able to wash and shave for the first time in a week and for the next three days got hot meals for the first time in a while also. Even though the meals were British rations, they weren't so bad when cooked properly.

As we enjoyed our respite we saw a British convoy passing. The trucks contained survivors from Arnhem, a few thousand men of the original 10,000 British and Poles who had gone in by glider and parachute. They were exhausted, looking dirty, unshaven and decked with bloody bandages. The survivors had been ferried across the Rhine by British and Canadian engineers. They were lucky to escape because, when dawn came, the Germans had stopped the evacuation with murderous artillery fire. We waved and cheered them as they passed, and, proudly, they waved back and shouted words of encouragement. The battle was over for them. For us the worst was yet to come.

The last glider flights had come in on D+6, four days later than planned. We had seen them come in with all the trauma of previous flights, the heavy flak, C-47s being shot down. The Troop Carrier Command did a fabulous job in Holland at a great sacrifice in men and planes. Whatever reservation we might have had before about the air force went by the wayside after Holland. The serials brought in the 907th GFA, guns which we sorely missed the first week of the campaign. At the same time our seaborne element joined us, chiefly motor vehicles but also some men who had been left at Brock for one reason or another. Our 1st Sergeant, who had been left behind because of illness, did not come.

The battle for Veghel continued on D+8, +9 and +10 with the Germans sending a crack force of paratroopers to cut the road. All these troops had seen service in Russia. This force cut the road at Koevering, about three miles south of Veghel, then consolidated its positions with tanks and self-propelled guns. While the 501st, 502d, and 327th consolidated their positions in a perimeter defense line, the 506th plus some British armor and troops were left to remove the roadblock.

We moved out at midnight in a drizzling rain, across a deep canal and east where the 401st was to take a stand against Germans reported moving on Veghel. While the rest of Company C dug in along ditches and small canals, Lt. Kohl gave me the job of patrolling a large area to our front, mostly woodland where the 506th had fought a bitter battle just days before. My men complained about always getting "the shitty end of the stick," but I explained to them that the other two squad leaders were new at the game and we would have to bear the brunt until they had more experience.

I selected a deserted farmhouse for my CP and had my men dig positions in the rear by a cattle pen. However, during daylight hours I wanted them in the house, because I didn't want them to be spotted by the enemy. I had been given a map of the area with the patrol route and places where the enemy had been seen by the last squad which occupied the position. I picked four men at dawn, Gardner, Helton, Vigus and Reid, and we took off carrying the minimum of equipment.

We approached the woods cautiously because the enemy could still have been there. There were, but all of them were dead. Great gaps had been blasted in the trees by artillery fire, and bodies of Germans were sprawled as if tossed by a giant hand. We saw a heavy mortar position that had taken a direct hit, the mortar and crew blown to pieces. Dead horses still in their traces, wagons and destroyed equipment also greeted us. It was a sight as bad as the one that I had seen in the road cut in Normandy. There were also traces of American casualties, abandoned gear, bloody uniform parts and broken weapons. We threaded our way through the wreckage, my stomach nearly retching from what I was seeing. I picked up an Iron Cross from a dead German and wondered how the young man had gotten it. We passed through this charnel house and out into the fields, glad to be rid of it. Fifty minutes later we were back.

We mounted these patrols for three days, thankfully not running into anything more than the disappearing form of a German outpost. The enemy did make a probing attack on the 27th, bumping into Company A, but were driven off by artillery fire from the 907th.

We went back to Veghel to our previous positions where we pitched tents and got hot Limey meals once more. We also got our first baths since coming to Holland. We had to march over two miles to an old laundry in a steady rain. We stripped down, soaped up and tested the water. It was scalding hot, too hot even to think about getting under, so we splashed the soap off, donned our wet uniforms and hiked back to the bivouac area.

We were called to the company CP the next day, all the NCOs, and told there had been a reorganization because of 1st Sergeant Long's absence. Tech. Sergeant Claude Breeding, the weapons platoon sergeant, was to be top kick until Long returned. We could have cheered, because Breeding was one of those rare Army men who knew what he was doing. In combat in Normandy, his machine guns were always where they were needed, his mortars in position to support any attack or defense. Robust and taciturn, he commanded the respect of every man in the company. Staff Sergeant Irving Turvey was to take over the weapons platoon. Tall, dark, thin and wiry, he was an enigma in the company. Later I learned he had been in prison when the war broke out, was released to enlist, and found a home in the Army. The government got a bargain and he found his niche. When he returned home after the war, he got into his old habits, winding up in prison again. Released because of Colonel Allen's intervention, he continued his illegal activities and was sent back to prison, where he died of tuberculosis.

We went back to the front again the next day, setting up a roadblock on an auxiliary road. My squad dug positions on either side of the road overlooking a large open field. About 800 yards away where the road made a bend was a large farmhouse with the usual outbuildings. We were told the enemy occupied it. My line of foxholes was on the edge of a deep ditch, so we could move around without being seen easily. The platoon CP was right behind us in a barn, the 1st squad on the outpost line and the 2d in reserve behind the CP. Our view of the road was somewhat limited because of deep ditches filled with brush which paralleled it, so I put two men on duty at all times to watch the road. The 2d squad sent two men up to alternate with mine.

All during the day I could see Germans around the farm and reported it to Lt. Kohl, requesting artillery fire. He got back to me after checking with the company CP and said none was available, just to keep a check on the enemy in case they tried to move up the road. I passed on these orders to the guards at the road. The day passed uneventfully although I thought about requesting some mortar fire on the house. I changed my mind when I saw Dutch children around the place. It was quiet during the night with a heavy mist over the ground at dawn.

We were busy cooking rations over Coleman stoves shortly after daybreak, concealed in the ditch behind our foxholes, when someone let out a shout "Germans!" We dropped everything, grabbing for weapons and facing the road. Three German paratroopers were just yards away, pedaling toward us on bicycles. They heard the yell, turned, and tried pedaling away. Someone opened fire, then another. One of the Germans tumbled over, the other two leaping from their bikes into the heavy underbrush. I called to Hanss and Reid to follow me and we took off down a lane to the right, which led to another farmhouse, thinking to head the Germans off. But they had disappeared in a field of kohlrabi so dense with growth that it was impossible to find them. We went back to the road and found four men around the man who had been left behind. He was a young blond lieutenant. A bullet had hit the back of his head and come out the cleft of his chin, killing him instantly. PFC Arvin White got the credit for killing him and was busy looting the body when Trudeau came up. Trudeau got a Luger and a Colt .45 automatic pistol; White got the man's wristwatch and a smaller Walther pistol. The German had been doing some looting himself—an American gas mask case filled with toilet articles was slung over his shoulder.

After storing away his treasures, Trudeau raised hell with the men on guard, White, George Lolley and Dudley Diggs, telling them any more carelessness on their part could mean a court martial. Those Germans should have been spotted sooner regardless of the mist. Men could have died because of the incompetence of our guards.

That night it was dark and moonless with a heavy mist. Even though we kept a third of our men on guard, somehow a German patrol slipped by them. We never knew it until the next morning when Trudeau told me the CP had had some night visitors. PFC Stanley Clark, the platoon medic who was on guard, heard the noise of hob-nail boots on the brick pavement outside the barn, then men speaking in German. He quietly awoke the others, Lt. Kohl, Trudeau, and PFC Norman Labbe, the radioman. There was little they could do but wait, because a grenade thrown into the barn would have set it on fire. The Germans checked the inside of the barn using flashlights, missing the loft, then left to check the nearby house before they moved away. Trudeau wasn't upset with our sentries in this instance because he knew they were alert. The company had been assigned a large area with its platoons and squads holding isolated positions with great gaps between units. It was easy to slip through the porous network.

Trudeau and I checked the other squads. It was still very hazy with poor visibility. We stopped to talk to Staff Sergeant Thomas Leamon to see if he had heard anything during the night. While we talked the haze lifted and we were shocked to see a group of Germans approaching from the distant farmhouse. There were about 25 walking in a column of twos with rifles slung. We couldn't believe our eyes. We dashed away to warn the other squads and a 30-caliber machine gun team attached to us. We waited breathlessly as the unsuspecting enemy got closer. When they were about 200 yards away, we opened fire, bowling them over like ten pins. When the firing ceased, 18 bodies lay in the field. We had seen some making for a nearby ditch, so they must have escaped. Pretty soon some German medical corpsmen carrying Red Cross flags cautiously approached. We held our fire while they gathered up eight wounded and helped them from the field. Minutes after they left mortar shells began dropping on our positions. We were well dug in and it would have taken a direct hit to harm anyone, so the only casualty was Leamon's rifle and pack which were torn apart by a near miss.

Dutch civilians came up the road later in the day, telling us that the German section had been lost and that they had told them that the company they were seeking was where we were dug in. The civilians said they had also told the three Germans on bikes the same thing. The Dutch were very patriotic and hated the Germans with a passion for the way they had been treated during the occupation.

Trudeau got word of a combat patrol being sent against the Germans around the farmhouse. Hanss volunteered to accompany the patrol composed of several jeeps armed with 50-caliber machine guns and some mounted men. I told Hanss that he was foolish, the patrol would get nowhere, but he went anyway. Just after the jeeps passed our outpost on the road, they came under heavy mortar and machine-gun fire. After expending thousands of rounds of ammo, the patrol withdrew with a few casualties, feathers ruffled and feeling hurt. Trying something like that in broad daylight with so few men was ridiculous. Not long after the jeeps went back to the battalion command post we got another pasting from German mortars.

The next day Company C got orders to attack and occupy the distant farmhouse. We jumped off at about five in the afternoon with my squad on the left side of the road and Leamon's on the right; Rafferty's brought up the rear. PFC Jimmy Shoemaker from Olive Hill, Kentucky, and Frank McFadden were sent down the road as scouts. We followed, eyes glued on them and the farmhouse around the bend. No sooner had the scouts reached the bend, than they froze for an instant then leapt into the ditches as a burst of small arms fire whistled around them. Leamon and I hustled forward to see what was up. We met the scouts crawling toward us in the ditches. They had run into a platoon of Germans who were heading in our direction; we had nearly bumped head on.

Lt. Kohl and Trudeau met us as we got back, telling Leamon to take his squad to the right flank, and me to take the left in an effort to catch the enemy in enfilading fire. I led my squad down a slight drainage ditch and set up a firing line while Leamon did the same. I could see a German machine gun, its muzzle spurting orange flame in the twilight. I directed our fire on it and put it out of action. The noise was deafening, especially when our mortar began tossing some rounds into the road cut. Then, for some reason I never knew, the order came to cease-fire and withdraw. Perhaps it was the coming darkness when control was difficult, or some other reason, but we started to pull back.

Hanss and I covered the withdrawal, the last to leave. When we got back to our former position along the ditch, there was no one there. I couldn't understand it because the order was to withdraw to our former positions, and that position was the only block between the enemy and our company CP. Where the hell had everyone gone? Had there been a general withdrawal? We waited for a while, and then I sent Hanss back to see what the score was. He seemed to be gone forever, as I lay on the side of the road peering into the darkness with all sorts of deplorable thoughts running through my mind. Finally I heard the rustle of boots on the road behind me, my men were coming back. One man had misunderstood the order, which caused the rest to panic. I knew who it was and was determined to get rid of him as soon as I could.

The next morning when a heavy fog was still over the area, Trudeau sent a couple of scouts down the road. They came back shortly saying there were a number of German dead in the road and ditches. Later in the day we were relieved by the 1st Platoon and put in company reserve, an orchard near the CP. The 1st hardly got settled when a terrific mortar barrage dropped on them, causing a number of casualties. The company was relieved the following day, going back to Veghel where we dug in around a large field. After pitching tents, digging foxholes and latrines, we got a hot meal and a rum ration, as the British did. After being without alcohol for so long, some of the guys got drunk. We got our first mail from home and I had many letters. My wife wrote every day, and I did too, provided it was possible. Someone spread the rumor that the Germans had pulled back and for us the campaign was over; we were going back to England. John Gardner, my BAR man, looked at the rumor spreader and said, "I'll believe it when I see pigs fly." And he was right.

On September 28th, instead of returning to England as everyone hoped, we were placed under the control of the British XII Corps because the British needed help holding the ground they had captured south of the Rhine.

CHAPTER 11

The Island

After our fighting around Veghel, during the first week of October we moved onto what we called the "Island." It was called the Island because it was a long narrow neck of land between the Lower Rhine and Waal Rivers, low and flat with no rise in the ground apart from the towering dikes holding back the great rivers. It was a land of farms and orchards, cut by many drainage ditches and small canals. The dikes were 20 feet high with roads on top, the sides varying from steep to gradually sloping. Men lived in built-up foxholes or slit trenches most of the day, raised because to dig more than three feet down meant a water-filled hole. From their positions in the hills on the north side of the Rhine the Germans had a perfect view of our lines. To move about invited an instant artillery barrage. During October and November when the winter rain moved in, unimproved roads became mud holes and the foxholes and trenches turned into wells.

We knocked down our tents and boarded trucks, which headed north past Uden, Grave, and Nijmegen where furious battles had been fought in the first phase of the invasion. The roadsides were littered with the carnage of these battles, trucks, jeeps, tanks, weapons carriers, and the white crosses of the British dead. Homes and buildings were destroyed, yet civilians still clung to their remains. Everywhere we got friendly greetings, offers of wine and cider, admiring looks from young and old. They had paid the price in dead and wounded as well as we, and would continue to as long as the Germans remained in their country.

We moved up the road of bloody battles and across the bridge over the Waal, which had cost the 82d many casualties. It had been captured in the nick of time, just before it was to be blown, because of a young Dutch boy who led Americans to the demolition wiring. The bridge stood out like a sore thumb and efforts had been made to camouflage it with netting, but it was still a favorite target of the Germans and had been hit many times. When we crossed it in our convoy we heard shells coming over followed moments later by the

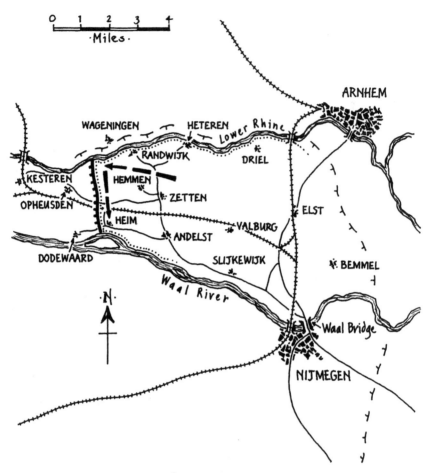

0 1 2 3 4
·Miles·

WAGENINGEN   HETEREN   Lower Rhine
RANDWIJK   DRIEL
KESTEREN   HEMMEN
OPHEUSDEN   ZETTEN   ELST
HEIM   VALBURG
DODEWAARD   ANDELST   SLIJKEWIJK   BEMMEL
Waal River
·N·   Waal Bridge
NIJMEGEN
ARNHEM

·THE DEFENSE OF 'THE ISLAND'·
·OCTOBER 5th 1944·

Waal Bridge : This bridge, secured by the Allies,
remains a key target for German
artillery attacks.

Movements of the 401st.

Line held by battalions of the 401st
and 506th.

Area of Allied presence.

German positions.

DS·
·2001·

boom of the guns, but the shells dropped in the river. Everyone breathed a sigh of relief when we were safely across.

Once across we unloaded from the trucks and moved into an orchard where we dug in. The trees were loaded with delicious apples, golden and red and ripe. We feasted on them, a delicious change from the British rations of bully beef, heavy puddings and tea we had been subsisting on.

We were put in division reserve while the division got settled in after taking over from the British 43d Infantry Division. The 502d held the eastern sector from Driel to Randwijk, the 506th from Randwijk to Dodewaard and the southern flank along the Waal was guarded by British troops. Unknown to us at the time, the German 363d *Volksgrenadier* Division was forming in the west with the mission of clearing the Island of all Allied troops. Only a stroke of luck stopped them from doing it, a blown bridge over the Rhine. The Germans had to ferry regiments across piecemeal, sending them against us as they arrived, instead of attacking as a division. A series of bloody battles began. We moved up on October 3d for our role in the coming bloodbath.

We left late in the day by trucks, which took us near the small village of Groote Hel where we unloaded and prepared to continue the advance on foot. The trucks were driven by black drivers from the 397th Quartermaster Truck Company, which had been assigned to our division to bring in supplies. These were the days of segregation when blacks were put in black outfits and whites in white. Some of the rednecks in our outfit called the drivers "airborne niggers," a joke most of us thought not to be very funny.

It was dark when we got to Groote Hel and the village was being pounded by artillery and was burning. Ahead as we moved down a secondary road, I could hear the crump of mortars and the rattle of small arms fire. We ran as best we could through the town, burdened by weapons, packs and much ammo. Soon we were sweating in the cool night air. I heard someone hit the ground ahead, then passed someone with medics bending over him. It was Pappy Bates who had been injured in the crash the day we landed and had gone to the aid station for treatment. The doctors there did not find his broken ribs, taped him up and sent him back. He must have been in great pain for a week, yet said nothing. Now he lay with a rib puncturing his lung. He died later that night.

Most of the fighting had died down when we reached our sector. After a long delay while our officers were getting their assignments, we moved north of some railroad tracks near the village of Opheusden in an area of deep ditches and sparse vegetation overlooking large fields cut by drainage ditches with woods in the background. Lieutenant Kohl told the squad leaders there had been heavy fighting in the sector just the night before when three men had been killed and six wounded. The 506th had taken a beating overall, 6 officers and 86 men killed or wounded the first day, 11 officers and 91 men the second, and 3 officers and 95 men the third. It promised to be hot for us, too.

I was instructed to put out two outpost teams. I placed Gardner and Helton in one, Larry Reid and Harold Zimburg in another. Zimburg was Jewish and from New York City, a dapper man of nearly 30, short, dark-haired and with a thin moustache. He was a good soldier, but had fixed opinions about everything. The rest of the squad took over the 506th's foxholes and slit trenches. Jerry Hanss and I shared one with the platoon CP and an artillery observation post (OP) right behind us.

Around noon I was called to the CP and told to take out another outpost team, PFC Paul Deliberto, of Waterbury, Connecticut, and PFC Orr H. Wallace from West Virginia. Lieutenant Kohl showed his lack of experience by giving the men a negative view of their situation. The lieutenant's pessimism put them on edge before they ever got to the outpost. I tried to reassure them that all they had to do was report enemy movement and, if endangered, to return. I gave them a sound powered phone to report to the CP and said I'd have rations ready when they came in. (The sound powered phone was merely a receiver, like a regular phone with thin wire connecting it to a receiver at the other end. To get the listener's attention, the sender simply whistled into his piece.)

It was quiet until late afternoon when the enemy dropped a heavy mortar concentration on our sector. We believed an attack would follow and got ready. A fierce firefight broke out as the enemy hit the 1st Platoon's area. The Germans were driven off leaving dead littering the fields and ditches. Afterwards we could see the Germans reforming in the woods in front of our positions and called for artillery support. A short time later, we heard shells screaming toward us, but instead of dropping in the woods, they exploded along our defense line. Kohl and the observers of the 377th Field Artillery tried to correct the range but Colonel Allen interfered, saying the shell bursts were from German guns, an old trick to deceive us. He ordered another salvo. Same results. The ground around our sector erupted. In the outpost, Deliberto was frantic as one of the shells had been a near miss. Lt. Kohl told him the shells were ours. "Oh, that's okay then," Deliberto said, "I thought they were German."

Colonel Allen was up to our position shortly after the last salvo, not believing our shells were dropping short. He ordered another salvo, standing near my foxhole with binoculars focused on the woods. The salvo came screaming in, again short and this time sending Colonel Allen into a muddy ditch. He was furious, cursing the gunners and telling them to raise the range. The woods rocked with exploding shellfire at last, breaking up the enemy formation.

It began to rain at dusk while I was picking up rations at the CP. I distributed them to the men on the line and took some to the observation posts. Zimburg was really raising hell about being left out there, and I tried to calm him down. It was a duty everyone had to pull with no favorites shown. I was up all night answering frantic calls on the sound powered phone from the two observation posts. Every sound brought visions of German patrols, rifle fire or an explosion of a grenade. Nerves were on edge, as bad as I had ever seen them, especially after Company B got hit again.

We were pulled out of the line before dawn and rushed to support the other two companies who were up to their necks in Germans. A battalion of infantry supported by tanks had tried to break through along the railroad tracks. A raging firefight developed with heavy casualties on each side. We moved in on the left flank of the two companies, setting up a defense line to keep their flank from being turned. The enemy was driven off leaving many dead on the fields.

Captain McDonald sent battalion a request for help to evacuate some of his wounded. Trudeau grabbed my squad and we took off along a deep ditch filled with a foot of water. Moving along in a crouched position because showing ourselves meant bringing mortar fire down, we finally reached Company B. All the wounded had been assembled and we helped these men back to the aid station.

Company A had been hit badly and Company B had suffered more than 38 dead and wounded. We moved up screened by a big dike and tree-lined ditches. We dug in around a farm and put out outposts. Hanss asked to go to one and I had Helton, Gardner and William Smith, a lanky Tennessee boy with a fine sense of humor, go with him.

The Germans took a breather in our sector but not in the others. All day we could hear the sound of fierce firefights. The 1st and 2d Platoons had dug in along a weed-choked ditch with a foot of water in it. A huge dike protected us from observation from the distant hills.

The company CP was in the rear, hidden by more brush. Our defense line overlooked a large open field and some woods where the 506th was dug in. Hanss' outpost was on the north side of our perimeter overlooking an unimproved dirt road.

Night is a scary time in combat for men on the outpost line or the main line of resistance. The enemy might sneak up and kill you while you are sleeping if one of your sentries falls asleep while on guard. It is an easy thing to do, falling asleep on sentry duty, because for weeks you have been under the stress of combat and the body and mind are nearly numb with fatigue. I have caught men sleeping on guard, even had trouble keeping awake myself when it was my turn. Usually we pulled a one-hour shift with two hours off. In a critical situation, half the men might be on duty all night. After weeks of either regimen, the body refuses to take any more. And it wasn't only us, as anyone who has ever taken a patrol through enemy lines can tell you.

The quiet in my sector was broken by a volley of rifle shots around midnight, coming from Hanss' outpost. Because it was in such an exposed position, I was reluctant to call on the sound powered phone, feeling confident he would call me if he needed help. Later, when I visited his outpost, I saw a German ration wagon standing 50 yards or so down the road. The horse pulling it was dead in its traces, and the driver lay sprawled in the dirt. Hanss said he heard it approaching, challenged it and opened up when he got an answer in German. The man had evidently gotten lost in the rain and wandered into our lines. The wagon was filled with good food, canned meat, butter, bread, cookies and little cigars. We unloaded it and distributed the booty to the rest of the company.

In the meantime we improved our positions. After much work we felt fairly safe against a tank attack. I say fairly because nothing worries an infantryman more than the threat of a tank attack. While it was true that most rifle platoons had three bazookas, we had little faith in their ability to stop a tank. The gunner had to let the tank get practically on top of him. We depended on anti-tank guns, the 37mm with the muzzle booster or the 57m guns in our 81st AA Battalion, to knock out enemy armor.

The enemy appeared out of the heavy ground fog, more than a company strong, hitting and rolling back a company of the 326th Airborne Engineers on our left. Fortunately, a company of the 506th had thrown up a defense line behind the engineers and called for artillery fire. The subsequent barrage routed the Germans and sent them streaming back across the field to our front. We cut the remnants to pieces. When the firing finally died down, the field was littered with dead and wounded. Some of the wounded wandered around in a daze either to be shot or to be waved over to our position and taken prisoner. Two came into my area, one shot in the side of the head and the chest, the other with a large chunk of mortar shrapnel in his leg.

Meanwhile, Lt. Martinson, who had taken over the 2d Platoon when Lt. Armstrong was hit, took a small patrol along the ditch in search of strays. Suddenly he dropped, sitting down and firing through his spread legs at a German sergeant who had popped out of the ditch. He killed the German and his patrol shot down two others.

Frank Trudeau was a great souvenir hunter and after the attack was broken up set out on a collecting trip. As he was searching the ditch where a lot of German dead now lay, nine live ones popped up, one a captain. Rather than attacking Trudeau, who was alone, they surrendered.

When Trudeau got back he wanted to kill the two prisoners who had surrendered earlier, but I talked him out of it. I told him I would take them back to the aid station. However, the one shot in the chest and head couldn't walk, so Trudeau told me to take the other one back. The man was average in height but stocky and could put little weight on his injured leg. However, I managed to get him back to the company CP where Captain Towns saw me and instructed James Turner, from Vienna, Illinois, one of our cooks, to help me. Turner was big and powerful, built like a weight lifter. We followed the ditch to a group of farm buildings nearly 800 yards from our positions, dropping the German off at the aid station. He was filled with gratitude, thanking us and showing us a photo of his wife and two children. Turner thought I was a fool to go to the trouble of bringing the man back, but it was something I had to do.

Dusk was now falling as we headed back along the ditch. The area was saturated with dead Germans. They lay in the water and along the alder-choked sides and I couldn't take my eyes off of them. Suddenly two shots rang out. My ears rang as if someone had fired a pistol near them. Turner and I hit the ground. The shots came from the ditch but it was so choked with brush it was impossible to tell from where. We waited for a few minutes then went forward cautiously, weapons ready. We never found the sniper. He could've played possum until we left, posing as one of the dead. We weren't about to root among the corpses to find him.

We left after dark, moving to relieve a battalion of the 506th south of the railroad tracks between Dodewaard and Heim. Companies A and B went on the line with C in reserve. We walked for what seemed like hours with the sky filled with cumulus clouds that blocked much of the light of the moon. The 3d Platoon had the point as we neared a large dike. Suddenly the fast firing of a machine gun split the quiet and we went to ground. Captain Towns came up, telling Lieutenant Kohl no enemy had been reported in that area. He suggested sending a patrol to investigate. I was picked.

I took Hanss, Gardner, Helton, and Naegle to the base of the dike where we formed a skirmish line and started climbing the steep bank, keeping as low as possible. We got separated in the darkness and I got to the top first, crawling the last few feet and peering over the top as the moon broke out of the clouds. I froze. Something was staring at me just a few feet away, a round shape looking just like a man's head. My heart was in my throat as I tried to get my Thompson in a position to fire. Then the shape elongated and I saw two big ears. It was one of those big European hares, and it had scared me out of my wits. I collected my men, heart pounding. The German gunner had pulled out, sliding down the dike and into an orchard we had been slated to occupy, as we found out when he opened up with several bursts from his gun, sending us to ground. We retired to where the company waited with our information. Captain Towns was told to hold where he was for the night and move up the next morning.

Before dawn Lieutenant Kohl was nervously pacing near the CP. I asked him what was up. He had to send a patrol into the orchard ahead and didn't know whom to pick. I volunteered the squad. We stripped down to weapons, grenades and cartridge belts and moved out in the morning mist. We went around the dike and across fields cut by ditches, approaching the orchard without any trouble. We formed a skirmish line and went through it, finding a foxhole where the Germans had been but little else. I called Lieutenant Kohl and told him the orchard was clear. He said to form a defensive line and cover the platoon as it came up. There was a shallow ditch near the forward edge of the orchard and we had barely reached it when I heard a loud swish and the explosion of a mortar shell. We hugged the ground. Shell after shell rained down, sending apples tumbling about us. We froze, unable to move.

Ray Vigus, a Normandy vet who had been shot through the leg and returned to duty, lay just ahead of me. He started to mutter, then yelled, "I'm getting the hell out of here." Panic was in his voice.

I grabbed his foot as he started to rise. "Get down, you damned fool. You'll be killed," I shouted.

He tried to tear himself away. "We'll be killed here. I'm leaving."

The shells were crashing all over the orchard, fire from more than one mortar tube. "For Christ's sake, Ray. Use your head," I said as calmly as I could. "Stay put. It'll be over in a minute."

He did and it was. Lieutenant Kohl had been burning the batteries up on the radio, wanting to know if we needed supporting fire. I couldn't answer until the barrage was over. When the shelling ended I told him to bring up the platoon. He did and we dug in, barely in time because another barrage soon came tumbling in as bad as the first.

Meanwhile, the 2d Platoon had relieved Company B, moving into an orchard overlooking a double canal and a road running west to east. Two two-story homes were on the other side of the road, some ten feet in elevation lower than the 2d Platoon's orchard. The 2d Platoon put a squad across the road into the orchard and a light machine gun covering the road to the west. They stationed a bazooka team in a pit beside the road, Privates Floyd "Red" Adkins and Willard Burgmeier from company headquarters. Adkins was from West Virginia, good-natured and an addict of country music who had listened to it on Armed Forces' Radio most of the time we were at Brock. Burgmeier was a solid, quiet sort of person, formerly a cemetery worker in Milwaukee. Neither had much experience in the field as they had spent most of their time in the supply room.

The 2d Platoon barely got settled when the attack came. It was preceded by an intense artillery barrage all along the front of the 401st and to our left flank where the 1st Battalion 327th was dug in. Over 2,000 rounds fell in the 1st Battalion's sector in 15 minutes. Company A was hit hard, too, and reported tanks and infantry moving across the fields toward us; we learned later that it was two regiments of infantry supported by eight tanks.

The assault ran headlong into 2d Platoon, which called for support from our 81mm mortars and from the guns of the 377th Parachute Field Artillery, the 81st AA Battalion and the 116th Regiment Royal Artillery. The din of the battle echoed over to us as we waited nervously for an attack across the fields to our front. It didn't come, only heavy mortar fire, which kept us down in our holes.

The tanks came down the road, pouring fire into the 2d Platoon's position. There were two, coming at high speed. Adkins and

Burgmeier fired two rockets at them, which glanced off their hulls, then saw the tanks race past followed by a wave of infantry. Both men sprawled in their pit playing dead, as the infantry overwhelmed them. Burgmeier was fluent in German and heard the enemy talking as they examined the pit. One said, "Good, they are both dead." And then moved on.

Meanwhile, a machine gun, with Henry Condor, a lanky, craggy-faced hillbilly from Harlan, Kentucky, behind it, poured belt after belt of bullets into both tanks and the infantry behind them. A shell from one of the tank's guns made a direct hit on Condor's gun, disabling the entire crew. Tech. Sergeant Irving Turvey, the jailbird who had taken over the platoon, rushed up, salvaged the gun and continued to fire at the infantry. The tanks had passed, heading down the road for the battalion CP where they ran head on into a 37mm anti-tank gun, which put one out of commission and ran off the other one.

The combined small arms, mortar and artillery fire broke the back of the attack and the enemy withdrew later in the day, leaving 2d Platoon's position badly mauled. Tech. Sergeant Larry Donoho, who was acting as platoon leader, had been mortally wounded. Sergeant James M. Lovelett, mortar section leader, had been shot through the head while observing. There were about 20 casualties in all to be evacuated. The 1st Platoon sent men up to help under Yeiser O'Guin's leadership. He narrowly escaped death himself while withdrawing when a German with a leveled machine pistol jumped out of a ditch just yards away. O'Guin kept his cool, motioned for the German to drop his weapon and surrender. O'Guin's M1 was slung over his shoulder, impossible to retrieve but to his surprise the German did as ordered.

Meanwhile Adkins and Burgmeier lay in the pit as the enemy retreated past them. This time they were both captured for a time, but managed to escape.

The 3d Platoon assembled in the darkness and moved out squad by squad, keeping noise to the minimum. Staff Sergeant Gerald Rafferty's first squad had been told to take over foxholes along the twin canals which separated us from the enemy. Staff Sergeant Thomas Leamon's second squad was to take over the northern border of the orchard we were to occupy. My third squad had a string of foxholes facing west. Meanwhile the machine-gun pit had been repaired, after a mortar round had demolished it, and a new crew under Staff Sergeant Amos Datwyler from Warren, Ohio, occupied the position.

The night was pitch black. A cold, wet misty curtain fell on the area as the platoon moved up to relieve the 2d Platoon. Slipping and sprawling over the uneven ground, we covered the open fields and ditches to "death orchard." I called it that because some of Company C's best men died there. Even in the orchard the earth was torn by craters. Finding one's way in total darkness without using a flashlight takes luck and experience.

Relieving troops in our outfit was normally done at night since moving about during daylight hours was suicidal. It had to be done in total silence, if the enemy was close by. And in the orchard, the enemy was just over the twin canals, possibly no more than 50 yards away. They were dug in and had posted men in the upper floors of the two houses where they had good observation of our position.

As my squad slipped into the muddy foxholes 2d Platoon had occupied, I whispered to my men not to move about during daylight and keep their eyes glued to the front. If the enemy decided to attack, it would come from that area. Also, I put out an outpost 50 yards away in an abandoned foxhole, connecting it with my position by using a sound powered phone.

I was up before dawn to check on my squad. Everyone was okay and well dug in. Lieutenant Kohl had his command post in the middle of the orchard alongside a forward observation position for our heavy mortars, one for the 161st Royal Artillery and another for our 377th Parachute Field Artillery. The officer in command of the British unit, a major, had been killed earlier and his body lay sprawled across the double pit, the top of his head gone. There were other bodies lying about as well and they were covered by GI raincoats.

I started to open one of the greasy British rations when Trudeau appeared at my hole. We had had a perfect relationship since I joined his platoon, never any conflicts despite the trauma of some situations.

"Bowen, I'm going to take a patrol across the canal to check out some of that abandoned equipment," he said. "I'll need a couple of your men."

Naturally I thought he had gotten orders from Captain Towns, so I said "Okay, I'll go with you. We'll take Gardner and Hanss." I had no way of knowing Lieutenant Kohl had given specific orders to keep to this side of the twin canals.

Trudeau picked six more men from other squads and we took off. The canals were about ten feet wide with a couple of yards separating one from the other. They weren't deep, no more than six feet, and both had some water in the bottom of them. A wide board had been thrown across and we went across in single file, a heavy ground mist obscuring us. We crossed the road and got in a shallow ditch, which ran outside the evenly spaced trees of the orchard. We went up the ditch bent over, anxiously looking through the trees. The ground had been chewed up by artillery, and deep craters, abandoned equipment and dead Germans littered the area. There was a shed at the rear of the orchard with baskets piled in it, a pile of equipment at the front, and German weapons scattered about. It was also marked by numerous foxholes with piles of fresh earth thrown up. We moved to the far end of the orchard.

I had good eyesight, sharpened by years of hunting, fishing, and bird watching and thought I saw some of those foxholes had men in them. I looked again, saw the flat tops of the helmets and grabbed Trudeau's arm.

"Frank, the Germans have moved back into this orchard. Those foxholes are occupied," I whispered hoarsely.

The patrol went to ground while Trudeau checked. He evidently saw nothing. "You're crazy. I don't see a damned thing."

I pointed to a hole less than ten yards away where a wisp of smoke curled skyward. "Bullshit. Your nerves are shot," he said.

"Wait here," I said softly, and crawled out of the ditch and over to the hole. A young German face popped up, eyes wide with surprise when he saw the Thompson I had pointed at his head. I motioned for him to come with me and we both crawled back to the ditch. Trudeau took the man back to the canals and turned him over to Rafferty while we waited. By now everyone had spotted Germans. Yet Trudeau was still not convinced. We had an argument in whispered tones until Hanss finally persuaded him there were just too many for us to handle. Trudeau gave the order to withdraw the way we had come.

We crept back, keeping low in the ditch until we got to the road south of the canals. Trudeau told me to cross over first and cover the rest of the patrol as they followed. He said he'd bring up the rear. I took three men and put them in slit trenches once we had gotten over, telling them to cover the others. I then went back to my hole to get something to eat. I had barely gotten a can opened when I heard rifle shots ring out, then a Thompson sub-machine gun started to chatter. I dashed back to the machine-gun pit by the canal. Hanss rose from a ditch on the other side and shouted. "Frank's been hit."

Small arms fire broke out as I jumped into the first canal, crawled over the ground to the second and through it to the ditch where Hanss and the other patrol members were firing into the orchard.

"What the hell happened? Trudeau said the rest of you were coming over," I said angrily.

Hanss pointed to the pile of equipment, mostly German, and some Schmeisser machine pistols. "He went back for those," he said.

I could see Trudeau, lying on his back with the Thompson near his extended hand. Abe Spector, probably the closest friend Trudeau had in the platoon, crawled over to me. He was tall and skinny, dark haired and dark skinned, a likeable fellow and one of the inveterate card players in the company. "We've got to get him out," he said, plainly upset.

A German machine gun was ripping off bursts, firing down the length of the orchard. It would've been suicide to cross the open ground to reach Trudeau and I told Spector so.

"I'm going over. I got to see if he's alive," he said. I knew there was no use reasoning with him.

"Okay, then, We'll try to shut down the gun. Go ahead, but crawl," I told him.

The three others and I opened up with a grazing fire, concentrating on the back of the orchard from where the machine gun was firing. Spector squirmed over on his stomach, felt Trudeau's neck, got his Thompson and crawled back. He was completely crestfallen.

"He's dead, Bowen. No doubt about it."

"Why'd he go back Abe?" I asked.

"For those damn machine pistols."

A lively firefight now sprang up. Meanwhile, Andy Mitchell, mortar squad leader in the 3d Platoon, had brought some men over. I had no idea why as our best bet was to get the hell out of there before anyone else got killed. One of the men was PFC Stanley Clark, the platoon medic. Someone sent him across the clearing to check Trudeau. He was struck by fire from the machine gun and tumbled into a shell hole. Bullets from the gun whipped by my face so close I could hear them. I ducked and yelled for Mitchell to pull his men out. It was too late. They couldn't hear a damn thing.

I looked back at the canals and saw Lieutenant Kohl running for the ditch beside the road where he stopped, peering into the orchard. "Get down, lieutenant. For Christ's sake, get down," I yelled. Too late. Puffs of dust erupted from the back of his jacket. He crumpled and fell to the road. I crawled down the ditch and over to him. He knew he was badly hurt and pleaded with me not to leave him. I told him I wouldn't and said I'd need some men to carry him out. I yelled across the canals to where Rafferty's squad was firing into the orchard, asking him for some help. He got three of his men and dashed across the canals with the German bullets kicking up dust around them.

While they tried to get Lt. Kohl off the road, I took Hanss and several others and crawled up the ditch beside the orchard. Andy Mitchell and his men were on the other side and we blasted the place with an enfilading fire while Rafferty's men were helping Lieutenant Kohl. PFC Lyle Appel, a young replacement from Volga, South Dakota, went down, shot across the stomach with his entrails popping out.

Meanwhile, 1st Platoon had heard the commotion and Lieutenant Robert Wagner, the leader, ran up the canal and saw what was happening. Spector crawled back into the orchard and checked out Clark. He had been killed instantly. Lieutenant Wagner advised me to get everyone out of the orchard and I did, using the ditches to communicate with Mitchell and Hanss. With Datwyler's machine gun raking the orchard with fire, we scrambled across the canals bringing Lieutenant Kohl and Appel with us. Andy Mitchell had been wounded also by a grenade fragment in his jaw.

We barely got settled when a red flare shot up. Within minutes a heavy German mortar barrage dropped squarely on the orchard. I couldn't believe my eyes. Did the Germans think we had moved in? It lasted for 15 or 20 minutes, and when it was over five Germans rose from their holes and came toward us, hands raised. Spector yelled at them in German and they hurried across the canals and into our hands. We searched them and sent them back to the CP under guard.

Lieutenant Wagner was as upset as I was about the casualties and asked Staff Sergeant Schwartz, the mortar observer, for some 81mm fire. Schwartz said it would be dangerous as the orchard was less than a hundred yards distant. But Wagner insisted and the rounds were soon on the way. They dropped right on target, exploding in great mushrooms of smoke and flame. Wagner also wanted artillery fire. The forward observer from the 377th refused, saying that we were within the safety zone. However, the British captain who had taken over from the dead major had no qualms. He radioed the range and within minutes we heard the shells screaming toward us. They burst with ear-splitting explosions, most were on target but a few landed in our orchard. Fortunately the only casualty we suffered was Gardner's helmet, which was caved in by a piece of shrapnel.

When the shelling ceased, we looked at the smoking orchard. Five Germans came toward us, hands raised. We held our fire. When they got to the deep ditch beside the road, they jumped in, out of our line of fire. We were furious. However, Howard Thornton, who had taken over Andy Mitchell's job, lobbed some 6omm mortar shells along the ditch. We saw some bodies in there later.

Wagner requested another salvo and it came in on target. When it was over, a white flag was waving in the orchard. Six Germans emerged heading toward us and the deep ditch. Rafferty's men gunned them down. Evidently the orchard was too hot for the Germans. Off and on all day, they pulled out, singly or in pairs, dashing for the ditch or out the back of the place. Rafferty's men killed some and missed others.

With the killing frenzy tapering off, we went back to our holes, unable to move freely because it would bring an instant mortar barrage. Hanss and I shared a double slit trench. We talked about the patrol and how useless it had been, especially when Trudeau had specific orders to avoid the place.

"He always believed he was invincible." Hanss said. "He thought he led a charmed life."

"Why, for God's sake?" I tensed with anger thinking about it.

"In Normandy he did a foolish thing, running headlong at a German machine gun position and wiping it out. It wouldn't happen again in a million years but he didn't believe that," Hanss told me.

"He thought I had lost my nerve because I wanted to get the men out of there," I said dully.

"You were right, Bob. There was at least a section of Jerries in there. Every one of us could've been killed. Frank was one helluva nice guy, but he was foolhardy. It got him killed, and Clark too. And from the looks of it, Lieutenant Kohl won't make it either. All over a couple of German machine pistols."

I was crushed mentally and physically, overwhelmed by guilt even though I couldn't have done more. I stuck to my hole most of the day, only leaving to see that my squad got rations and water from a dump we had set up at the back of the orchard. Off and on throughout the day, mortar barrages dropped unexpectedly on us, whenever anyone was seen moving around.

At dusk Lieutenant Wagner came to my hole, telling me that I had done well in the fight and that Lieutenant Kohl wasn't going to make it. "I just got back from the CP," he said. "Captain Towns wants you to take over the 3d Platoon." I couldn't believe my ears. I was just a buck sergeant, Leamon and Rafferty were staff sergeants. I told Lieutenant Wagner it just wasn't possible. "I've already talked to them. They agree that it's the best solution and will back you 100 percent,"

Wagner said. "If you need any advice or help just ask for it. I'll be only too glad to help."

We talked for a while about my duties and he left. I turned my squad over to Jerry and moved my gear to the command post. I visited every squad and was received happily by everyone. I instructed the men to be especially watchful during the night and not to move around. I didn't want any more accidents. When I got back to the CP, it consisted of just Norman Labbe and myself due to casualties.

PFC Earl Bacus, a mortarman from the weapons platoon, a small, wiry, quiet fellow from Indiana, a veteran from the early days of the company, was waiting for me. He told me that Captain Towns had asked for a volunteer to take Appel's place in the 1st squad and he was it. Because the mortars were always kept behind the main line of resistance, I warned him about moving around and to do exactly as his squad leader asked him. He readily agreed and I took him up the canal to Rafferty.

I had just gotten back when another mortar barrage blasted our orchard. When it was over, I was so tired that I fell asleep, only to be awakened later by Sergeant O'Guin shaking my shoulder. "Bowen, some of your men are buried alive," he said. He led me to the canal in the darkness. The hole had been dug deep and the men were struggling. It was pitch black, no moonlight. We finally began pulling men from the hole, Bacus first, because he had been perched on the side of the hole, then Ted Feldman and George Damato, both replacements. Bacus was unconscious, the other two unhurt. I examined Bacus as best as I could but could get no pulse. I decided to call the company command post for a medic since ours had been killed. Sergeant Bean didn't want to come up. I insisted but he said I knew what to do because of the course I had taken in battlefield first aid. I went back to where Bacus had been carried. Andy Mitchell who had had his face wound dressed and had returned to the platoon, examined Bacus also.

"He's dead, Bob. A large hole in the back of his skull." Mitchell said, "I tried to lift him and my hands went right in it."

I went back to my hole, crushed. A platoon leader for a half hour and I had already lost a good man. Despite being completely enervated, I couldn't sleep, so I took over guarding the CP. I couldn't get over how foolish Trudeau had been. Not only had he got himself killed, he had caused Lieutenant Kohl's mortal wounds and Clark's death. I cursed him for his disregard for others, the tragedy he had caused over something so trivial and swore to myself that as long as I had control of men nothing like that would happen.

Tech. Sergeant Claude Breeding, the acting top kick, brought up a detail of men around midnight with rations, water and ammunition. He congratulated me on my promotion then gave me some bad news. Tanks had been reported moving toward us along the road and we might be hit at dawn. After he left I checked and alerted all the squads, telling them to report immediately any movement to their front. We had three bazookas with three rockets, not much to stop a tank attack.

Rafferty's excited voice woke me several hours before dawn. He had heard tanks moving toward us. I rushed to his position and listened. I could hear them, too, some distance away. I went back to the British artillery observation post and awoke the forward observer. He invited me into his dugout. Covered by a tarpaulin to hide the light, I used his map to point out where the tanks were. Within minutes I could hear the screaming shells coming in. They burst along the road, great orange fireballs and thundering reverberations that split the night air. When it was over, I went back to 1st squad's positions and listened. No more tank movement was heard that night.

The following morning Ted Feldman reported on the sound powered phone that the Germans were moving back into the blasted orchard. A steady sniping fire broke out. The enemy had to cross an open field about 200 yards away to get to the orchard, and, when they did 1st squad or the machine gun under Datwyler's direction would open fire on them. By the time we were relieved nine German bodies lay in that area.

To our great relief, the tank attack didn't materialize but enough of the enemy had infiltrated into the orchard to make moving about to be suicidal. The only way we could get rations, water and ammunition to the 1st squad and the machine-gun position was to crawl along the ground and push or pull it along. On occasion I had to visit one of these positions and it was always scary, a mad dash greeted by a burst of enemy fire.

I got to Datwyler's gun near noon with some rations and to see what was happening in the orchard. Datwyler had asked for some rifle support during the night and I had moved some men around to his gun. He thanked me because it was isolated and the crew did not feel adequately protected at night. He was one of the old hands who had been with the company since its formation. Originally from Warren,

Ohio, he had done an outstanding job in Normandy. We talked for a while, about the situation, then home and civilian life. Before leaving, he mentioned that he had to take fuel for the Coleman stoves to his other gun stationed at the other end of the orchard. I warned him about moving around, then crawled behind the gun pit and back to my hole.

A short time later I got a call on the phone; Datwyler had been shot by a sniper. I hurried to the gun pit. His body was being pushed out the back with a hail of bullets peppering the dirt parapet near him. We dragged his body back to the orchard while Norman Labbe, my radio operator, called for a litter. A bullet had pierced his forehead; gray matter drained from the wound. Sergeant Breeding, one of Datwyler's closest friends, brought the litter bearers. We got him out of the orchard and back to the battalion aid station from which he was taken to the main hospital in Nijmegen. He lived in a coma for 17 days before dying.

Our belief that there wouldn't be a tank attack was short lived. We could hear tanks moving up late in the afternoon. The British artillery captain contacted his headquarters, which relayed a message to a British airfield near Eindhoven. A short time later some British Typhoon fighters came in fast, low and spitting rockets. We could hear the explosions and louder ones and black rising trails of smoke when the fuel tanks on the Panzers went off. The Typhoons left orchards and roadsides littered with burned and wrecked German armor of all kinds. They were our main line of defense against tanks for the rest of the campaign.

When night came we could move about, bring up water and rations and improve our defenses. Andy Mitchell had to be evacuated. The wound in his jaw had become infected. He would be missed. He came from Rogers, Arkansas, and would return home after the war and become a school principal. A storm blew in near midnight, deluging us with rain while the wind tried to tear the apple trees apart. In the middle of it, an artillery barrage blasted our orchard, causing some casualties who had to be evacuated.

During the night an unusual thing happened, a German wandered into our position looking for his outpost. Ted Feldman was lying asleep in a slit trench under a raincoat with his rifle outside the trench. He was awakened by someone softly calling in German, "Karl, where are you?" Unfortunately for the German, Feldman could understand him. He felt helpless with his rifle outside the hole and took a chance, lying quietly until he heard the German moving away. Then he threw the raincoat aside, grabbed his M1, and blasted away at the shadowy figure. Evidently there was another man with the first because Feldman heard him running away, but the first man went down. I saw his body the next morning when I got up, lying with knees drawn up and a Schmeisser nearby, just a few yards from Feldman's slit trench. He was a big man and his body was draped in a shelter-half.

Sniping began as soon as it was light, worse than it had ever been. For anyone to leave his hole to answer the call of nature was impossible. Something had to be done about it. Turvey believed the sniper was in the nearer of the two houses across the road, high up where he could look down on our position. The artillery forward observer was especially worried because a bullet might strike the exposed radio, our lifeline against the tanks. Sergeant Schwartz tried to flush the man out with a mortar concentration, but to no avail. He continued to plague us. I got one of our bazookas and a bag of three rockets and wormed my way to the front of the orchard while Turvey lay behind a tree with his binoculars focused on the house. He told me he had seen some movement in the attic window. I wired the bazooka, set the sights, aimed at the window and fired. The rocket left with a roar, burning my face. But it hit the limb of an apple tree screening the window and exploded. I reloaded the tube and fired again. This time the round hit right beside the window, tearing a hole through the side of the house. I fired a third rocket. It hit the eaves under the window. We weren't bothered any more by that sniper.

Mortar barrages still plagued us, coming without warning. A loud swish and an explosion was all the preparation we ever had. If anyone was out of his hole he became a casualty. We were particularly vulnerable to tree bursts which sprayed the shrapnel into the holes.

Captain Towns called me to the CP in the late afternoon to see how I was conducting things. I said everything was going fine, expecting him to replace me with an officer from battalion. He said none were available and he was certain I could handle the platoon until one would be. He also said, knowing the problems we were having with mortar attack, that he was going to send the 2d Platoon to relieve us that night. I thought for a moment then told him I didn't think it was a good idea. With the noise involved and the nearness to the enemy, we could have men caught in the open when the mortar attack began. I volunteered to hold the position until we were relieved. He was surprised but grateful.

The 2d Platoon had lost more than half of its men and was in no position to lose more. In the back of my mind was the thought that somehow we could recover the bodies of Clark and Trudeau, lying across the canals in plain view. Every time I looked over and saw them, a wave of desperation went through me. But it wasn't going to happen. The sector was too hot. The bodies lay there and added their stench to the terrible odor coming from the dead cattle and bodies of the enemy. It is a smell one never forgets, an odor that permeated my clothing and my mind.

We continued to be harassed by sniper fire, mortar barrages, and the threat of a tank attack. These annoyances plus hours of sitting in foxholes with depressing thoughts running through our minds, eating the cold, greasy British rations and thinking about the deaths of men we had served with for years, were beginning to get everyone's nerves on edge. I wondered if we would ever get out of that orchard alive and if I had made a mistake in taking on the responsibility of leading the platoon. But salvation came that night when Captain Towns asked me to send a couple of guides back to lead in another unit. We were being relieved.

The company pulled out after dark, leaving us in the orchard waiting for a platoon of the 327th which was late. They moved in, making a terrible racket in the darkness. I warned the officer in command of the nearness of the enemy and the barrages which had caused so many casualties. To make matters worse, his men were using flashlights. He said, "The hell with the dumb bastards. If they're that stupid let them pay the piper." I got out of there as fast as I could, taking Hanss and Labbe with me. I got hell from Captain Towns for being late but didn't mind that. All I wanted was to get away from that place. We had barely begun our march to the rear when a terrible mortar and artillery barrage dropped in our orchard. We heard later that the unit that had relieved us had horrendous casualties.

CHAPTER 12

Debilitation

The German attacks on the Island lasted until October 15th. When the attacks tapered off, the enemy heavily mined the Opheusden sector. Most were Schu-mines, plastic boxes the size of a brick containing a pound of explosive. They were buried in the ground with only a half inch of the tiny trigger mechanism showing. Unless the rain washed away the ground around them, they were nearly impossible to see, especially at night. One patrol of the 502d lost an officer and seven men to these mines. This, plus the constant mortar and artillery barrages if anyone was seen during daylight hours, was what we had to contend with for the next month and a half.

Our night hike from the Island ended in Zetten at a building that had been a primary school. It was a brick, one story affair with a play yard and an orchard. We fell out of ranks in the dripping darkness, wet, muddy and dead tired, entered the gym room and flopped on the floor. Within seconds everyone was asleep. Zetten was about 2½ miles from the defense line, under artillery observation by the enemy and had been heavily damaged. To move about in daylight was to invite instant shelling.

We were given a hot meal the next morning, better this time because we had become accustomed to it. We got mail and our barrack bags with personal things. We got clean uniforms, too, and a chance to take a shower. We had to go to Nijmegen and that meant crossing the bridge, but most of us thought it was worth it. We loaded 2½-ton trucks with rifles, web belts, soap and towels and took off. It was only about ten miles, but most of the way we could be seen by the enemy in the hills, so the convoy was strung out and took a circuitous route. The ride over the bridge was scary, just ahead of some shells, which dropped in the river, and we pulled into the yard of a large monastery where the engineers had set up showers. There isn't much that can feel better after living in holes in the ground for two weeks than a good hot shower and a change of clothes. Afterward, we saw a movie, had a chance to read *Stars and Stripes* and some recent issues of popular magazines. We stayed inside because the place and surrounding buildings had been bombed by planes and hit by artillery. The Germans had a big railroad gun hidden in a tunnel in the hills, and used it for distant shelling. We had a meal and returned to Zetten, feeling like different men.

The Zetten respite was the beginning of a new schedule for us where we would be four days on the outpost line, four days on the main line of resistance, and four in reserve. At no time were we ever more than 2½ miles from the front.

On the fourth day, Captain Towns took all platoon leaders on a reconnaissance of the new sector we were about to occupy. It was near Opheusden again. We pulled out after dark in pouring rain, hiked the road going to the town and dropped off short at another orchard. Somehow I got the squads squared away and dug in, an almost hopeless situation in a strange place, in the dark and in the middle of a storm. My command post consisted of PFC Norman Labbe, radioman, "Doc" Grapes, the medic, and myself. Normally we three would dig in near the 6omm mortar squad so that we could help with guard details at night. Now that Andy Mitchell was out until his wound healed, PFC Howard Thornton took over that squad. Slim and dark haired with a friendly face, he was from Covington, Kentucky, and a good mortarman.

Called to the company the next morning, I was told by Captain Towns to maintain three roadblocks while the rest of the company was in reserve behind Company B. I moved my men out, dividing Hanss' squad in two; one half in an abandoned farmhouse from which they had to run nightly patrols, and the other half blocking a road. As Hanss was without an assistant, I moved Elmer Felker into that spot. Young, blond, and German-speaking, he came from San Francisco and had been a good friend of Trudeau. In fact, Trudeau had nicknamed him "Goat" for the chin whiskers he grew after not being able to shave for a week or so. I put Leamon's squad in the orchard where we had been so heavily shelled and Rafferty's along an exposed position by a dike where a 37mm anti tank gun was located. The platoon was spread over a half mile, out of a decent range for our radios. We stayed there for three days, protecting the left flank of the battalion.

On the fourth day I was summoned to battalion headquarters. They had a job for me. I was ushered into Colonel Allen's office, a room with the CO, Major Angus the exec, and Captain Brouilette the S-3 (intelligence officer) waiting. The room was littered with supplies and wall maps. In another room of the building were communications, signal and supply personnel.

"Sergeant, I got a little job for you," Colonel Allen began. He wasn't tall, no more than 5 feet 5 inches, blond, trim and spunky, and spoke with a soft Texas drawl. He led me to a wall map of the Opheusden sector. "I want you to take a patrol out tonight using this route." It was marked in red on the map. He handed me a smaller map marked with the same route. "You'll leave from B Company's sector, follow this canal to this orchard, continue along this canal to this group of houses, where we believe an enemy command post is located, go north to this point behind the houses, and come back along this route to B Company's right flank position. You'll have a radio operator with a 300 set with you. I want you to call Captain McDonald every 30 minutes about your progress and any information you might pick up. I'm sure you've heard about the mines. We lost Sergeant Singleton in that area last night to one. So be extremely careful. Don't take obvious paths. Are there any questions?"

I had a million but didn't ask but a few. I returned to the company CP to find my platoon waiting. The company was dug in in a battered orchard strung with bits and pieces of equipment and men's bodies, bits too small to worry about. A wheelbarrow nearby held several bodies waiting to be picked up by graves registration. These were men from the 327th. We found slit trenches then I asked for volunteers for the patrol. Hanss was one, of course—he volunteered for everything— along with Leamon, Gardner, Helton, Smith, Wilson, Tishaw, and Shoemaker. Most were replacements; all had done well so far. Captain Towns sent me PFC Benjamin Molinaro as a radioman. He was from Chicago, dark skinned and with a Latin temperament.

It was just after dark when I checked in at Captain McDonald's command post. He went over the route once again and had guides take me to his outpost line. Just as we arrived a patrol was coming in, carrying two of their men on improvised litters. They had stepped on Schu-mines, losing their legs. It was a dismal start.

The night was typical for mid-October, fairly bright with fleecy clouds blotting out the moon off and on. I led the way, using the ditches instead of the path the other patrol had used. It was cold, wet, and noisy, but less likely to be mined. I took my time, stopping often to listen and rest. I checked with Captain McDonald after the first half hour, and then moved on taking the route I was told to. A noise to our left stopped us. We slid deeper in a ditch. Leaving the rest of the men there, Leamon and I crawled ahead softly, spotting a couple of figures in the darkness, a German listening post. We got the men and detoured around them, then back to the route. We came to a demolished house with a slate roof. More noise, hob-nailed boots walking on broken slates. In the house, I could hear men speaking in German. Another detour, this time around the house. When we were clear, I got the men in a ditch and called back again. We started down a path, feeling that it wouldn't be mined in the German positions.

Suddenly, several figures popped up, turned and disappeared. Had we been seen and identified? We took refuge in a shallow canal, waiting breathlessly. A loud pop, a stream of rising light, a bursting flare. It drifted down, swinging, lighting up everything. We froze, faces buried in water. Even though I was soaking wet and cold, sweat rolled down my spine. The flare descended slowly, burned out. I passed the order to stay down. Another flare went up, this time almost over us. We became part of the terrain. We waited for ten minutes and I was about to give the order to withdraw when I heard someone coming.

It was a German patrol, hob-nails crunching on the wet dirt. I could see them plainly less than ten feet to our left. Another patrol came from the right, joined the first group and sat, talked and ate hard cookies. I could hear their teeth crunching on them. We backed away, and took cover in another canal from where I called in again. Captain McDonald asked if I wanted mortar or artillery fire. I said "Hell No!" that was the last thing I wanted because we would be in the middle of it. He advised me to withdraw because we had been seen. We took a different route back, always sticking to the ditches. It was slow but it was sure. Fortunately, I spotted Company B's guards first, softly giving the countersign for the day and leading my patrol in. No one had told the guards one of our patrols was out. We were lucky not to have been fired on.

I reported first to Captain McDonald then to the battalion CP, giving them the information we had picked up. We hiked back to Company C where the men went back to their positions and I went on to Captain Towns. After I gave him my report, he told me to take off my wet clothes and wrap in a blanket. I made a bed in a hay loft and fell sound asleep.

We relieved Company B the next morning, moving up beside the railroad tracks. The 1st and 2d Platoons occupied a line north of the tracks, the 3d on the left in what remained of a tree farm, rows of saplings that were losing their leaves. When the morning fog lifted and I looked over the immense field to the front, I was startled. A wrecked Lancaster bomber lay on its belly 100 yards away, several dead crewmen still in it. There was a .50-caliber gun pit, destroyed by a direct hit with dead Germans around it. There were knocked out tanks, German and American, dead men in them, and bodies of both sides scattered over the field. One was an American paratrooper less than 50 yards from our lines, a young redhead whose hair shown like a flower when the sun hit it. My platoon was put there to cover the tracks and a road beside them, and an anti-tank gun, right behind my CP. The position was very exposed so I warned all the squad leaders to make sure any movement during daylight hours was absolutely necessary and kept to a minimum.

Using the information we had gathered on the night patrol, 1st Platoon sent out a combat patrol after the fog lifted. It didn't get very far before it ran into trouble, near the house where the slate roof had been knocked down. A heavy firefight broke out, and then mortars and artillery barrages were called in to cover the patrol's withdrawal. The patrol brought back three casualties, carrying them on shutters ripped from the house. One was a British forward artillery observer; the other two men from the 1st and 2d squads, PFC James Gilstrap and PFC Louis Dokupil. The two Americans had stepped on Schu-mines, losing legs. Dokupil was short, heavy-set and wore thick glasses, coming from Chicago. He was talkative and opinionated, the center of most arguments in the platoon. Gilstrap came from Douglasville, Georgia, a young nervous boy who was hanging in there despite having obvious problems coping with the trauma he was going through. Someone told me later he actually seemed relieved to have been wounded because he now had a ticket home.

Because there was a wide space between my platoon and the 506th on my left, I had to send a two-man patrol once every hour throughout the night to where the bomber sat in the field. I let Rafferty's squad handle that. Meanwhile, I had the men reinforce their foxholes and slit trenches because the position was so vulnerable to a tank attack. That became a problem because, after digging more than a foot or so, water began seeping into the holes. We solved this by building dirt parapets around them and making roofs with abandoned lumber.

The next morning just after dawn while a low-lying fog covered the field before us, I picked up the mail and rations at the company CP and returned to distribute them before the day cleared. I got back to the pit dug for our CP where Thornton and Labbe were heating rations on the Coleman stove. I had a 300 radio set, the kind you carried on your back, to communicate with company, and each squad had a 536 hand set to communicate with me. I had warned the squad leaders once again about moving about and knew they would follow the orders. We would be in that exposed position for several days, and I didn't want unnecessary casualties. As we began to eat the fog lifted as if a window blind went up. Suddenly we heard the scream of incoming shells and everyone buried himself in his hole. The barrage dropped right on our outpost line, tearing gaping holes in our little tree farm and shaking us as if an earthquake had hit the sector. Little did we know that someone from the anti-tank gun had wandered out in the field behind us and that the enemy had spotted him.

Someone was yelling my name as the barrage tapered off. It was Leamon, so I ran to his sector. A shell had dropped right into his BAR position among three men. Deliberto, the nervous one, was running around in circles, the net of his helmet hanging around his face like a veil. He stammered incoherently. Leamon tried to quiet him while I checked the others. Both were breathing their last breaths. Private Floyd Tishaw, from Long Island, Alabama, and Private Harmon Wilson, from Baltimore, were replacements. Although they were new to the company they had performed as well as any draftees could. Tishaw had a Christmas card in his hand, one with a big red feather on the front. Under it his sister had written "Red means danger, Floyd. Please be careful."

Someone was screaming at the top of his lungs in the field behind us. It was the careless anti-tank gunner who had caused all of this to happen. None of his crew would go out to help him, so I dashed into the field as another shell came whistling in. It was short. The man kept screaming that he couldn't move his legs. I tried to quiet him as I cut away his bloody pants and long johns. It was next to impossible with his wounds and the shells dropping not far away. I knew he was as scared as I was, but unless he relaxed, his wound could be fatal. I turned him over. A piece of shrapnel the size of a silver dollar had pierced both buttocks near the base of his spine. Thick globs of blood squirted out. I finally got him stabilized, calling to Labbe to get in touch with our CP to send the medics. His wound was beyond my limited ability to treat. I stayed with him until the shelling stopped and the medics came. We got him out without any more shelling, but I heard later that he went into shock and died.

I visited an outpost dug in on our right flank on top of the railroad later in the day when the clouds moved in. Doc Harrell was there along with some of his men. They had seen what went on in my area and were sorry to learn of the two deaths. Doc said, "You'd better clean up. You look like a butcher."

I looked at my hands and arms. They were caked with dried blood but there was no way to clean up out there. Water was too scarce. Doc pointed to a blasted gun pit nearby. Beside the wrecked 20mm gun there were two dead Germans in the waterlogged pit. One was a young lieutenant, blond and handsome, but with the top of his head cut through by a shard of shrapnel. Only a bit of skin kept the pate on and when the water in the shell hole moved it opened and closed.

We spent four long, tiring days there, pinned in our holes all day long. If a man had a bowel movement or had to urinate, it had to be done in a can and thrown out front. To move around during daylight was asking for an enemy barrage.

We pulled out in the middle of the night and hiked back to the school in Zetten, sleeping on the floor of the gymnasium again. We got our duffel bags, hot meals and our first Christmas parcels from home. My wife sent me one every week, cakes, cookies, candies, anything I requested. She made great sacrifices for me when certain foods were hard to come by at home and she'll never knew how much they meant to me at the time.

While resting in Zetten I was promoted to staff sergeant, on a level with Leamon and Rafferty. I had Hanss and Felker promoted, too, even though ratings were hard to get in my company because so many NCOs were in the hospital, but still officially on the table of organisation.

I was having problems with Rafferty's squad. As brave as he was—his behavior was impeccable in the orchard fight—and as good a garrison soldier as he was—no one gave close order drill much better—and as good as his deportment was—no one dressed better or had a neater locker—in the field, he lacked maturity. I talked with him about it, telling him the problems he was causing, but nothing changed. So I went to Captain Towns and discussed it with him, thinking a change to another platoon would be helpful. When Captain Towns talked with Rafferty about a change he absolutely refused, saying he would rather stay in the platoon as a private. I didn't want to allow it, but for the sake of harmony kept him, sending him to Leamon's squad. He served with distinction for as long as I was with the company, never causing any problems or holding his demotion against me.

We moved up to the Lower Rhine four days later, in the middle of the night as was the practice, to a position between the villages of Heteren and Randwijk. It was the north flank of the 327th's sector about six miles west of Arnhem, the scene of the British 1st Airborne Division's disaster. A huge dike ran along the south side of the river with a road running parallel to it at its base. Clusters of homes and farms bordered the road on the south side. On the other side of the Rhine, which was no more than 200 yards wide, but deep and fast, there was little concealment along the bank until one got about 600 yards north where a high tree-covered embankment provided cover for the enemy positions. The enemy stayed along the embankment during the day, then moved to the river's edge during the night to outpost it. Our mission was to outpost our side to prevent the enemy crossing over as they had done early in the month when the 501st held our sector. The SS troops who had made the effort had only been driven back after a hot fight.

It was now November 1st and the winter rain had set in in earnest. Secondary roads turned into mud holes because of the night traffic of our vehicles, our foxholes and slit trenches filled with water and our weapons picked up a rusty film unless they were cleaned daily. Needless to say we were continually soaked and, with the temperature dropping, spent one miserable day after another. Finally, after several days of this, I decided that enough was enough and did something that the other platoon leaders would probably not have done. I moved my men into abandoned houses during the days on outpost duty while maintaining the position with a reduced force. Guards were always on duty day and night with the main body of each squad billeted in nearby houses. In the event of alarm, the squads could move to their defenses in a matter of minutes. Not once did any of my squad members abuse the privilege nor were we ever caught off guard by any patrol action. In fact, by keeping out of sight during daylight hours, we had fewer casualties than any platoon in the company.

The 1st and 2d Platoons moved into orchards behind the houses while outposting the dike in front of their positions. We moved to the left flank setting up a defensive line around the edge of a farm, digging shelters and covering them with sheet metal and lumber we found around the place. While there I reorganized the platoon. I had Elmer Felker lead the 1st squad, Ted Feldman his assistant. Feldman came from Philadelphia, was married and had four children. He had been a carpenter before the war and left a well-paid defense job because he wanted to do his part in a war. Although he was a greenhorn as far as the service went, he was a resourceful person with a great deal of practical knowledge and common sense. I made George Naegle, the man who had acted as our copilot on the way into Holland, Leamon's assistant. He was from Salt Lake City, a quiet thoughtful person who handled his duties as if he were born to them. I got Joseph "Chicago" Kloczkowski, from 2d Platoon, another quiet competent fellow, to serve as Hanss' assistant. I never regretted any of the changes I made as long as I had the platoon.

The company spent eight days in this position, being shelled occasionally by the infamous 88s. They were terrifying and deadly. We were certain it was harassing fire as no one moved outside during daylight. One outpost was particularly hot, a large house on the riverbank opposite Wageningen. It was isolated, more than a quarter mile from any friendly troops, and could only be relieved or supplied at night. The men hated pulling duty in that spot because it was so isolated, as indeed were some of the other outposts along the dike. After taking several casualties, we pulled our troops from the outposts during the day.

About this time we were transferred to the First Canadian Army, a blessing because our rations improved considerably, not that we were going hungry. The gardens near the houses were full of vegetables, basement shelves were stocked, and cattle and hogs were always being killed by shellfire. Most of the homes were as the owners had left them, completely furnished with only valuables taken. Strict orders were sent down about looting and most of the men in my company adhered to them. However, there were notable exceptions.

Captain Towns informed me that an intelligence-gathering patrol from regiment was going to cross the river by rubber boats through our positions. He asked for volunteers to go along. Gardner, our husky BAR man, had just gotten word that his brother had been killed in southern France. He had a score to settle and asked to go, and where he went, Helton went. The night came for the patrol but it never showed up, going through Company A instead. Gardner and Helton were lucky. When the patrol reached the other side, it was wiped out.

Having nothing much to do must have gotten on Colonel Allen's nerves. He decided to make a feint attack across the river, moving up .50-caliber machine guns and arranging for artillery support. He asked for a squad to support the machine guns and I sent Hanss off at the last minute, I had just gotten the order, and he took off around 04.00 in a pouring rain with a mile to travel. The attack began at 05.00 preceded by smoke shells. We got a reaction all right, a counter-battery fire as bad as anything we had ever experienced. Hanss got there too late and caught hell from Colonel Allen. Hanss told me about his difficulties in the rain and mud and said when he moved through Companies A and B, all the guards were asleep. However, when he reached the 81st, he was nearly fired on because no one told them a patrol was coming to help. When Captain Towns began to chew me out on the matter, I took up for Hanss and pointed out the lack of communications, which could have killed him. The matter ended there.

We moved back to Zetten during the night. The shelling had gotten worse and most of us felt safer behind the dike. The Germans were using their big railroad gun and tossed a few shells at us each night. When the shells went over they made the noise of a passing freight train. One just missed the building my platoon was in, crashing in one across the street where the company CP was located. Fortunately the shell was a dud, smashing through three walls to fall in a room of sleeping men. However, PFC J.B. Roberts, a driver, was crushed to death and several others were badly injured.

Four days later we were back on the line, this time taking over from a battalion of the 327th. My platoon went into an orchard behind a house still occupied by civilians. Our mission was to support a 57mm anti-tank gun and block a road while protecting the left flank of the company.

After we tidied up the defense line to our satisfaction, I selected places the men could use to dry out and clean weapons. In the rear of Felker's squad was a small shed that had been used for storage. It was dry and close to their line. Behind the other two squads was a garage, which would serve the same purpose. The main thing was to keep the men out of sight as the position was easily seen from across the river and from the west where the enemy had his defense lines. During daylight hours there was no traffic between the line companies and the battalion CP. Any movement brought an instant artillery barrage.

Captain Towns called early one morning saying I was to have some visitors to inspect my platoon. It turned out to be General McAuliffe, second in command of the 101st, and Colonel Allen. I took them to every squad sector, explaining fields of fire, outposts, patrols and neighboring units. McAuliffe was a fine officer, one the men respected and admired. Later, Sergeant Breeding told me that he had overheard the general telling Captain Towns that I was the best informed platoon leader he had talked to in his rounds, which made me feel good.

There were several families living in a nearby house where, in the attached barn, I had settled my CP. One of the older women there had been wounded in both arms and one of our medics would visit occasionally to check and dress her wounds. There were also several teenage girls in the house, which caused some problems as some of the single men had eyes on them. While I didn't mind fraternization, I wasn't about to let a situation develop which might cause repercussions, from their families or the company. So I limited relations. Some nights the Dutch would invite me to bring some men in for refreshments. Doc Grapes, the medic, could play piano and organ, and was always invited. While he would play an old foot-pedal organ, the women would sing Dutch songs. I'm sure the Germans could hear the music across the river but they never interfered with our singing.

The enemy did continue his harassing fire, dropping intermittent barrages on us for no other reason than to let us know they were still out there. Many of the rounds would be duds, which still scared hell out of everyone when they dropped nearby. We called the engineers and they would usually mark them with white tape to be removed later.

During one of our stays Captain Towns decided to try to supply two hot meals a day. Before dawn and after dark the kitchen brought up large cauldrons of food to the CP. We would send the squads back to eat, but somehow the Jerries got wind of it after a few days and began blasting the CP area.

Each trip back to the outpost line became increasingly nerve-racking. In one sector I had to run nightly patrols along the river for nearly a mile every two hours. When one patrol got in, another left. One never knew what to expect on these excursions and it wasn't long before I was like a zombie because I rarely got a night's sleep. If it wasn't checking my squads, taking out patrols or checking outposts, it was trips back to the company CP for the latest information. My body finally rebelled, my nerves as raw as a skinned knee. During one of these changes of position, when the 327th was taking over, there was a lot of racket outside my CP. I went out, warning the men about a mortar attack. My warning, however, fell on deaf ears. As soon as I went inside, the noise began again. I called Felker's squad in and really blew my stack. In the middle of my tirade, mortar rounds began dropping outside, wounding some of the relief men. When the barrage ended I was shaking all over.

Near the end of November we moved back to the Opheusden

sector, the scene of so many deaths and casualties. We dreaded going near the place. Both sides had pulled out of the town, but we maintained a presence by putting a platoon of men in it every 24 hours. The relief was always done at night. The town had been devastated, with destroyed building, shell holes, abandoned equipment, burned tanks with charred bodies in them and an odor that turned one's stomach.

Company A got first crack at the place, moving up in the darkness over barren fields and narrow canals. At one of the canals, a German patrol was waiting. A sharp firefight ensued and three Company A men lay dead including Staff Sergeant John Gacek, the pro wrestler. All the Germans were killed, but one of the 401st's heroes was, too. Once in the town the platoon was subjected to constant mortar, artillery, and sniper attacks. Wounded could not be evacuated until dark and many died before this could happen. Company B followed with no better luck than A. Then it was C's turn. The 2d Platoon went in first and was luckier than its predecessors, escaping with some minor wounded casualties.

At that time I was sent to a post in sector along the Rhine where there had been a lot of patrol activity. My squads occupied 2d Platoon's old positions, one an outpost right on the river's edge. This position was connected to my CP by phone. During some shelling the wire got cut and the two men at the outpost, Harold Zimburg and Chester Stempkowski from the 2d, were worried because they could hear the Germans on the other side of the river talking. I went back to the company CP and got a roll of wire, returning crawling along the riverbank to the OP, stringing new wire as I went. As I was hooking up the phone, the Germans opened up from the far bank, lacing the position with machine-gun fire. While the gun was firing I took a compass reading, and when the gun stopped firing, went back to my CP where I relayed the azimuth readings to Captain Towns. In minutes a salvo was on the way, but fell short, nearly dropping into a hole occupied by Gardner and Helton. I adjusted the range and the second salvo dropped right on target. For good measure, I asked for another salvo and got it. The gun didn't bother us any more that night.

A day later I was called to the CP and told it would be my turn to occupy Opheusden when 1st Platoon got back. We had heard a sharp firefight there during the day and I wasn't looking forward to any more of my men being killed occupying a town of no strategic value. Fortunately, providence intervened.

Captain Towns, Sergeant Breeding and Lieutenant Wagner were at the CP as Staff Sergeant Grayson Davis, leading 2d Platoon, and I reached the CP. Their faces were all smiles. We were going to be relieved that night by a battalion of the Scots Guards! I returned with the good news. Everyone was ecstatic. Even old Amos Darmon, a dour Kentuckian from Robinson Creek who never ever had a good thing to say about military life, smiled and got into the flow.

That evening after dark we were relieved. I handed my position over to a young, untried officer and warned him about the obvious dangers. Squad by squad we pulled out to form up on a paved road in the rear. We marched away in absolute silence, the last remnant of the company to leave. We hiked for nearly an hour, the moon shining bright over us. A guide met us at the bridge. He told me where the company had assembled and we started over the concrete structure, not knowing that the enemy had zeroed in on the thing. Suddenly we heard the scream of an approaching shell. We hit the road, waiting. A gigantic explosion nearly deafened us, ringing in our ears and covering us with flying earth. We got up and into ditches as fast as we could run. However, it was an encore for us, a parting shot by the railroad gun in the tunnel. Those gunners would never know that they came within 50 yards of wiping out what was left of the 3d Platoon, some 20-odd men.

We joined the company in an abandoned school for the night, marched a short distance to waiting trucks and left the Island, headed for some unknown place the following morning. We went down the road the way we had come, passing the carnage of the battle for the Netherlands. We reached a large city in France around midnight. Someone shouted to a civilian, asking where we were. "Reims," the man answered. But we didn't stop there, going on 20 more miles to Mourmelon-le-Grand, once a French artillery center, but more recently the base of a German Panzer unit. It was November 27th.

CHAPTER 13

Bitter December

Tired, hungry and battle weary, we unloaded the trucks and stumbled into low, stucco barracks, which weren't in the best condition. Hot chow was waiting for us, good American food that beat any of the British and Canadian rations we had been eating for the last 72 days. Afterwards, we returned to the barracks for the first sleep uninterrupted by gunfire in more than two months. Word slowly got around that we were in a place called Camp Mourmelon.

The previous German occupants had sabotaged everything that they could before they left, breaking stove grates, punching holes in water boilers and stopping up drains. They left the inner walls alone because they had been decorated with beautiful drawings of German troops in action. As an artist I admired whoever had done the work; it was outstanding. Rumors circulated that we would never go back to Brock. This was our new home.

Our two-story building held the entire company with each platoon having its own room. The NCOs were separated again, three or four in a room. My roommates included Tech. Sergeant Cecil Caraker, 2d Platoon sergeant, Tech. Sergeant Irving Turvey, weapons platoon sergeant, and Sergeant Andy Mitchell who had returned from the hospital after the wound in his jaw had healed. We were compatible and had no problems. Master Sergeant Long returned and Sergeant Breeding became leader of the weapons platoon again.

We resumed garrison life, expecting to stay at Mourmelon for the rest of the winter. We checked clothing and equipment and slipped into a light training schedule. We had a belated Thanksgiving Dinner, turkey with all the trimmings. Passes were issued to Reims and Paris. Red Cross clubs were set up. Some of the men wounded in Normandy and Holland returned, a few on hospital leave, others on duty.

Tony Guiterriz got back. He had picked up two Purple Hearts and was only a shell of his former self. He came to my platoon. Deliberto, who I called "the nervous one," also returned. He had miraculously survived when a shell dropped into his BAR pit wounding him and killing his companions. Appel returned. He had been wounded while helping evacuate Lieutenant Kohl. And Leroy Beezley, who had been seriously wounded in Normandy. He had been the spark of the 2d Platoon, one of those humorous people who maintained his positive outlook no matter what the circumstances. Guiterriz was the only one to stay, the others soon pronounced unfit for further combat.

The weather was typical for December in my home state of Maryland, cold, rainy days with blustery winds. However, we didn't complain. Anything was better than the front. Our barracks were chilly despite the pot-bellied stoves. There was a coal shortage but plenty of pinewood. Most of the wood, however, contained shrapnel and was green. No matter what we tried, we were unable to get the wood to burn properly.

Finally, Turvey hit upon a solution, "The damned kitchen's got plenty of coal. What say we borrow some?" he said.

"Impossible, That's been done before so now they've posted a guard on it," I replied.

"If he's a typical guard he'll be screwing off," Mitchell pointed out. "I think we should do it."

"What say we flip to see who gets the first load?" Turvey said, pulling out a British shilling. Andy and I matched him for it. I lost.

Slipping into a field jacket, I took my helmet liner and sneaked through the blustery night to the coal pile. Andy was right. The guard was in the kitchen drinking coffee so it was an easy matter to reach the pile and fill my helmet with coal despite the bright moonlight. Back in our room, I dumped part of the coal in the stove.

Turvey looked at me in disgust. "Dammit, Bob, you brought coke," he said.

"So?" I said, not knowing the difference.

"How the hell you gonna get it to burn?" Turvey said, explaining the properties of coke.

"No problem. Put some wood in first, dump a little gas on it and presto, instant blast furnace," Mitchell said.

Turvey thought for a moment. "Be right back." He left to return with a number 10 can filled with gas. Meanwhile, Andy and I had rearranged the wood and coke. Turvey poured a liberal amount of gas in the stove and, taking out a match, stood back.

"This is gonna be tricky," Turvey said, knowing more about such things than we did as he had ridden the rails during the Depression and spent many a night in hobo jungles. "When I light it, one of you slide the lid on." Andy picked up the lid and Turvey tossed in the match.

We stood waiting. Nothing happened for a few seconds then the stove seemed to explode, sending the lid all the way up to the ceiling. The noise brought a crowd to our door. We had scrambled for cover meanwhile as a belch of smoke poured from the stove.

"Jesus Christ! What kind of gas was that?" Turvey said.

"High octane. Aviation gas," someone said at the door.

"Sure has got a kick," Andy said, watching flames pouring out the open top of the stove.

"Yeah, but who's going to light it tomorrow night?" I said.

Each evening we did the same thing, swiping coke and lighting it with the aviation fuel. A couple times the lid barely missed one of us, making Andy ask, "I wonder if we'd qualify for a Purple Heart if that thing hit us?"

On December 12th, I was told by Matt Pas, the company clerk, that my name had been drawn for a pass to Paris on the 23d. The men who had already been to the city raved about it. They were, however, upset by many of the civilians who, they believed, were mercenary and distant with the GIs. However, I wasn't interested in people, only in seeing the sights.

The next day I went to Reims on pass with Elmer Felker, and Jimmy Clark, a mortarman in the 2d Platoon. Reims was the largest city on the continent that we had been in, its cathedral the former coronation place of French kings. It was also the center of the Champagne region. We spent the morning sightseeing and shopping. We bought perfume to send home, and I bought a pipe, having broken mine in Holland. After finishing our shopping we decided to try the local champagne.

We stopped in the bar of a large hotel. Champagne was 300 francs a magnum and it was delicious, as smooth as silk. Needless to say, we drank too much, four magnums, in fact. The rest of my time in Reims was an inebriated dream. It was near dusk and we were hungry, I recall, so we wandered about until we found an army kitchen set up for men on pass. I recall standing in a long line until I was given a sandwich. I went outside, dark by now, and an old woman with a shopping bag grabbed the sandwich out of my hand and disappeared in the night. The others wanted more drinking but I declined, setting off to find the trucks that had brought us but with no idea where they were or where I was. I recall wandering into an MP station for information and giving them a hard time because they wouldn't tell me where our trucks were. I got sick and threw up, wandered some more and saw a line of trucks parked by a curb. I crawled in back of one and went to sleep, having no idea which outfit it belonged to.

I was awakened by someone shaking my shoulder and calling my name. It was Willard Burgmeier, the fellow who was nearly captured at the houses near Opheusden when the Germans overran his bazooka position by the road. He told me he'd get me back to the barracks, and he did, for which I was grateful.

The next day back with the company wasn't much fun. I took the morning report with a head full of cotton and a mouth full of green persimmons. When I got back to my room, Merle Smith, my cousin who was in the 463d Parachute Field Artillery, was waiting for me. His outfit had just been transferred to our division after fighting in North Africa, Sicily, Italy and Southern France.

Our easy time around Mourmelon came to an end on the morning of December 18th when word of the German breakthrough in the Ardennes reached us. The German offensive had come like a bolt out of the night, catching the Americans manning the thinly held defense line completely by surprise. The troops had sent reports of a buildup to First Army Headquarters but the reports were either ignored or improperly analyzed. At 05.30 on the morning of December 16th, with six inches of snow on the ground, the Germans burst out of the pine forests of the Schnee Eifel behind a screen of artillery fire. They quickly overwhelmed the 28th, 99th, and 106th Divisions and began advancing toward Antwerp. If they had succeeded, they would have split the Allied armies in the West in two. The 82d and 101st Airborne Divisions were alerted on the evening of the 17th and by the next day were on the way to Belgium, right in the path of the German drive.

"All platoon leaders report to the orderly room immediately. That means now!" Matt Pas sang out as he went through the barracks right after chow on that fateful morning. Red Adkins had one of the few radios in the company. All morning it had been blaring out about a German offensive in the Ardennes, a region along the Belgian-French frontier that I knew about from the 1940 German offensive that drove the Anglo-French armies into the sea at Dunkirk. It was 100 miles north-east of us and I couldn't imagine how it could involve the 101st. I soon found out.

We weren't a very happy group when we received the news. Instead of passes to Reims and Paris I suspected it meant another trip to the front. With memories of all those we had lost in Normandy and

Holland fresh in my mind and with a body run down from too many sleepless nights, improper nutrition from the greasy British rations and the stress of performing in a job which I had little training for, I certainly wasn't looking forward to more of the same.

Besides, the company was under strength with three of the four platoons being led by NCOs. First Lieutenant Robert Wagner still led 1st Platoon but First Lieutenant Martinson had moved up to exec, with Staff Sergeant Caraker supposedly taking over his platoon, but Caraker was absent, arrested in Reims and in jail over an incident in a bar. No replacements had arrived aside from the few with healed minor wounds like Andy Mitchell. There should have been 45 men in my platoon with a platoon lieutenant and platoon sergeant. Instead we had 28 with no officer to lead us. Some of the other platoons were worse off.

Captain Towns' face was abnormally grim as he began telling us about the situation in the Ardennes, so sketchy and convoluted that even he was puzzled by it. There had been a breakthrough by the Germans and the 82d and 101st were being sent to stop it. He asked for questions and got plenty, most of which he had no answers for. He concluded by saying, "That's as much as I know, or anyone else here, for that matter. I do know we'll go into corps reserve to be used only in the event of emergency." I believe he actually thought that was true.

Then, as an afterthought, he said, "I know you've got men in your platoons who are not at their best. I don't think we should take them. Give me their names and we'll leave them behind."

"What'll happen to them, Captain?" Claude Breeding said.

"It's my understanding that they'll go to a rear echelon outfit. You know, quartermasters or something similar. Anyway they won't see any more combat."

Then it was back to orders. "You can draw ammo and rations from supply. Instruct your men to take overcoats and overshoes. There could be snow where we're going. Trucks are supposed to pick us up at 18.00. If there are no more questions I suggest you get cracking. We've got one helluva lot to do and no time to do it in."

I assembled my platoon and told them the unwelcome news. They took it a lot better than I imagined. However, when men are programmed to follow orders and accept the inevitable, in most cases they'll do what is asked of them provided they have faith in their leaders. At least that was my experience in situations where normal people would say, "No way." Being trained to be a warrior is not what most Americans look forward to. Men get killed and maimed in wars, especially in the infantry where about 80 percent of the casualties occur. My thoughts drifted to John Aspinwall, Howard Kohl and Howard Hill, now dead and leaving children that they had never seen. There was Frankie DeMarco with two children and Ted Feldman in my 1st squad had four and another on the way, and I believed the odds against his escaping death or wounds were about 100 to 1.

I asked the squad leaders to pick men who they thought should be left behind. It was a hard choice to make. The platoon was only at half strength to begin with. Three men were obvious picks. Private Morris "Pop" Zion, a veteran and an old friend. Pop was an older man from Chicago who had pushed his body to the limit to keep up with the younger ones. When I hear anti-semitic jokes I think of Pop Zion, the Jew who gave everything because he was willing. George Damato, another older man who should have been in the kitchen instead of a rifle platoon, a clown whose humor kept sanity in insane situations, was another. The last was Ken Schnese, an outstanding high school athlete whose nerves had reached the breaking point in Holland. Later I called the three to my room and told them their new assignments. While all were sorry to be left behind, I could detect relief on their faces. However, Utopia wasn't to come that easy for them. Because of the horrendous casualties in the Bulge, all three men were pulled from the Repo Depot and sent to the front as replacements; Zion and Damato died among strangers.

We packed everything, as if we would never return to Mourmelon. I insisted that every man take an overcoat and overshoes as ordered. Most men detested both and would discard them at the first opportunity. The overcoat seemed to weigh a ton after being soaked by rain, and the overshoes were like anchors, especially in deep snow. I also insisted on taking an extra blanket in the bedrolls. We left behind two platoon sergeants, Irving Turvey and Cecil Caraker. Turvey had reported to the aid station with a pulmonary infection. A spot was found on his lung. Caraker was still in jail, the victim of a con game by a civilian.

Latrine rumors were circulating like water in a whirlpool. Radio reports from the fighting front were grim and confusing. There was talk of a massive breakthrough by the enemy, a monumental Allied defeat. We formed on the company street where Turvey said goodbye, tears flowing on his cheeks. I envied him. We marched to a waiting convoy of open-bodied trucks as darkness fell. Jammed aboard like olives in a jar, we left for Belgium.

It was a long cold ride with a biting wind chilling us to the bone.

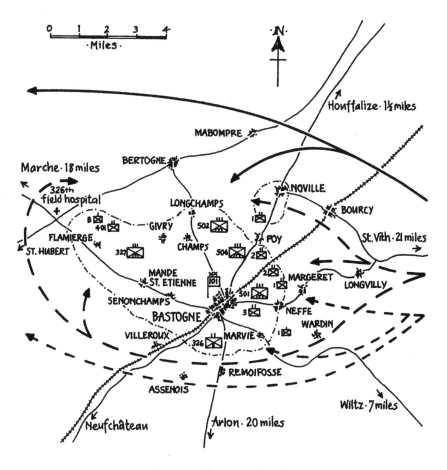

·THE BATTLE OF THE BULGE·
·TROOPS DEPLOYED IN DEFENSE OF BASTOGNE·
·DECEMBER 19ᵗʰ 1944·

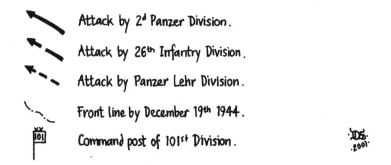

Attack by 2ᵈ Panzer Division.

Attack by 26ᵗʰ Infantry Division.

Attack by Panzer Lehr Division.

Front line by December 19ᵗʰ 1944.

Command post of 101ˢᵗ Division.

The headlights of the trucks were on despite being in a combat zone. We raced through small towns and we headed north-east, civilians with anxious faces cheering and waving to us. Were we to be their saviors again, I wondered? After five years of war, I was sure they'd had enough.

Although we did not know it then, Bastogne was our destination, though inadvertently. Actually we were supposed to defend Werbomont, 20 miles north of Bastogne, but we were re-routed to Bastogne while we were on the way. It was cold, rainy and foggy when we passed through the town near daybreak. We took a main road to the west, over rolling hills, through sleeping hamlets and patches of woodland and farms. The trucks pulled on a side road just west of the hamlet of Mande St. Etienne. Cold, hungry and stiff from hours of cramped riding, we unloaded silently, moving off the road to await orders. In the distance I could hear the boom or artillery, really not that far away. Corps Reserve? Hell, that wasn't more than a few miles to the north, I thought, and I was right. No sooner had the 501st unloaded than it was engaged in a firefight with an enemy column.

Captain Towns called me on the 300 radio set and I was soon on the way to the CP. I could see Companies A and B moving out and knew they had been committed. The CP was in the garage of a small stone house off the road. Men from the headquarters platoon milled about as I pushed my way through. The other platoon leaders were there, gathered around Captain Towns. He had the only map of the area and pointed out the positions we would take in the defense line.

He told us what he knew about the German drive, which was more serious than he had been led to believe at Mourmelon. We heard that the defense line held by the 28th and 106th Infantry Divisions had been shattered by enemy spearheads headed in our direction. He said that German troops dressed in American uniforms had been captured and warned us to challenge everyone regardless of dress. "Make goddamn sure before you let anyone in," he said adamantly. He had a boyish face for someone in his mid-20s, but now it was as grim and worried as I had ever seen it. He answered as many questions as he could and then sent us away.

I led my platoon to part of the defense perimeter on the right flank, while the 1st and 2d Platoons set up roadblocks on the main road. As it turned out we were thrust out on a salient, an egg-shaped line, which reached Flamierge in the west, about eight miles from Bastogne. To the west a great hill ran roughly north and south. Another ridge ran west to east to my front. Behind us, where the battalion CP was located, was a dense pinewood. There were secondary roads I had to cover, so I had Hanss set up a block at one crossroads while I put Leamon's squad outposting the ridge to our west. I settled Felker's squad alongside of Leamon's because it was too much ground for one squad to cover adequately. Andy Mitchell's mortar squad went back with the company mortars in a defilade position. Companies A and B were on our right. I set my CP in the rear of my three squads.

Company C held a very vulnerable sector of the defense line with the greatest gaps between it and the other companies. The 2d Platoon held the westernmost roadblock in the division, dug in on the slope of a rise among some trees, with rolling hills and patches of woods to the front. In its rear on slightly higher ground was a great stone house with outbuildings surrounding a sunken courtyard. Tremendous fir trees bordered this area, as they did along the main road running between Bastogne and Marche 18 miles or so to the north-west. A 37mm anti-tank gun was set in the trees facing down the road, and a Sherman tank and two tank destroyers moved into the courtyard. The roadblock appeared strong enough to stop anything coming down the road.

Meanwhile the 1st Platoon moved into a copse of trees some hundred yards or so to 2d Platoon's left flank, covering large open fields and bits of woods to the south. Some riflemen were dug in on the embankment along which the main highway ran.

The weather was cold, especially at night. During early morning hours heavy fog and ground mist covered everything until the sun burned it off in the late morning.

During the afternoon I went back to the company CP to pick up rations and learn the latest news. I took PFC Ted Feldman and PFC Gerald Helton with me. Even though Feldman was an assistant squad leader, he still hadn't gotten his sergeant's stripes. Nor had I gotten Tech. Sergeant's stripes despite holding down the job for more than two months.

Men of headquarters platoon had dug in around the house and an adjacent garage where an old automobile was parked. Inside the car Captain Towns and Lieutenant Martinson were scanning a map. Both men had faces with the most woebegone expressions I had ever seen on them. After they gave me the latest reports I soon knew why. The enemy was probing the defense line to the north and east, hitting hard with armored units in an effort to find a weak link. Saboteurs had been captured wearing American uniforms, infiltrating our lines then killing or capturing our men. Armor was reported on the roads leading to our positions.

I tried not to let my depression show as we headed back to our roadblock. Fighting tanks with bazookas is a crapshoot with the odds against surviving, especially in open country where it is difficult to get a close up shot. Of course, we had mortar and artillery support and the 37mm anti-tank gun. The Sherman and two tank destroyers were unknown quantities to us, as the only tanks we had worked with in Normandy and Holland had been more or less road-bound, doing their thing there while we took off across country.

Dawn came and men began heating rations on the portable stoves while I checked the squad leaders. Thomas Leamon reported hearing tanks on the far side of the rise facing his positions but, because of the heavy fog, I could see nothing through my binoculars. However, I reported the observation as soon as I got back to my CP. About the same time, Hanss called to report men moving through the woods to his front about 800 yards away. I rushed to his roadblock.

I could see them through my glasses, stragglers dressed in olive drab and moving south in a single file. Hanss volunteered to take a patrol and contact them. As he moved out I called Captain Towns, telling him the situation and asking for mortar and artillery support if I needed it. I watched grimly as Hanss' men moved up a draw and into a wooded area. I had confidence in him, knowing he could handle the situation if the men were saboteurs. Soon he emerged with a stream of men behind him. When he got back, he brought survivors from the 28th Infantry Division who had been overrun two days before after a two-day battle in which they had interrupted the German drive. All were cold, hungry and demoralized. I directed them to the company CP and they were later sent on to Bastogne to help bolster our defenses.

It was much the same all day. Groups of disorganized stragglers with hair-raising stories of thinly held lines collapsing under overwhelming odds kept dribbling in. All were thankful we had picked them up, because, had they continued on their southerly course, the Germans would have rounded them up for sure. These men were taken to Bastogne, given weapons and ammo and organized in a reserve pool nicknamed Team SNAFU. They were used to bolster weak spots in our defense line.

Meanwhile, on our left flank in the town of Marvie, the 2d Battalion of the 327th moved in, relieving men from the engineers. They were hit hard on the 20th by tanks supported by infantry. The

Germans got all the way into town but were driven off, losing three Mark IVs, a self-propelled gun and more than 50 men. The same night the division hospital just north of Noville was overrun. Southwest of Bastogne, the road to Neufchâteau was cut, isolating Bastogne.

In our sector, Company B was sent down the St. Hubert road to attack a German unit that had destroyed a convoy from the 28th Infantry Division. Company B attacked at midnight, killing more than 50 Germans and liberating a light tank, some trucks and men who had been captured. Early on the morning of the 21st Company B was hit in return by nine half-tracks, seven 75mm guns and seven light vehicles. All were captured or destroyed except one that managed to escape. A little later in the day, two tanks and some infantry attacked again and were driven off. Company B then moved back into the defensive perimeter on our right flank.

The weather changed for the worse on the 21st with the temperature dropping sharply and a heavy gray overcast blanketing the sector. I was called to the CP and again found Captain Towns and Lieutenant Martinson using the car in the garage as their HQ. I was instructed to take a squad of men and support Company A, which held a roadblock south of our positions. I withdrew Felker's squad, spread Leamon's dangerously thin along the ridge, and headed for the new position.

Company A had two squads dug in around a large stone house north of the main road, supported by a light machine gun. Tech. Sergeant Robert Bradley, Fayetteville, Tennessee, was the platoon leader, an excellent NCO with a good record. He showed me his position and thought my squad should be dug in along a row of fir trees on his left. Just down the road a couple of hundred yards on the south side was a small hamlet surrounding a large courtyard. It was still occupied by civilians, as was the house in back of Bradley's line. In back of that house was a large barn. After getting Felker's men in place, I went back to my position, over a quarter mile away. It was bitterly cold and snow began to fall, slowly at first then like a dam bursting.

All around I could hear the sounds of fighting, sometimes muffled, other times just over the next hill. The snow began covering the ground and quickly got deeper. Foxholes now became freezers and no amount of stamping around could get one's feet warm. The cold had more serious effects, too. The actions on our weapons froze and all the lubrication had to be removed. Men who had foolishly discarded their overcoats and overshoes now suffered horribly. They spent a miserable night, wrapped in blankets, shelter halves and sleeping bags and still cold. I checked my squad several times during the night, mainly to keep warm.

A sharp fight awoke me at dawn on the 22d. It came from Company A's roadblock. Matt Pas called me immediately, instructing me to report to Captain Towns. When I got to the CP, it was in a frenzy. The road behind us had been cut. Captain Towns told me to get over there fast and appraise the situation.

I plowed through the knee-deep snow, glad to have overshoes even though they weighed a ton. When I got to Bradley's CP he said the Germans had moved into the hamlet during the night. He had been sending a two-man patrol east on the road to the battalion CP every two hours. Just before dawn it had been fired upon near the hamlet and one of the men had been wounded in the hip. The other had managed to get back through a hail of small arms fire, telling Bradley the enemy had occupied the hamlet and blocked the road with farm equipment. Because of the twin row of huge fir trees along the road, all I could see were two Germans lying in the road screaming. Every time someone tried to retrieve them, Bradley's men would fire on them. I decided to check with Felker to get an idea of the disposition of the enemy.

It was easier said than done. To reach him, I had to cross over 50 yards in perfect view of the enemy. I mustered my jaded nerves and took off through the snow, using a row of firs as a screen. A fusillade of small arms fire came from across the small valley, knocking off pine needles and splattering me with snow. Felker saw me coming, making room for me in a BAR pit. I dove headlong with bullets ricocheting off the frozen ground around me. I attributed my good luck to the cold weather. Evidently the Germans' hands were as cold as ours.

A lively firefight had started between Felker's men and the Germans, who were dug in around a farm shed and a huge mound of potatoes. Bobbing my head up and down over the dirt parapet, I could see enemy foxholes along the road, also two *Panzerfaust* positions and a machine gun. I had seen enough and passed the word to Felker's men to cover me. I dashed back the way I had come, bullets cutting the limbs off the trees acting as my screen.

I plowed through the snow back to the CP, reporting everything I had seen. As cold as it was, my body was covered in perspiration. Captain Towns thanked me then said, "Bowen, we've been surrounded for two days. Nothing getting through to us. Pass the word to your men to conserve food, water and ammunition. However,

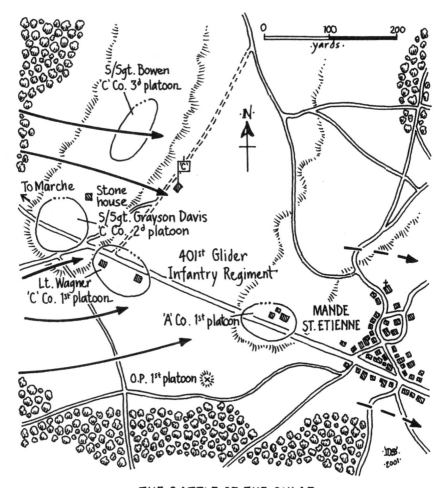

·THE BATTLE OF THE BULGE·
·THE 401ˢᵗ GLIDER INFANTRY REGIMENT HOLDS POSITIONS·
·ALONG THE BASTOGNE-MARCHE ROAD·
·DECEMBER 23ᵈ 1944·

⟶ Direction of German assaults on December 23ᵈ.

--⟶ Retreat of U.S. forces.

Bowen's 3ᵈ platoon joins forces with the 1ˢᵗ and 2ᵈ platoons of Company C,
in a blockade of the Marche road. While being led into position by
Sergeant Bowen, 3ᵈ platoon is called to a halt by Captain Towns,
resulting in Bowen's isolation, and subsequent capture by enemy forces.
▨ The Stone house functions as a hospital and shelter for soldiers and
civilians alike. This is the site of Bowen's injury in a shell attack,
and capture by German troops.

Third Army's headed our way. Should be here in a day or so. If your men see or hear tanks approaching, check if they're ours because they could be headed down that road. That's all for now. I'll call your report in to Colonel Allen."

I barely got back to my CP when Captain Towns was on the phone, asking me to report to his CP again. Once more I took off, accompanied by Norman Labbe, my radioman. Word of our situation had leaked to the men in the headquarters platoon by the looks on their faces. Captain Towns and Lieutenant Martinson were still in the car.

"That enemy roadblock has to be taken out, Bowen. Colonel Allen wants you to do it. Take Hanss' squad and one from Bradley's platoon. His machine gun can give you some support. I've already contacted Hanss. He should be up there by now. Get together with Bradley and coordinate your attack. Good luck."

Short, sweet and scary. As I headed for Bradley's CP, my mind was filled with doubts. I imagined all of us being shot down as we tried to cross those snow-covered fields. I was mad, too, thinking an officer should have been in command of something so important. However, being a slave to orders, by the time I got to Bradley's roadblock, most of my anger had dissipated.

Bradley was a soft-spoken Tennessean who had been with the 401st since its activation. He had been a platoon sergeant in Normandy and now led the platoon because his officer had been lost in Holland. We discussed the situation, trying to take the right course with the fewest risks. There had to be another way than just charging down the road. It came in the form of a tank that had been at 2d Platoon's roadblock. It stopped beside us, a husky sergeant getting out and saying, "Colonel Allen told me to run down the road and shoot the shit out of those houses." I told him about the *Panzerfausts* and his mood suddenly changed as he had run into them before. "What've you got in mind then," he asked.

"We decided to send a squad down each side of the road supported by enfilading fire from a squad on the left. Those Germans in the hamlet could make things hot for us because I don't think our firepower is enough to drive them out," I told him.

"Suppose I took care of the houses with my gun?" he said after appraising the situation. "My 50-caliber could deal with those foxholes dug in around them. Okay?"

"Okay man, you've just come from heaven," I replied.

I told Bradley I'd have to tell Felker his part in the plan. He readily approved and we set the idea in motion. Not trusting the scheme to be discussed over the radio, I told Bradley as soon as I gave Felker's men the order, I would begin firing and the attack could begin. He agreed. I dashed across the open courtyard to the music of German small arms fire, sliding into the BAR pit and passing along the plan. When everyone was ready, I gave the signal and Smith's BAR began to chatter.

It was a textbook attack, working better than anything we had ever done in practice. The tank began throwing shells into the hamlet, raking it from end to end while its heavy machine gun hammered away at the enemy foxholes. Felker's men poured small arms fire on the enemy along the road and around the shed and potato pile across from them. The two attacking squads went down the road, ducking from tree to tree with hardly a shot being fired at them, because the Germans were pinned in their holes. Germans began to flee from across the way and we shot them down without compunction. Hoarse cries of "*Kamerad! Kamerad!*" ended the action less than a half an hour after it had begun.

When I reached the hamlet 12 dead Germans had been taken from the houses, most killed by the tank's guns. There were more in the fields, some screaming in pain. I had them brought in, one a kid of 17 whom I had shot in the hip and who kept screaming "*Nicht Schiesen*" ("Don't shoot"). Felker could speak German and assured him he would be taken prisoner. We rounded up 26 in all, but others got away and began sniping at us from a copse of trees. I asked the tank sergeant to throw a couple of shells at them and that was the end of that. Most of the prisoners were young, from the *Luftwaffe* or naval units and were dressed partially in American uniforms. A few begged us not to kill them, saying they wore our uniforms because they were cold. Felker told them they would be taken to Bastogne as prisoners.

We had one casualty, Jerry Hanss. He had been accidentally shot through the calf of his leg and lay on the icy road covered in a blanket while we waited for a jeep to take him to the aid station. I knelt beside him until the jeep came. We had been friends since the day I had come into the company, and shared a secret which no one in the company except he and I knew about. He was an ardent communist, so zealous that it had separated him from his church and his family. I had even written to his mother, praising him and telling her it was something he had to get out of his system. He was a good friend and a credit to his country.

The tank sergeant was euphoric, unable to believe what we had accomplished. He joined me on the road saying, "I've been in this shit since D-Day plus 12 and seen a lot of things. But I never saw anything like this. You guys are tops in my book."

I got Captain Towns on Bradley's radio and reported the outcome. He told me to bring the prisoners to his CP. I selected a few men and we took off over the snow-covered fields, chilled by the cutting wind. First Sergeant Long met us on the way, relieved me of the prisoners and told me to get back to the roadblock. I defied him, saying I wanted to give my report to Captain Towns personally. Some of the men deserved a decoration for what they did that morning. Besides, the tank commander needed ammunition and I didn't want his wishes lost in the flush of the moment.

Afterward I went back to the roadblock and set up the defense as Captain Towns instructed me to. As I passed the dead Germans sprawled in the foxholes along the road, I noted how young they were, nothing but teenage boys. The dead lying in the courtyard were bloody and torn up by the tank guns, some of them middle aged. I wondered about the paradox of the situation. The night before they had probably been flushed by the sense of victory after driving their enemy back. Now they lay dead in the snow, freezing and lost forever to their families and friends. I felt sorry for them.

I became horribly depressed. They had been struggling for survival the same as us. But they had lost and we had won. How much more of this could we go through before we might be the ones stacked like poles ready to be loaded on a truck? I wondered about religion. Germany was not a godless nation; most of the people were either Catholic or Lutheran. Was nationalism more important to them, the righting of old wrongs, than the lives of these young boys? How could this be rationalized either morally or religiously? None of it made any sense to me. I went back to the CP as downcast as I had ever been.

We set up our defenses, using captured MG42s along with our own weapons. The tank went back to 2d Platoon, the crew pleased with their contribution. If it hadn't been for them, American bodies would have been lying alongside the Germans. Not long afterward, a jeep came down the road and stopped by the hamlet. General McAuliffe and some of his staff got out. He seemed to recognize me immediately as I saluted and told him about the action. He had complimented me in Holland when we were in positions along the Rhine. He did again, congratulating some of the men individually as well. His visit helped improve our morale and steady our nerves.

With Jerry Hanss gone, Joe Kloczkowski took over the squad. I went to check Leamon's squad on the windswept ridge. They were freezing, most without overcoats or overshoes. Wrapped in blankets and shelter halves, they stamped in their holes against the bone chilling cold. I delivered a few rations—we were down to two Ks a day—and told them the latest news. I also promised to relieve them as soon as possible.

A civilian lived in a large stone house near Bradley's CP. He was a burly man with a beard. His ears had been frozen during World War I. He was very kind to us, inviting us into his kitchen to cook our rations on his stove and to warm ourselves. We took advantage of it during the day, but at night had to man the foxholes. Nothing I could do, however, could keep me warm. The night passed like a horrible dream.

A burst of fire from the 2d Platoon's roadblock, the rattle of small arms fire and the bark of cannon startled me awake on the 23d. A heavy ground fog had reduced visibility to near zero and the Germans had used it to good advantage, moving close to the roadblock before they were identified as the enemy. More moved against 1st Platoon, opaque figures in snowsuits emerging from the pines. A 1st Platoon outpost spotted them first, fired then tried to withdraw. The two men from the outpost struggled through the snow under a hail of German fire. One of them, PFC Ernie Howard, Marion, Ohio, a veteran of Normandy and Holland, and one of the finest men I had ever known, was killed before he could reach our lines. The other, PFC Steve Horkey, another veteran, from Cudahy, Wisconsin, a troubled person who was worried about family affairs at home, had his thumb shot off but managed to get back.

After being wakened in this way I checked my squad but found that nothing out of the ordinary had been seen or heard, other than the movement of tanks in the distance, something which had been normal every night. I was heating K rations on the Belgian civilian's stove when Labbe got a message for me to report to Captain Towns immediately. I had no idea what was going on at the other roadblocks except for the frenzied firing. I hiked back through the snow and got to the garage.

Captain Towns and Lieutenant Martinson were still in the old car. "Bowen, 2d Platoon's under heavy attack. They don't know if they can hold. They've had some casualties and need help. I want you to take Felker's and Kloczkowski's squads and move to 2d Platoon's roadblock to support them. Lieutenant Wagner will meet you near the intersection of the main road and the one out front of here and lead you into position. I don't have to tell you to hurry. Good luck and do whatever you can," he said. I noted how drawn his face seemed to be. It was the last time I would ever see him.

I collected the men and their gear and went across the field close to the raised embankment of the main road to shield us from the Germans I could see near the pines to our left. A cold biting wind whipped across the field, scattering the snow like breaking sea foam. Wagner didn't wait for us, coming nearly to Bradley's block where he met us. He took off at a fast clip, too fast for us weighted down by arms, ammo and blanket rolls. I kept near his heels, but my men began to straggle. I urged them on. Tanks shells and mortar rounds were dropping in the field to our right, tearing black holes in the snow. No one hit the ground. We kept going. We passed a foxhole in the embankment; the torn and bloody fragments of a body in an American uniform littered the remains of the hole. I didn't know it then, but it was all that remained of my close friend Homer Johnson, formerly of Company B and recently sent to C, the same Johnson I had been with at the British hospital after Normandy.

Wagner continued to get farther ahead. He reached the secondary raised road leading to the company CP, turned and motioned me to follow. I looked back at my straggling squads. Only Joe Kloczkowski and Harold Zimburg were close. Wagner dashed over the road, joined by Joe Damato and Frank McFadden of his platoon who had been sent by Yeiser O'Guin. They followed at Wagner's heels, flinching as the shells burst in the field beside them but continuing on. I called back for my men to follow me and dashed after the others. Ahead I could hear the sharp bark of cannon, the rattle of small arms fire, and the crack of mortar shells. Nearly exhausted from the more than half mile hike through the snow, I put my head down and ran as fast as my legs would carry me, oblivious to anything but reaching the outbuilding behind the 2d Platoon's line. I finally got there, collapsing against the wall of one of the buildings with my lungs on fire. Zimburg and Kloczkowski came up on wobbly legs and dropped beside me. We all fought for breath.

When I got up and looked back across the field, I could see Labbe, my radioman, and Felker staring over the bank of the secondary road. I had no way of knowing it then, but Captain Towns had changed his mind and halted the rest of my platoon before they crossed the road. I missed Labbe and his radio especially. I had no contact with the company CP with him gone.

I looked around. Lieutenant Wagner had gone around the

building and into a sunken courtyard behind the big stone house located in back of 2d Platoon's position. I joined him and we learned that the situation was very bad. The tanks that had supported us the day before sat beside the house but had been severely damaged. Some of the crew had been wounded by shrapnel. The burly sergeant had painful wounds in his face and hands. He had been firing the tank's .50-caliber machine gun when an anti-tank shell had hit the turret just under him. Although wounded, he was lucky to be alive. He had been moved into the cellar of the big house where an aid station had been set up. The 37mm anti-tank gun which had been positioned in some tall firs was out of action, its wheels frozen in the ground and unable to fire at the 11 German tanks which sat in defilade positions and poured shells into 2d Platoon's defense line. German infantry in snowsuits were scattered in a semi-circle some 200 yards away, firing directly into 2d Platoon's foxholes. There were dead and wounded men lying in the snow all along the line. The only obstacle keeping the Germans from overrunning the roadblock was the 76mm gun on a tank destroyer.

The tank destroyer was commanded by Staff Sergeant Chester Sakwinski, Milwaukee, Wisconsin, a stout blond fellow with a ready smile. There was a second tank destroyer at the roadblock but it was out of action, its turret so frozen that it couldn't be moved. The TD platoon's commander was there, too, a Lieutenant Gwyn, who had been given a battlefield commission that very day.

Gwyn tried desperately to thaw the frozen turret but had no luck. Finally, he told the disabled tank destroyer to take off to battalion to have the turret repaired. It pulled out of the courtyard and made a dash for the rear down the elevated main road. Fortunately, most of the German tanks did not have a clear shot at it, but those that did threw several shells at it. As it disappeared over a ridge near Bradley's position, I thought I saw a pile of blanket rolls on the back of the tank destroyer fly into the air, helped along by a German shell.

Sakwinski's tank destroyer was holding the enemy tanks at bay, rising from the sunken courtyard to fire at the enemy then backing down to escape enemy shells, which were soon to follow. Gwyn directed the action, selecting the targets from a rise in the ground.

Despite its perilous condition, the 2d Platoon was keeping the enemy infantry from advancing. Two machine guns from our weapons platoon were also helping. However, one was soon knocked out and its crew killed. Colonel Allen sent observers from the heavy weapons platoon of the battalion, Staff Sergeant Schwartz in command. All through the day he directed 81mm mortar fire on the enemy line and into a wooded area where he evidently believed their reserve might be located. We could hear the screams of the wounded over the din of small arms fire and ordnance. However, because of an ammunition shortage, we were denied artillery support from division. Shells were being rationed. Only sure targets were being fired on. There were plenty out there but we had no forward artillery observer to select them. Evidently our word wasn't good enough.

I put the men Wagner and I had brought in a line along the main road in back of 2d Platoon's position. On the icy road was a string of bicycles with luggage racks packed with clothing and personal things. They belonged to civilians who had been caught up in the battle at dawn, people who had been fleeing down the road from St. Hubert one step ahead of the Germans. They had dropped the bikes and run into the cellar of the house at the outbreak of the battle. Now they were talking excitedly with Wagner, who spoke some high school French, pleading with him to have someone recover the valuable bikes.

I told Wagner I would see if it were possible. I dashed over the snow-covered lawn in front of the house to the main road and was greeted by a burst of small arms fire, which tore up the snow around me. I flopped to the ground in the cover of the embankment, and then raised my head to see how far away the bikes were. Bullets ricocheted off the road and I knew I had been seen. There was no way I was going to retrieve that stuff and took off for the house again. I returned to the basement and told Wagner it was out of the question. When he told the civilians they burst into tears. I felt sorry for them but wasn't going to risk any of my men on so foolish a mission.

Some medics came up from the battalion aid station, four, I believe, including Tech. Sergeant Bonner, the ranking NCO, and Sergeant Bell, an old acquaintance. They went to work on the wounded. One was an old friend, Staff Sergeant Oakley Knapp, a rotund genial farmer from Portsmouth, Ohio, who had been painfully wounded by a bullet through his ankle. His machine gun position had taken a direct hit. The two men with him, Private Lorne Torrence, Plainfield, New Jersey, and PFC William Epson, Quincy, Massachusetts, had been killed instantly. Epsom was the platoon clown, one of those people with a natural bent to make others laugh. His clever imitations of Walt Disney characters had saved many stressful situations in the past.

I checked out the roadblock in an effort to see what could be done to preserve it and noticed a half-track pulled into the trees near the anti-tank gun. It belonged to the 10th Armored Division and somehow had gotten mixed up in the battle while trying to locate others from its unit. Its crew of ten or so men had taken cover behind the big house.

Next I crawled to the crest of the rise overlooking the sunken court and checked 2d Platoon's defense line. Some of the wounded lay in the snow, one babbling incoherently and another screaming. More were sprawled in contorted positions, obviously dead. The screams got to me. I returned to the aid station and asked Bonner if we couldn't bring the wounded back. He told me his men had tried, but were fired on as soon as they showed themselves. I said I would like to try. He asked Private Everett Padgett, Phoenix, Arizona, an aid man often assigned to Company C, if he would go too. Padgett readily agreed and we dashed through the snow to the main road.

Small arms fire from the Germans, as well as mortar and tank fire was sweeping the area. We looked down the forward slope of the hill, sucked in our guts and started down. It seemed to me that the volume of fire increased, with every German there personally interested in ending our military careers. We soon knew it was useless but we were lucky. We got up and sprinted back to the cover of the crest of the rise. Padgett told me to stay put, that perhaps the Germans would honor the Red Cross emblems on his helmet. He went back down the slope. It was one of the bravest acts I had ever witnessed with enemy bullets plowing up the snow around him until he reached the wounded men. Then the German fire slackened and he tended the two men. A short while later he crawled back, still plagued by some rifle fire from diehards. But he made it and I thought of the wounded Germans who lay in the road the day before and how Bradley's men had tried to kill whoever went out to help them.

Padgett said the men were beyond help, both had been shot through the head and were hysterical. One was Private Joseph Cammarata, Detroit, Michigan, who we called Peppernose for obvious reasons, a prankster who constantly played practical jokes on men in his squad and whom his friends accused of overburdening the post office with his steady stream of letters home. Another was Staff Sergeant Fred Poling, Fairmont, West Virginia, a veteran of the 401st's activation, solid as a rock in combat and a friend to almost everyone. One of the dead lying near them was Staff Sergeant Robert Rehler, Circleville, Ohio, a young dedicated fellow who had only recently received his sergeant's stripes.

Above: Bedraggled members of Company B, 401st Glider Infantry Regiment, pose for a quick photograph at the height of the Battle of the Bulge. The icy conditions of the fighting are apparent. (Carmen Gisi)

Left: Sgt. Richard Gill (left) poses with a fellow member of Company B. Gill had been in hospital with Bowen following the D-Day landings. (Carmen Gisi)

Left: The town of Bastogne was virtually destroyed during the Battle of the Bulge, even though the Germans did not gain entry into it. (US Army)

Below: Members of the 101st leave the relative safety of the ruins of Bastogne for positions on the front line. (US Army)

Above: A glider infantryman cleans his rifle during a short break in the fighting. (US Army)

Left: Two glidermen fire on German positions near Mande St. Etienne. (US Army)

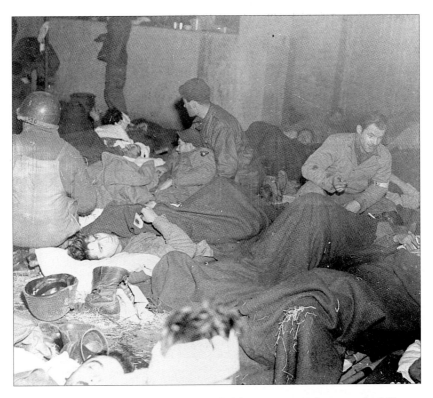

Above: Wounded members of the division are treated at a makeshift hospital in Bastogne. It was in just such a temporary hospital that Bowen was captured on December 23d. (US Army)

Above left: Members of the 401st inspect an abandoned German staff car. (Carmen Gisi)

Left: The 101st Field Hospital captured by German troops on December 19th, 1944, photographed during a patrol made by members of the 401st. (Carmen Gisi)

Above: The ones who made it: (L–R) PFC Leonard Waddlington, PFC Robert O'Mara, and SSgt Ted Feldman survived the fighting and are pictured here at the 101st's camp at Mourmelon, France, in 1945.

Above left & left: Stalag XIIA, photographed on March 28th, 1945. Bowen spent some time at XIIA as a prisoner of war.

Right: (L–R) SSgt John M. Garrett, PFC August L. Fortuna and Ted Feldman in Sens, France, July 1945.

186

Above: The division, minus the thousands of men who had been killed, wounded, or taken prisoner, finished the war at Hitler's Eagle's Nest retreat. (US Army)

Top left: A Company C member, Robert C. Lott (pictured here on the left), later decorated for his role in the Battle of the Bulge, relaxes in the Alps after the seizure of Adolf Hitler's mountain retreat at Berchtesgaden, April 1945. (Robert Lott)

Left: Two members of the 401st have their picture taken beside a wrecked American halftrack at Berchtesgaden. (Robert Lott)

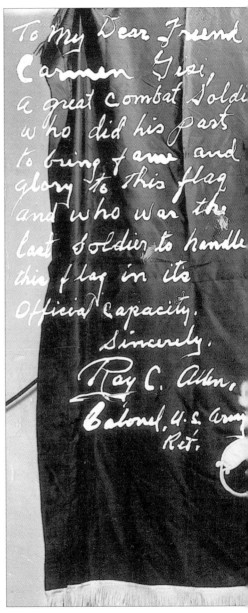

To my Dear Friend Carmen Gisi, a great combat Soldier who did his part to bring fame and glory to this flag and who was the last Soldier to handle this flag in its Official Capacity. Sincerely, Ray C. Allen, Colonel, U.S. Army Ret.

Top left: Robert Bowen wearing a British battledress jacket obtained at a British hospital in Liège, Belgium, in May 1945.

Left: Bowen during his post-war recovery at White Plains, New York, in September 1945.

Above: Colonel Ray C. Allen, commander of the 401st Infantry Regiment, stands in front of the Regimental flag after his return to Marshall, Texas. (Carmen Gisi)

Attendees at a post-war dinner, held for members of the 401st Infantry Regiment in 1955. Robert Bowen appears in the front row, second from right, wearing a patterned shirt. Also pictured is Bob Bradley (seated in the second row, third from left, wearing tie), the platoon

sergeant who commanded the position from which Bowen did much of his Bastogne fighting in December 1944. Contact remains strong among many surviving members of the 401st Regiment, who have been active in the 101st Association.

Above: Robert Bowen at home in Linthicum, Maryland, in early 2001.
(Christopher Anderson)

Below: Bowen with Christopher Anderson in early 2001.
(Christopher Anderson)

I told Wagner that perhaps the gun on the disabled tank might help out and that I had some experience in artillery. He suggested talking to the tank commander and I did in the aid station. He said it wasn't possible; the gun was out of commission.

The 2d Platoon bore the full brunt of the attack although the 1st Platoon was taking fire from Germans in a wooded area to the front. The German tanks edged closer to 2d Platoon and were now firing directly into foxholes. Sakwinski's tank destroyer kept the tanks to the front at bay, but others in defilade positions to the side couldn't be touched. The 2d Platoon's casualties mounted and ammunition was getting scarce. Staff Sergeant Grayson Davis, Charlotte, North Carolina, had been blown out of a foxhole by a direct hit and was severely wounded. Even though no one had taken over from him the squads stayed in place and held off the enemy grenadiers.

Wagner, Gwyn and I met behind the main building, agreeing that something had to be done about the tanks the tank destroyer couldn't align on. I noticed a bazooka and some rockets in the half-track and suggested that I take it and try to get in a shot. Wagner agreed, so we got the weapon and loaded it. I had to cross the front yard of the house that was being swept by small arms fire. However, I managed this without being hit, even though my heart was in my mouth the whole time. I settled behind the embankment and looked through some trees for a target. A tank was sitting in a little draw some 200 yards out. I set the sights, took a long careful aim after making sure the pin was pulled in the rocket, and pulled the trigger. Without a shield on the weapon or protective glasses, the blast from the rocket nearly blinded me. However, I kept my eyes on the tank. The rocket grazed it without exploding. The tank hurriedly backed out of sight. I ran back to the house and told Wagner about what had happened and said I'd like to go back in case the tank moved forward again. "I think we should save the rockets. We might need them later," he said, noting that only two were left.

The 2d Platoon was taking a terrible mauling and the ammo was running out. PFC George Kalb, Baltimore, Maryland, a lanky, quiet fellow from Highlandtown in the eastern part of the city, was a BAR man. I didn't know him well because he was a replacement after Normandy and our paths hadn't crossed that often. He fired clip after clip until his ammo was gone, then watched helplessly as the Germans inched closer. When darkness fell, he and PFC Frank A. Marine, Philadelphia, Pennsylvania, isolated and without any direction from an NCO because of the casualties, made a mad dash over the snow to the rear. But the night was crystal clear with a bright moon, and the enemy saw them. They were fired on and Marine was killed, trapped by a wire fence he was trying to cross. Kalb miraculously got away.

Our heavy mortars were helping Sakwinski's tank destroyer, but the shells were being rationed as the battle wore on. The house, outbuildings and courtyard were coming under increasingly heavy fire. The tall firs around us were being hit, the tops tumbling to the snow with flying needles, branches and cones raining on us. Staff Sergeant Louis A. Butts, Gorrardstown, West Virginia, a short stocky veteran, one of the original members of the company, managed to wriggle through the snow and reach the big house. His heavily whiskered face wore a stunned expression as he came over to where we were standing.

"Half my squad is either dead or wounded. And we're nearly out of ammunition. The rest of the platoon is no better off. I think we should pull back," he said in a bewildered way, his soft drawl slurred. Wagner was on a spot, unable to talk directly to Captain Towns, his only orders, "Hold as long as you can." Moreover, from where we were, we couldn't see the extent of the damage to 2d Platoon's defenses. Something else he had to think about was what would happen to the men if they withdrew along the forward slope of the hill in full view of the enemy. Wagner looked Butts in the eyes. "Sergeant, my orders are to hold this position. Until there is a change in those orders, that's what I plan on doing. Now, you go back to your men. You'll be notified if we are to pull out."

Butts stared at us, a look of disbelief on his face. However, he was too good a soldier to argue with an officer. Even though his face was flushed with anger, he gritted his teeth, turned and somehow got back to his squad's position.

It was getting to be late afternoon with a gray curtain of clouds settling over the area. Even though the battle still raged, 2d Platoon's resistance was faltering because of casualties and the ammo shortage. Joe Damato came back from his position on the main road, telling Wagner, Gwyn and I that he didn't think 2d Platoon could hold out much longer. The tempo of the German fire had increased, small arms rounds, mortar and artillery shells sweeping over us or dropping in the courtyard. I saw the top of a huge fir disintegrate, the debris dropping around us as we stood in back of the basement of the house. It should have been a warning to us, but we were inured to such things and careless. Trying to bolster our sagging defensive line was more important at the moment.

Suddenly the world seemed to explode in my face. I felt myself being tossed aside as if a giant bubble had violently burst at my feet. My ears rang, my vision was blurred, my body felt as if it was on fire, and my nostrils filled with acrid smoke. A shell had dropped less than ten feet from us, bowling us over like pins in a bowling alley. All four of us were down. My chest was on fire and my arm numb. Gwyn lay in a crumpled heap, Wagner, Damato and I got up and limped closer to the wall of the house. Medics rushed outside and helped us to the temporary aid station.

Gwyn was the most seriously wounded, chunks of shrapnel tearing holes in many parts of his body. He was placed on a litter and taken inside. Wagner was the least wounded, with a piece of steel through the toe of his boot and into his foot. After having it dressed, he returned to direct the resistance. Damato had a painful gash in the back of his right thigh, a piece of shrapnel the size of a silver dollar having torn into it. I was lucky, my ammunition belt suspenders slowed up a chunk of shrapnel, which still buried itself just below the ribs on the right side of my chest. It was the size of a half dollar and the medics picked it out. But they couldn't do anything with the piece in my right wrist, a jagged shard that had buried itself in the bones. The medics dressed our wounds, gave us shots of morphine and told us to lay on a pile of straw with other wounded. For us the battle was over. With the effects of the morphine making me dreamy-eyed, I couldn't have done much anyway.

Darkness falls early in late December and soon enveloped our fateful roadblock. Unbeknownst to us, the survivors of 2D Platoon were withdrawing any way they could. We didn't know because none came back past the big house, but followed draws in the terrain on either side. Wagner had come to the aid station, trying to round up men from the half-track, anti-tank gun and armor, men who hadn't been wounded, but without any success. They simply wouldn't follow his directions, probably, I assume, because he was an unknown officer, and they weren't about to put their lives under his command in such a tense situation. Anyway, he left without motivating them to form a defense line along the main highway and it was the last I was to see of him.

Time dragged on with only random firing coming from the enemy in front of us. Damato and I were worried, wondering why Wagner hadn't come back and ordered the aid station to be evacuated. (He couldn't. Germans had moved in and cut him off from the place, so he had gone back to 1st Platoon to find the platoon gone, withdrawn to a line closer to the battalion.) We got up and went outside. The gray cloud mass had moved away, leaving a bright clear night with few clouds in the sky. Joe looked across the field to our rear and said, "Bob, I don't think Wagner is coming back. I think we should make a break for it."

I looked at the distance we would have to go and thought about his leg wound. He could hardly walk and I knew he would never make it. As for me, my wrist was extremely painful but the wound in my abdomen nothing to speak of and I knew I could move in a pinch. However, there were other things to consider. We had no way of knowing that the 2d Platoon had pulled out, we didn't know whether Wagner would come back, there were wounded, medics and men from the mortar observation crew in the basement, and, more importantly, Captain Towns had told us to hold until ordered differently. In retrospect, it was flawed logic. Towns had no way of knowing what was happening at the roadblock without radio contact. He didn't realize the desperation in 2d Platoon, that they were in an every-man-for-himself situation with no one in command, and he assumed Wagner had control. In other words, the roadblock was a disaster waiting to happen. And it did!

I helped Joe into the basement, which had become complete chaos. The civilians were hysterical, crying, praying, and screaming. The medics were unable to quiet them. Some of the wounded were in much pain, hiding their torment but still groaning despite the morphine. Men from the half-track, tank and tank destroyer, many moderately wounded, waited for orders as to the next move, orders that never came because all the officers were casualties. I wondered what had happened to Lieutenant Wagner and waited anxiously for him to return with orders to evacuate the place.

The small arms and tank fire to the front petered out. Something told me we had been abandoned and that those who were able should make a break for it. But that meant leaving the wounded behind, something we had never done. I put the thought out of my mind. I felt for the .38 Smith and Wesson I carried in a shoulder holster. After hearing about the massacre at Malmédy, I wasn't going down without a fight.

Sam, a German-speaking medic, went outside in the darkness to hunt for Lieutenant Wagner. Lying by the doorway I heard him talking to someone. "Nothing but wounded," I heard him say in German and knew that the worst had happened. The door was shoved in with a kick and a big German in a snowsuit came in, machine pistol leveled. He had a flashlight, which he shone on the medic and the litters. I raised my pistol, ready to fire if he did. Instead he said gruffly, "Yes, they are all wounded. That's good." I put the pistol away. He walked along shining the light about and nodding. Then saying, "For you the war is over."

Sam spoke with him a moment, then told us we were prisoners of war and would be treated as such. I breathed a sigh of relief.

CHAPTER 14

Into the Frying Pan

The ambulatory wounded were marched through the knee-deep snow with a biting wind tearing our uniforms. Most of the men had discarded overcoats during the battle and were now paying for it. We were taken to a hillside from which the German infantry had been firing into our positions. The snow was trampled, torn and blackened from mortar and artillery shells and some German corpses lay sprawled in the snow. At other places were bits of uniform and bloody stains left by the wounded who had been taken away. We were lined up by angry Germans who shouted such things as, "*Verdammt Amerikaner Schwinehund*," "*Unser Kameraden kaput*," and "*Scheiden die Amerikaner Bastarden*." It was a tense moment for us. The enemy soldiers were so angry, anything could have happened. After all, just days before, one German unit had shot down nearly 100 American POWs in cold blood at Malmédy and other Germans had killed numerous Belgian civilians, many of them women and children, for little or no cause. However, a sergeant suddenly appeared and calmed his men. He allowed them to strip us of any valuables and I lost a nice, but broken, wristwatch that my wife had sent me. It had stopped running during an artillery barrage, which had shaken my foxhole. Fortunately I was allowed to keep my wedding band.

The enemy had surrounded the position and began rounding up stragglers who were brought over to us. Two were from my 3d Platoon, Sgt. Joseph Kloczkowski, third squad leader, and PFC Harold Zimburg. Among the other prisoners were Sergeant Oakley Knapp, Joe Damato, and Lieutenant Gwyn. Tech. Sergeant George Bonner, S/Sgt. James Z. Bell, Sgt. John Semel, PFC Cloyd R. Brotherton, Pvts. Edward Melanz, Herbert Lawhorne, George Miller, Rinehard and PFC Milan, were also captured. The crew of the disabled tank and the crew of the TD including its commander, S/Sgt. Chester Sakwinski were prisoners also. There was a lot of random shooting and explosions as the Germans consolidated the position. I thought the wounded who couldn't walk were killed but they weren't. However, Semel, who was Jewish, was killed later that night.

The moon was bright and full, bathing the countryside as if a huge spotlight had been turned on. Many of 2d Platoon's men who had survived now tried to escape over the snow. PFC George Kalb, my friend from Baltimore who was a BAR gunner, fired all his clips, methodically put the empties back into his belt, and took off with Private Frank Marine. They reached a barbed wire fence, bullets kicking up the snow around them. George got over, Frank didn't. His body hung in the wire.

The scene around the large house in back of the roadblock was eerie. Fire from a burning haystack lit the area along with what remained of the burning tank; it had been blown up. The TD and half-track were being driven away by rowdy Germans. The enemy had thrown caution aside. They acted like boy scouts at a jamboree, boisterously shouting and acting as if they were in no danger of being shelled by our troops.

After rounding up all the Americans, the Germans marched us to some captured trucks and weapons carriers and we took off. Eventually, we reached a small town, which was bustling with motor traffic moving toward Bastogne. Surprisingly, there was a complete lack of blackout discipline. I wondered if the Germans knew about our ammunition shortage?

We were taken to a row house, probably the regimental CP, searched, then questioned by an officer who spoke perfect English. Afterward, we were taken upstairs to a dismal, dark attic and told to find places on piles of straw that covered the floor. It was jet black with only the light of a small candle near a guard with a tommy gun. Our medics, who managed to keep their medical kits, gave all the wounded shots of morphine. Sammy, a medic from the 99th Division who had been picked up, helped. Then, being Jewish with parents from Germany, he talked to the sentry in his native language, establishing a good rapport with him. Damato, Sakwinski, and I curled up and tried to sleep, but couldn't.

During the night the guard was changed. The first sentry left soon to reappear with a bottle of schnapps. It was passed around until emptied. Shortly thereafter an officer suddenly burst into the room, red faced with anger. He began cursing at the sentry because we had been given the schnapps. Sammy finally managed to placate the officer, denying that the sentry had brought us the liquor. However, the hot liquor in our empty stomachs seemed to have a soothing effect. I had managed to hang onto a D ration chocolate bar and shared it with Joe before we got some sleep.

At daybreak on the 24th we were loaded aboard a truck and a weapons carrier, though our number had grown as more men were brought in. We were packed like sardines in a can, with the wounded put in the truck where they weren't as vulnerable to the icy wind. Our driver had been thoroughly briefed as to our route yet continually got lost. Over winding roads through the hills and forest covered with snow, our journey was as rambling as a drunk's. A heavy mist still covered everything but wore away as the day lengthened. On all sides was left the carnage of the battle. Burned trucks, tanks and jeeps, destroyed homes, some still burning and smoking, and the dead, frozen in the snow, like fish in a box of ice. In the distance, I could hear the crash of artillery shells and knew the battle was still raging.

The sun came out as we finally reached a small village which had recently been bombed and strafed by our planes. Fires blazed, huge craters were in the road and fields, and German soldiers were crouched in roadside ditches. They looked anxiously at the sky, searching for the P-47s which had just left the village a mess. We unloaded the trucks, with the wounded being taken to a dressing station where we were examined and had our dressings changed. The return of our planes sent the Germans scurrying for cover while we cowered in the house with the bombs dropping outside to be followed by long strafing runs from our planes. A bomb dropped nearby. The house shook and plaster came down like snow. Even though I reveled in the Germans' terror, I realized that we were just as vulnerable as they were, but the attack was short-lived. Our wounds dressed, we were taken to a nearby house and put with the other prisoners.

It was a typical Belgian farmhouse with a barn attached to the house. We went into the barn, so crowded with prisoners that you could hardly turn around. The floor was covered with straw wet with urine and smeared with feces. Anxiously we waited until the enemy soldiers came and took us away several at a time for questioning. Fortunately, the officer who questioned me seemed to know all he needed because his questions were curt. I tried to follow the instructions given to us in training and that seemed to be satisfactory. Back in the barn, others said the Germans had a detailed knowledge of the units trapped in Bastogne, as well as those trying to break through to them.

Additional prisoners kept being added to our number, including the crew of a C-47 that had been shot down on a supply run to Bastogne. The fliers gave us the latest news of the battle, which wasn't that much, and said Patton's army had reached the outskirts of Bastogne.

Late in the day the Germans brought us a large kettle of steaming hot noodle soup. No one had any mess gear except some spoons, something an the infantryman keep as handy as his rifle. By passing the spoons around, everyone got some of the hot soup, the first warm meal some had had in nearly a week. There was a small egg stove in one end of the barn, which was freezing cold, and a robust German began shouting something which none of us understood. Finally, Harold Zimburg spoke up, telling us that the German wanted some of us to go out in the yard and fetch some coal for the stove. Several men volunteered and soon a fire was going, giving those near it some warmth. Straw was pulled from the loft and thrown on the floor, but the barn was so crowded there wasn't room for everyone to lie down. Most of us stood or sat throughout the night, saying little but despondent about our fate.

On Christmas Day we woke hungry and cold, the coal in the stove long since having been consumed. Everyone was flushed from the barn to be lined up and counted. Assigning five guards to watch over us, the enemy herded us onto a hard road for the long trip to Germany. The soup had long since been digested and my stomach growled with hunger. Also, my wounds hurt, especially the one in the wrist. The sky was clear and bright, ideal for our planes, as we hiked along the icy road. We walked past the usual carnage, burned and wrecked vehicles, one a German ambulance well-marked with the Red Cross. Bodies were still in its smoldering wreckage. Several times the road was blocked and the able-bodied prisoners made to remove the wreckage left by our planes.

Our guards made the prisoners carry their rucksacks. The guard near me was munching on fried chicken legs. Several times, he waved a leg in front of me, saying, "*Das ist Gut, Ja?*" Then he would laugh and take a bite. At that time I couldn't understand his hatred. In all my experiences with prisoners, I had tried to be compassionate, one time nearly being killed by a sniper when I helped one back to our aid station. However, after seeing the damage our bombers did to their country, I began to fathom the depths of their animosity. Ahead we could see and hear our P-47s, which the Germans called Jabos, and our P-51s, going about their missions with a vengeance. It never entered my mind that we would be their next target.

The guards became very agitated by the planes, but we weren't worrying. After all, we were American; they wouldn't bother us. We were wrong. The American planes seemed to come out of nowhere and the guards began shouting "Jabos" and diving for the ditches. Some of the prisoners foolishly stood and waved at the planes as they came in from the side of the road with machine guns blazing. I dove right for a ditch. It was too shallow but provided some cover. I could hear the guns hammering and saw their bullets tearing chunks out of the macadam road, sparks flying. It was scary, as fearful as being caught in an artillery or mortar barrage. One plane made a pass, zoomed up in a wide turn and came back. I saw streams of tracers coming right at me, puffs of exploding road and sparks. A couple of medics jumped up, shouting and waving their arms frantically. The plane must have gotten the message and it broke off and left.

There were people down in the road. Our medics went right to work on them. One was Tech. Sergeant Bonner of our 326th Medical Company, hit in the hip by a bullet which came out of his leg near his knee. He was bleeding profusely. The chicken-eating guard was also down, within an arm's length of me. He still clutched the chicken leg in his hand, but a bullet had passed through his chest and he lay in a pool of blood.

The guards had the POWs carry the dead and wounded as we continued on our trip. Not for long. Each time we made some progress, the planes came back, strafing and sending us to the ditches. We finally reached a small village, with the dead and wounded Germans being taken to a hospital and the rest of us to a building which, evidently, was a Nazi headquarters. Herded into a large hall decorated with banners, photos of the *Führer* and other political paraphernalia, we were told to find places for ourselves. Most of us wearily flopped on the floor, especially the wounded, and waited for further developments. I was famished and my wounds ached. Joe Damato was in a similar state. The large wound in his thigh was giving him trouble. Hunger pangs knawed at our stomachs. For six days we had been living off one or two cold K rations a day and had burnt a lot of energy performing our duties. Most of the other men were no better off.

We were free to walk around the hall and inspect the Nazi propaganda lining the walls. It seemed inconceivable to me that the German people could swallow such garbage but such must be life under a dictatorship. Finally, a German brought a large box into the room. It was our meal, a cartoon of rotting and half-frozen apples. Very few of the men touched them.

Our medics, now under the command of Sergeant Bell, had been attending to Sergeant Bonner. In vain they had tried to have the Germans take him to a hospital in one of the ambulances which was going through the town. Bonner was barely conscious and bleeding badly. He would surely die if he didn't get surgical attention in a hurry. But the Germans were adamant and Bonner eventually died because of this indifference.

A German staff car going to the rear stopped in front of the building. After a short discussion with our guards, it was agreed that the car would take some of us wounded to a clearing hospital. Sakwinski and I were led outside and into the car. We began a cold ride with a driver, an officer and a guard to look after us. We reached a small village near dark and were taken into an inn. We were in Luxembourg. A bright fire burned in a large fireplace and the inn was crowded with civilians and Germans. The officer with us ushered us to a table and instructed a waitress to bring us something to eat and drink. She brought a sandwich and some *ersatz* (wartime substitute) coffee, the first I ever tasted and it wasn't very good. Meanwhile the officer sat with us, conversing in perfect English. He told us that Bastogne had fallen and all the Americans in it had been killed, wounded or captured. He said the German offensive had been successful, Liège had been taken and Eisenhower was a prisoner. The German drive was now close to Antwerp. None of it was true, of course, our captor was simply another victim of the German radio broadcasts.

The officer ordered a bottle of wine and shared it with us. He was very amiable, nothing like I had pictured German officers to be. Another German officer joined our group, and the two sat discussing something over a map. Meanwhile, our waitress, a middle-aged woman with a kindly face, rubbed against me and pressed something into my hand. I slipped it in the big pocket of my baggy combat trousers. She did it a second and third time. Later I discovered they were cookies from C rations.

An hour later we were taken outside and told to climb on the top of a stake-bodied truck with a canvas cover. A guard climbed on with us. Damato had come up with a GI blanket and the three of us lay huddled together, trying to escape the biting cold wind whipping over the top of the cab and eyeing the guard on the back who was just as cold but holding a machine pistol. The truck drove over the snowy road under black-out conditions, snaking through one fir forest after another. It took me a while to fathom that beside us he was carrying a load of Jerrycans filled with gasoline. There was another guard on the front fender who anxiously scanned the moonlit sky. Suddenly, he shouted a warning, the truck made a dash for another clump of trees and slid to a halt. Moments later a low-flying British Mosquito fighter-bomber zoomed just a hundred yards or so over us, evidently hunting for fat targets like gas trucks. However, he was gone in a flash and we continued on our journey.

Hours later, we reached a small village, so stiff with cold that we could hardly move. There was no need for the guard. We couldn't have escaped if we wanted to. We pulled into a courtyard with large buildings on each side. We were taken to the building on the right, upstairs to the second floor to a room with a dozen or so American prisoners in it. The floor was covered with straw and an egg stove threw out enough heat to keep the place warm. We went right to it, gradually thawing out.

I met one of the C-47 pilots who had been shot down on a supply run to Bastogne. He was about 25, small and blond and he was badly burned on hands and face with one leg in a cast. He also had a dislocated shoulder from landing in a tree before hitting the ground. After picking him up, the Germans took him to their CP for questioning, doing nothing for his burns, shoulder or broken leg. When he refused to tell anything about his mission or unit, he was made to sit in a chair in great pain and with no medical attention. The next day he had undergone more questioning, but still refused to talk. Understanding that they had a hard case on their hands, the Germans eventually relented and took care of his injuries.

Joe and I settled down to sleep but hardly closed our eyes when a guard came for us. I had taken off my shoes to rub my feet warm. The impatient guard keep shouting "*Kommen! Vorbeitkommen!*" His machine pistol under my nose, I left the boots and followed him. We went down the stairs, across the courtyard nearly knee-deep in snow and to the other building which was serving as a temporary hospital. When we walked into the operating room, I nearly gagged. There were a half dozen tables surrounded by doctors in white rubber aprons splattered with blood. All the tables were occupied with German wounded or men with frozen limbs. Buckets on the floor held toes, fingers and other appendages. The men on the tables had been given a local anesthetic, but were still screaming and groaning as the doctors worked. Sammy, the medic stood by, acting as an interpreter. He said I would be operated on, but not Damato.

When it came my turn, I felt like running, but climbed on the table anyway. A rag with ether was held on my face and I dropped off. I was awakened by slaps on my face and saw my right wrist was heavily bandaged and painful. Back across the courtyard I went and into the room. Some German wounded had been brought in, most with frozen limbs. They sat huddled around the stove, cold, wet, dispirited and looking nothing like supermen. Sammy came back too, saying Bonner was in the hospital at last but not expected to live. He didn't, dying during the night.

At daybreak we were awakened and given a black bread sandwich with some cheese on it. Ravishingly hungry, we savored every bite. Later, a doctor came into the room, talking to us in English. He seemed to be a veteran of many campaigns with battle ribbons and the Iron Cross decoration. He didn't try to pry any information out of us, just chatted amiably and told us what he could about the battle raging in the Ardennes. He seemed less optimistic than the first officer who talked with us. After he left, a German NCO visited the loft. He was a typical Nazi, full of propaganda and belligerent. He spoke poor English which he had acquired while working as a seaman. We were glad when he went away.

That evening some local girls visited the loft, passing out chocolate bars gotten from our rations and sandwiches made with rye bread and salami, absolutely delicious. We thanked them warmly for their kindness.

The following day Joe Damato and I were taken out and put on a truck loaded with German wounded. Although some of them looked at us with daggers in their eyes, most were so disconsolate that all they seemed to want to do was to be relieved of their pain. It was another long cold ride with the freezing air cutting right through our uniforms. The ride was interrupted off and on because our planes, which circled in the sky like vultures hunting for food, were attacking any vehicle they saw. It was dark when we reached a small town and were taken right to a temporary hospital for military cases.

We were put in a hallway on benches and given a bowl of soup and a sandwich while the Germans were taken to rooms. As we ate we met five medics from an American outfit who had been kept at the hospital to carry litter cases. They said they worked from six in the morning until eleven at night, receiving as pay two sandwiches apiece for breakfast and lunch and a bowl of soup and cup of *ersatz* coffee for supper. Later they took us to a room.

Mine was small, the floor straw-covered with blankets. All the other wounded were Germans and I was put between two SS troopers. They did not seem hostile, in fact, it looked as if they wanted to talk. However, as I spoke no German and they no English, our conversation amounted to sign language and pidgin English. The man next to me had been an anti-tank gunner and told me about knocking out two American tanks. However, the third got him, killing everyone in his crew but him. He even got a small metal case out of an inner pocket. It contained half-smoked cigarettes and he graciously offered me one. Even though I was never a cigarette smoker, I took a butt and smoked it with him.

Later that evening a nun visited the room, handing out some cookies and a chocolate bar to each man, a gift because of the Christmas holidays. In the distance I could hear other nuns singing Christmas carols and my thoughts turned to home. Would my wife and parents know that I had been captured? Due to the confused nature of the fighting, would they believe me killed? I wrote a letter to my wife most every day possible, and she wrote too. How would she take my being "missing in action?" As much as my wounds pained me, my emotions did more.

The next day I walked the hall looking for Damato. I found him and we stood talking about our situation. Was it possible to escape? There were no guards at the entrance, but where would we go? We didn't have the slightest idea where we were or how far were the American lines. Just then an elderly priest came by and spoke to us in English. He was kindly but seemed terrified of the *Wehrmacht*. When we mentioned escaping, he begged us not to, telling us there was no chance because of the weather, the deplorable condition we were in and our inability to speak German. He also said some other POWs had tried it and had been killed.

At nine that evening Joe and I were taken to an ambulance. After being put aboard, we heard a lot of confused talking and we were unloaded, marched down the street to a small building jammed with mostly German wounded and told to sit on a bench until we were registered. Then we were taken to an overcrowded room and left. There was no place to sit or lie so we stood, wondering what was coming next. Suddenly, American voices came from the back of the room and we went to meet three GIs who lay in a corner. Making room for us, they were anxious to hear our versions of the battle. One called Tex was from the 106th Infantry Division, an outfit that lost two complete regiments in the initial phase of the German breakthrough. He had frozen feet. Another, Clarke, was from a tank outfit, wounded and captured during the first days of the German offensive. Detroit (whose first name I have unfortunately forgotten) was a combat engineer and must have had dozens of pieces of small shrapnel in his lower legs. His pants were torn off at the knees and he had no overcoat. He had suffered miserably in his trip to the hospital due to the cold, yet seemed happy and good natured. He said he and Clarke had lain in the basement of a house for eight days with little food or water before the Germans evacuated them, all the while being under constant artillery fire as the battle raged around them.

The following day, December 29th, we were awakened by a loud explosion and a screaming noise. Detroit informed us that we were near a buzz-bomb launching station which was sending rockets into Liège and Brussels. Joe and I went to a window in time to see one taking off from behind a copse of trees. It looked like a small plane and spouted flame from rear exhausts. People on the streets cheered as they roared away, confident that the rockets, one of Hitler's secret weapons, were going to win the war for them.

Late in the morning, sirens started to wail and the German wounded nearly panicked. Those who could rushed from the room and across the street to a shelter. Those who couldn't stayed and prayed, their faces locked in terror. Going to a window I looked up and saw the myriad vapor trails of a formation of B-17 bombers. I couldn't see them release their bombs, but I heard the explosions. Evidently, the rocket base was the target. The town rocked as if hit by an earthquake, the building shaking and the noise deafening. It didn't take a genius to figure out that we were just as vulnerable as the Germans and we sat on our beds of straw praying that the bombardiers' aim was bad. A second bombing group followed the first and once more the town shook. Our German wounded were nearly insane with terror, shouting and screaming things which we didn't understand. When the bombers finally left, the Germans cursed us, calling us swine and other choice obscenities. I really couldn't get mad at them because hundreds of thousands of civilians were killed in those raids. One thing was certain as far as I was concerned—the sooner I got to a POW camp, the safer I would feel.

We stayed in the building for three days, one a carbon copy of the other with the daily raids. I don't know why the Germans didn't attack us, they were that mad. But most were badly wounded so all we got were vindictive stares and curses.

Some of us wounded were put on a truck several days later. After a ride that lasted all day and well into the night we arrived at the town of Euskirchen about 20 miles west of Bonn. We were taken to an abandoned school for disabled people which had been turned into a clearing hospital. It was crowded with German wounded, so crowded that many slept on the floors in the hallways. It was a heart-wrenching sight to see so many seriously wounded, amputees, men in bloody casts, screaming and groaning. I didn't care whether or not they were my enemies, my heart bled for their suffering as we passed them on the way to be checked in. We were registered and led to a dark, damp basement with no lighting. There were some wooden dining room chairs lying around and we pushed them together and lay across them. A little later, a German entered with a candle, handing each of us a sandwich.

As the German when around handing out the food, more candles flickered on and we saw the basement was full of German wounded who slept on temporary double-deck bunks with straw mattresses. There were others on straw pallets on the floor. I didn't understand the reason for putting men in a damp and dingy place until the next day. It was an air raid shelter and most of these men were on litters. It was a horrible existence for them, cold, damp, dark and they had to stay there until places could be found for them in hospitals which were just as vulnerable to the bombs dropped by our planes.

At noon the sirens began to scream and ambulatory German wounded rushed to our basement. Soon it was so packed that no one could move. Bombs began dropping outside, the building began to shake and some of the wounded began screaming. Sitting on a chair in the flickering light of the candles, I looked at several Germans who sat just a few yards away. Dirt, dust and flecks of paint showered us from a near miss. One of the Germans glared at me, pulling a Walther automatic pistol from his holster. At that moment anything could have happened. But soon the bombers were gone, the all clear sounded, and the German put away the pistol. When the Germans began leaving, I felt a breath of relief and prayed we'd soon be taken out of that place.

A little later an SS trooper came over to talk to us in halting English. He was from Hamburg, had spent six years in the army, fighting in Poland, Russia, Normandy and Holland. He showed us pictures of his parents and 14-year-old sister. All had been killed in bombing raids. Nevertheless, he seemed to have taken it philosophically and I sensed that he had had enough of war. Others around the trooper added their opinions through him. From what they said, I think the bombings had hardened their resolve to fight to the finish.

We endured another bombing the following day. I was sure we would be attacked by the Germans in the basement, perhaps killed, if we weren't removed from that basement soon. Fortunately we were the following day, being led up five flights of stairs to the attic by an English-speaking doctor. Taken to the far end of the place, we saw a small room with an egg stove and the floor covered by straw with blankets on top. As I was the ranking NCO, the doctor said that I would be in charge of the POWs. He also said, with a smirk on his lips, that the reason we had been placed in the attic was because, if the building were to be hit by bombs, we would be the first to know it. He added, however, that if any more wounded Americans were brought in, I was to check their wounds and, should any be in immediate danger, I was to let him know immediately.

Our attic had large windows at each end so that we could look out over the snow-covered city. It was beautiful, but marred by gutted buildings, deep bomb craters and blackened ruins. I couldn't understand why it had been bombed so heavily until later when an American airman was brought in and told me it was in the bombing pattern for attacks on Bonn. As our B-17s were often over 20,000 feet up and their targets often covered by clouds, bombs were released using instrument readings, almost haphazardly.

More men were added to our loft every day. We were served a breakfast of black bread and *ersatz* coffee, sometimes with cheese or jam. The meager rations were never enough to sate our appetites. We also had a noon meal of soup and for supper there were black bread sandwiches. Because my wounded arm hurt so badly and I had developed a fever, I had little appetite and gave my sandwiches to Damato or Detroit.

Even though we were in a hospital we had none of the amenities associated with one. We never received any medical attention until I went to the English-speaking doctor and demanded it. There was a toilet in the attic and a wash basin, but no soap or towels. We ate the soup out of cans with spoons we had to steal from somewhere. There were no linens, shaving items, or medicine for pain, nor were there any means to wash our filthy clothing. Most of us had just what we had with us when we were captured. We managed to wash our faces with the icy water in the restroom, but it wasn't enough to remove all of the dirt and crud picked up in combat and our travels since. Under these conditions, it wasn't long before many of us had diarrhea.

Nothing was more terrifying than the bombings. Several of the men tried to leave the attic for a ground floor during one of the raids but were quickly sent back. The building would vibrate from near-misses, windows shattering and the screams of the wounded downstairs reaching us. Once Joe and I were called downstairs before a raid and on the way up a raid began. Standing crouched in a doorway with bombs dropping outside, I saw the long and broad windows by the staircase bow in nearly a foot without a break when a concussion wave hit the side of the building.

Morris Gerwitz, a medic from the 99th Infantry Division who spoke German, had been working in the hospital carrying in litter cases. He was sent to the attic and was a welcome addition. Short, chubby and good-natured, he took over care of the wounded. He had been captured the first day or so of the German offensive in the Ardennes, awakening in his slit trench one morning to find all the other members of his company gone and the Germans on every side of him. He helped lift our despondent spirits with his funny banter, making life a little more bearable. Our helplessness during the bombings was beginning to erode our willpower and everyone wished that he could be shipped on to a Stalag (prisoner of war camp).

By January 4th I had been a POW for nearly two weeks and my arm was swollen, red-streaked and full of pus. I could rarely sleep and ate very little. Morris went to the doctor in charge and demanded treatment. An artillery officer had recently been brought to the attic with a hideous wound in the back of his thigh. It was split open like a dropped melon and the crêpe paper bandage put on by the Germans had loosened and fallen to his knee, leaving the wound totally exposed. I helped him down the five flights of stairs to the operation room on the first floor. The English-speaking doctor and a nurse were in the room, put me on the table and had the officer sit on the floor.

While the doctor was treating my wound, the sirens began to scream and I could hear the ambulatory wounded rushing down the hallway to stairs leading to the basement. A short time later, bombs began to drop, some less than several hundred yards from the hospital. The nurse began to scream when a near miss shook the building, running to a corner of the room and cowering like a whipped puppy. The doctor's face turned purple with rage. He grabbed me around the throat and began choking me. I tried to fight him off with my good arm but he was young and strong. Fortunately for me, the artillery officer struggled to his feet and pulled the doctor off me. The raid was short-lived, probably accidental because the target was Bonn. And, once the planes had gone, the doctor regained his composure, apologizing to me for his behavior. He said that the raids were almost daily and that several patients had died because of them. The bombing, he admitted, had also pushed his nerves to the breaking point.

The days dragged on and we were still confined to the attic. Our group had grown to about 17 with several from the 101st Airborne. Sergeant Carl Robare and PFC Leo Lewandowski, both paratroopers who had been in all our units' campaigns, were brought in as well as a trooper from the 82d Airborne and an Indian from the 35th Division. Someone made a checker board and another had a deck of cards. So, aside from the air raids, life wasn't too bad. Potatoes were stolen from a cold storage basement when men were asked to perform minor fatigue details and they were fried on the stove pipe.

Things, however, weren't going too well for me. My wounded wrist was so painful that I couldn't sleep and I was depressed. Not only had the lack of medical treatment and the bombing affected me but my thoughts kept drifting back to my being captured at the roadblock. I kept asking myself what had gone wrong? In all our combat experience, never had a situation been so overwhelming and confusing that we hadn't been able to salvage something out of it. Why had the rest of my platoon been kept from joining me? Had they been there, the roadblock could've been held—at least until the aid station was evacuated. Why had Lieutenant Wagner left and never returned? (He told me later that he had been cut off and couldn't get back, and I believed him.) Why hadn't someone seen the 2d Platoon withdrawing and warned those in the aid station?

I later learned, from men who survived that day, that the 2d Platoon's defense line had been so badly mauled by the tank guns that all semblance of order was lost. When nightfall came, it was every man for himself. The survivors fell back and the company withdrew a mile and a half closer to Bastogne to make a final stand, which came on the 25th. At 03.00 18 Mark IV tanks and two battalions of infantry from the 77th Panzergrenadiers struck in a "do or die" attack. When the battle ended at 09.00, all 18 German tanks had been destroyed by a combination of fire from four TDs, the guns of the 463d PFA and the weapons of the 401st GIR. Captain Preston Towns was mortally wounded that evening. Little did we realize then that by being captured we may have had our lives spared. The wounded from those fights had been taken to the division hospital in Bastogne. On the 26th the hospital was badly hit by German bombers and many of the wounded were killed, including men who had escaped from our roadblock.

In our attic we had little knowledge of the scope of the battle. New arrivals brought us local news, and the English-speaking doctor brought us the German version which was mostly propaganda. He visited the attic most every day, more of a social call than medical as very little was ever done for our wounds. A case in point was the young soldier who was brought up with the side of his forehead missing and the brain exposed. He had been bandaged with a paper bandage which had fallen off and his body was covered by powdery dust. It was said he had been in a building struck by a bomb—he was a medic who had been helping the wounded. Sammy and Morris cleaned the young boy and rebandaged his wound, but the fellow was delirious, tearing the wrapping away and crying hoarsely *"Wasser! Ich muss Wasser haben!"* ("Water! I must have water!").We did everything in our limited power to solace the dying man who seemed in great pain. I prevailed upon our doctor to administer an opiate and he sent up a nurse with morphine. The next day his suffering ended. With his last breath he asked for his mother. Some of our men took him down to a shed which served as a morgue. I kept a dog tag and his identification papers to turn in to someone in charge at our next stop. He was barely 20, blond and handsome, and came from Birmingham, Alabama. In his wallet were photos of his mother, father, sister and brothers. He had a beautiful girl friend. The experience bit into my psyche. What a terrible way to die, among strangers, and in a place where his body might never be recovered.

We carried water to the room and took helmet baths, without benefit of soap, towels or shaving articles. We even managed to wash our underwear and socks, drying them on the stove pipe. And we had our first experience with body lice; they were in the straw we slept on. Each morning after the meager meal, we would search our clothing for them, finding and mashing the opaque pests between our fingernails. Then a new arrival had a razor and we shaved for the first time, nearly ripping our skin apart because we lacked shaving cream and hot water. Every five days we went down to the dispensary and had the bandages on our wounds changed. Without any healing medicines, it took a long time for most to heal.

One morning a German sergeant came to the attic, asking for volunteers for a coal detail. The only way he could get anyone was to promise an extra ration of bread or a cigarette. Most of the men were inveterate smokers and took a turn at the details. I still had a pipe and lent it out as I no longer had the urge to smoke. The others smoked just about everything in it, including *ersatz* coffee grounds.

Some of the Germans who came to get a glimpse of American POWs were adamant Nazis. One, a sergeant, had been a POW of the British in World War I. A loud, belligerent sort, he told about how little the British fed him in this three years of captivity and how well we had it. He had completely swallowed the Nazi Party line, still believing Germany would win the war even as it was being destroyed by our bombers.

Our favorite "German" was actually a Ukrainian. In very broken English he would say to me, "I luff American," hugging me with arms strong enough to break into a cask. He had been captured in the Crimea and to keep from starving went into the *Wehrmacht* medical corps. Sometimes he would get drunk and come to the attic at night, laughing and cutting up like a kid. And what a thief he was, stealing cigarettes and pipe tobacco strong enough to make one's head swim, giving them to us without any remuneration. He said his joy in life was to steal from the Germans.

As the days dragged by, seeing that none of us had tried to escape, the Germans relaxed security. We sent men to pick up our meager meals, but didn't roam the hospital corridors because of the hostility caused by the bombings. Another 101st man came in, PFC Frank Tiedeman, 506th, from Patterson, NJ. He had been wounded and captured near Noville when his platoon ran headlong into a platoon of Mark IVs. He had a half dozen pieces of shrapnel in his face, arms and body, none life-threatening. Frank told me that he was all ready to go on pass to Paris when the alert came. He had drawn over $200 in back pay, dressed in Class As, and was waiting for the bus. He barely had time to get back to the barracks and get on his combat uniform when the trucks pulled out for Belgium.

During the raids the doctor told me to evacuate the more seriously wounded before anyone else, and this I did even if it caused hard feelings. No one wanted to stay in the attic any longer than he had to during a raid. A captain from the 101st came in with a severely damaged shoulder and a trooper from the 17th Airborne with a mangled hand and ripped-open thigh. I sent them out, getting some flak for it. Another fellow came in with a Band Aid on the side of his nose and another over the opening in one ear. He could barely speak, just mumble, and I thought he had been hit by shrapnel. When, two days later, he said a bullet had passed right through his head, I was stunned. He went right out. But the attic was getting crowded, about 30 men in all, and I leaned on the doctor to do something about it. He told me he would see what he could do.

A Russian slave worker was brought to the attic one morning by German medics. He had been horribly wounded in a bombing, and hadn't received any medical help whatsoever. He was in agony, moaning and groaning loudly and thrashing about. I begged the doctor for some morphia, but he refused, saying he treated the Russians the way he treated the Germans. The man died two days later and the Germans refused to remove his body to the morgue. None of our men wanted to either until the Germans offered some cigarettes in payment for conducting the odious chore.

During one of the raids a bomb dropped on an adjacent building housing some of the disabled people who had formerly occupied the building we were in. Twenty-six were killed and many wounded. After that none of us wanted to go down and pick up meals, the hostility from our captors was so bad. Then the doctor told me small groups of Americans would be leaving periodically for Stalags and convalescent camps. I sent out the worst cases first, then it became my turn to leave. Gerwitz, Detroit, Damato, Robare, Lewandowski (a member of the 502d PIR whose first name I no longer know), Tiedeman and I were put on a truck with straw placed on the bed. A young Italian worker was on the truck, and, through Joe, who spoke the language, told us how much better off we would be in a prison camp. Good food, clean clothing, cigarettes and Red Cross parcels would be available, he said glowingly. I never did know where he had learned that, because none of it was true. But we were free from the hospital in Euskirchen and the terrible bombings. All breathed a sigh of relief, feeling nothing could be worse. How wrong we were.

CHAPTER 15

Siegburg to Hoffenstahl

Euskirchen had been heavily bombed in the raids. As the truck wound through its cratered streets I could see the damage everywhere. On one street I saw something that reminded me of my civilian life, the remains of an engraving shop with milling machines and pantographs standing naked and unoccupied. Civilians walked the streets, many with baskets and shopping bags. When the truck passed and they saw Americans in back, they muttered angrily and shook their fists at us.

It was only a 20-odd mile ride to Bonn, but the cold made us miserable. Detroit suffered the most with the bottoms of his trousers gone and no outerwear except for a sweater and a knit hat, the rest having been taken by the Germans. We were unloaded in front of a bomb-damaged hospital, a guard herding us down several flights of stairs to a dark, clammy basement, which served as a shelter. There was no light and he left us to fend for ourselves. We did what most well-trained GIs would do, curled up on wooden benches and tried to get some sleep.

There were several air raids each day we were there. During each one anxious civilians streamed into the basement, women, children, and the elderly. When they saw us in the glare of their feeble candles or flashlights, they mumbled unintelligible but obvious damnations at the representatives of their tormentors. They had become terrified by the raids for good reason. When the bombs hit nearby and the building began to shake, their moaning and cries turned to screams. The men among them tried desperately to calm them.

We were in the shelter for three days, so cold that our teeth chattered. A German soldier, a Pole impressed into the German Army who had served on the Eastern Front until injured, brought each of us a sandwich for breakfast, dinner and supper. Through Lewandowski, who spoke the language, he repeatedly asked how long we thought the war would last. We told him six months, which he had trouble believing.

After what seemed like an eternity in that tomb-like place, we were finally taken outside and put on an old bedraggled bus. The rest of our group from the attic was on it—we had gained nothing leaving earlier. The bus wound through bomb-cratered streets and passed block after block of nothing but the shells of buildings and piles of mortar and bricks. We came to the Rhine River, dark and foreboding. Detroit joked about being the first American to lead the charge over the bridge, but I'm certain hundreds of POWs had preceded us.

The driver kept getting lost, an affinity shared by most German chauffeurs we ran into, but we finally reached the city of Siegburg and the 400-year-old monastery perched high on a cliff. It had been damaged by bombs near the end of December but still seemed formidable. Inside the walls, in rooms formerly occupied by monks for reading and studying, were scores of wounded. We were taken to one filled with Americans. A big burly sergeant was in charge, so healthy and well fed that I couldn't picture him as being a POW for any length of time. He told us right off that there was no room, obvious to see as every bit of space seemed occupied by a patient, and that we should have gone to Hoffenstahl lazarette. Nevertheless, he saw that we were given a bowl of thin soup and that our wounds were dressed.

One of our group, Keller might have been his name, had been hit in the calf by a shrapnel shard, which had worked its way near the shinbone. We saw the doctor searching for the piece of metal with a probe, unable to locate it. Keller had been given no anesthetic, was in great pain, but never uttered a sound. However, the ordeal showed on his face. When my wrist was dressed, the man beside me on another table, an airman, was having a thumb amputated. A third man, who was on the table before me, had a hole the size of a baseball in his back. The entire shoulder blade was missing and some sort of yellow disinfectant was poured into the wound. It was sickening to see.

We spent the night in the overcrowded, stuffy, smelly room and were later moved outside the walls to some wooden barracks occupied mainly by Italian POWs. There weren't enough bunks there either, so we had to sleep in shifts. The straw in the ticks of these double-deckers was so infected with lice that I wouldn't sleep in mine, I chose the floor instead, as did several others.

When the Italians saw that some of us had jewelry they told us about bartering with the guards for food. One of our guys got a loaf of black bread, a small tin of margarine and some honey for an $85 watch. Paper money had little value, however. Frank Tiedeman still had the money he had drawn for the Paris leave he never got but even he could buy nothing; the Germans wanted silver and gold.

The following morning about 30 of us were taken to the train station for the trip to Hoffenstahl. However, shortly after our arrival, the sirens sounded and we were herded into a cold, wet shelter to spend three miserable hours until the all-clear sounded. Some civilians were also in the place, friendlier than the others we had run into. They plied us with questions about the war. They claimed that they didn't understand why we were bombing their cities instead of war plants and refineries. And, naturally, they asked us our opinions of how long the war would last.

Finally we boarded the train and, after a ride through snow-covered country, we came to a small town. At least ten inches of snow were underfoot and we started a long hike to our destination. It was bitterly cold and a strong wind whipped the snow like foam off an ocean wave. Some of our group were without shoes, which had been taken by the enemy, and wore clogs instead. These men had tied rags about their feet and legs to keep warm. Others had frozen feet and suffered horribly during the march.

It was a long trek, considering our wretched condition, through a largely suburban area on roads that hadn't been properly cleared of snow. Accustomed to a ten-minute break after an hour's march, we complained to the guards because they kept prodding us to go faster without any breaks at all. Most of us were very hungry, three small sandwiches a day for the past three days having done little to satisfy us. But the guards were adamant, even drawing their pistols and threatening to kill anyone who dropped out. Finally, we prevailed upon them and they relented, allowing us a ten-minute break to rest and recover. We finally arrived at the wire-enclosed camp for Allied prisoners of war on a gray, overcast afternoon in the middle of January.

After being registered we were marched to a tent shower for the first real wash we had had in a month. After we stripped in the icy cold weather and tied our clothing in a bundle, we got a hot bath, being careful to avoid our bandages. Our clothing was taken to large steam cabinets for washing and delousing. After the bath we were dusted with insecticide, and picked up our hot clothing to dress and march to barracks where we were given a bowl of sauerkraut soup and two slices of black bread. We ate the soup from a small metal bowl. Those of us who hadn't stolen spoons along the way were given ones whittled from wood. Tiedeman and I went to the medical center because our wounds hadn't healed. It was a small, wooden, one-roomed shack with too many double deck bunks jammed into it.

There was a long table in the middle of the room and an egg stove at one end. There were 30 or so men assigned to the room, half of them Polish with the rest Americans. The Poles had been working in German war production plants, which were being heavily bombed and had been sent to the camp because of illness. All the Americans had been wounded, some very seriously. There was quite a difference in physical condition between the two groups, the Poles being well fed because they had been receiving extra rations as volunteer war workers, the Americans under weight because of the meager diet provided to prisoners.

The rations were just enough to keep us from starving. Breakfast consisted of *ersatz* coffee or tea. At noon there was one bowl of barley, cabbage or turnip soup per man. The first couple of weeks we were there, we received another bowl of soup for supper, but this was later discontinued and coffee or tea was substituted. There was also a ration of an eighth of a loaf of black bread daily and a tablespoon of sugar and a small pat of butter. Four times a week we got a spoon of jam. Everything was meticulously weighed. On Sundays and Thursdays we were given several tiny potatoes and a spoonful of gravy. Another reason the Poles were in much better condition was that they had been receiving American Red Cross parcels, discontinued shortly before we arrived because the bombing raids knocked out transportation, and could swap with the enemy highly prized items like cigarettes and chocolate.

A Pole was in charge of our barracks, a short, fat and amiable man of about 40. He had been in the ground crew in the Polish air force. Someone said he had had seven intestinal operations and he wore a colostomy bag that had to be changed daily. When it was, the odor was enough to knock you over. We Americans called him Pop and liked him much better than the others of his nationality who were clannish, selfish and so full of communist propaganda that we soon lost any desire to converse with them.

I can't remember any of the names of the Americans who were there when I arrived, in fact I never knew any but their first names. Some had been in the camp a long time like Bill, a tough hillbilly with an obsession for pancakes. He had been captured near Cherbourg, liberated, and captured again before he could be evacuated. Like all the others, he was severely underweight and had wounds that refused to heal. He complained about the way the Germans issued the Red Cross parcels, giving them to the Poles and French who had worked in war production but not to the Americans who had battle wounds.

Jack, a Ranger who had been captured in Normandy, had assumed the leadership of the American prisoners. A nice looking blond, he had a serious wound in his right arm which refused to heal. It had to be cleansed and irrigated daily causing him much pain and discomfort, but he still stood eye to eye with the Polish communists countering all the ridiculous assumptions and propaganda harangues the Reds tossed his way with patience and benevolence. He wasn't understanding about the way he had been captured, thinking like many of us that our outfits had let us down. It wasn't until later that we understood the feeling of guilt many POWs experience in being put in such a situation and how we try to rationalize it by attacking others for our misfortune. For me it meant going deeper and deeper into a shell of denial, burying all the terrible things I had seen and experienced only to have them come back to haunt me later.

The medical center was only one of many wooden, one-storied huts in Stalag 6G, which contained compounds housing different nationalities segregated by high wire fences. A double wire fence with guard towers, sentries and guard dogs surrounded the entire compound. Most of the British, French, Poles and Russians had been captured early in the war and were old hands at POW life, leaving the camp on work details which gave them a chance to meet and barter with civilians who swapped staples for chocolate, candy and cigarettes. The Russians were the worst off physically, many nothing but skin and bone with deaths nearly a daily occurrence. The other nationalities knew how to barter or buy through the guards and could survive much better than the newly-captured Americans who could not live on the meager POW rations. As a result, in less than a month, most of the Americans began losing weight. The weight loss increased if one caught dysentery. We all dreamed of food, Christmas and Thanksgiving Dinners, until the thought nearly became an obsession; a mania in many cases I know of. It was especially difficult for us to sit around in the barracks around noon or supper when the Poles were cooking mouth-watering bowls of stew and soup without any hope of ever getting a spoonful.

The constant pang of hunger in your belly made you do desperate things. Men traded all their valuables—watches, rings, pens, lighters, if they still had them—with each having a certain equivalent in bread, margarine, potatoes, and so on. Money counted for nothing until the end of the war.

At 6G we were kept in touch with the battle fronts to some extent through a radio in the camp commandant's office. Frenchmen who worked there would bring back the latest from German broadcasts, almost always victory after victory for the *Wehrmacht* but somehow an ever-shrinking defense perimeter to go with them! The Allies were nearly to the Rhine on the Western Front with the Russians deep in Germany at the Oder River, near Danzig in the north and Budapest in the south. Even though the days and nights seemed endless because of the misery of our wounds and the insatiable hunger gnawing at our stomachs, this news and the incessant air raids gave some ray of hope that the war was reaching a climax. The German guards denied imminent defeat, saying Hitler was about to unleash secret weapons that would win the war.

We who were ambulatory would stand outside in the snow and watch the vapor trails of hundreds of bombers as they traveled to Bonn, Cologne, and Koblenz. The sky would be a mass of exploding flak, so thick it seemed nothing could penetrate it, and all the planes didn't. Sometimes we would see the tiny white orbs of parachutes, and as time passed, would get burned and wounded crewmen in our Stalag.

During the raids, except for the Americans who must have considered themselves to be invulnerable, most of the POWs would make a dash for the shallow slit trenches which served as shelters—as if they would do much good against an exploding 500-pound bomb. The Germans mostly did, too, but made sure the guard towers were still manned. Doctors even left patients on the table in the middle of operations. During the night, when the British did their bombing, we would be awakened by the thump of hob-nailed boots and hear the Germans running for the shelters. Our huts were locked; none of the POWs could leave even if they had wanted to.

There was little for the Americans in the medical center to do aside from talking to one another and dreaming of home. The Poles had decks of cards, reading and writing material, chess sets, and they spent a lot of time preparing meals with the staples they had bought. The longer I was there the more I despised them. I knew it couldn't have been because they were Poles, and wondered if it wasn't because of the manner in which their country had collapsed and their struggle to survive ever since. At any rate, I can't remember much that was good about most of them who were in my hut.

However, the hut was warm and dry thanks to them, as they paid the Russians to bring in wood, huge pine logs which they went outside the camp to cut and haul back—under German guard of course. The guards were also bribed. All was paid for in our standard currency—cigarettes from the Red Cross parcels. Also, we could take baths in our helmets with water heated on the stove. But there were no towels, soap, shaving articles or dental things. Our wounds would be cleaned and wrapped with paper bandages, which soon stretched and fell off. We were free from body lice for a while at least, a blessing because they were as hungry as leeches. Occasionally I would visit Joe, Detroit, or Frank Tiedeman, who were in other huts.

As the days dragged on, most of us were getting thinner and hollow checked. Tempers flared over the most inconsequential things, arguments ensued, especially with the Poles, who looked on us as an unruly bunch of barbarians. But then a ray of sunshine came into our lives when we learned the Americans would be moved to other Stalags. Joe, Detroit and some others from Euskirchen were among the first to leave and happy to go. They marched out of camp one morning, many still with bandages on their wounds, with a meager ration of food in their pockets. I waved good-bye, praying that I would be in the next batch.

Shortly after they left a report circulated that the Stalag where Joe's group was to go had been bombed and destroyed. We heard this report first hand from men who had been there, 500 who had been moved into 6G after the bombing. They said most of the huts had been destroyed and many men killed. To make room for them men who had recovered from their wounds were moved out. I was in the first group to go even though my wrist was still unhealed and running with pus.

It was now after the first week in February. We were issued a tablespoon of salty fish paste and a quarter loaf of black bread as rations. We left 6G about 09.00 one morning on foot with a guard who claimed he knew a short route to Siegburg, our destination for the first leg of our journey. We left in a ragged column with armed guards at our sides. The snow was beginning to thaw some under the sunny sky but it was still cold. The back roads we took were still ice-covered in shady places and men fell and had to be helped along. At least the guards were more understanding, not whacking anyone with a rifle butt or cursing him for being slow. Still, it took about four hours to cover the 14-mile or so march and we arrived while an air raid was in progress. As there was no room in the monastery, we were stuck in a cold, wet shelter where we shivered until our teeth began to chatter even after being given a hot bowl of barley soup and a couple of thin slices of black bread. Fortunately, just after dark, we were led to the monastery and told to find a place in the hallway. It was a lifesaver as none of us had any blankets.

I found an unoccupied straw pallet and shared it with a fellow named King from our 502d whom I had met earlier at Euskirchen. He had a wound in the hip that had nearly healed. We moved out of the hallway into a large room with a low ceiling and massive pillars. Double-decked bunks were jammed into the room almost like herring in a tin, a veil of smoke hovering over everything, giving the place a ghostly look. The lice outnumbered the patients a thousand to one. Men with casts on arms and legs used long strands of wire to scratch the bites. And the odor of putrid flesh and corruption overpowered all other smells.

The same American sergeant was in charge, the big beefy fellow who looked as if he'd never missed a meal. Most of the men I talked to weren't very happy with him. As for me, I thought he had too much power for his rank, even telling officers what they had to do. I believe the others called this fellow Moose. To be fair to him he was in a stressful position with so many wounded and very little in the way of medicine to help them.

The next morning, after being given a cup of *ersatz* coffee and a sandwich, we were assembled in front of the monastery, about a hundred of us in all. Carl Robare, Lewandowski and Joe Damato, were in the group. We marched to a railroad station and loaded aboard small boxcars, 40 men or so to a car. An hour later the train pulled out, making an uneven progress because of frequent air raid scares. Although it was only about 50 miles to our destination in Limburg, it took most of the day. We marched from the train station to a camp surrounded by high wire fences, with innumerable one-storied barracks made of either wood or concrete. This was the infamous Stalag 12A, a transit camp which had been bombed by our planes on December 26th, 1944, a raid which killed 26 American officers.

CHAPTER 16

The Bottom of the Pit

Marching through the main gate to a compound of single storied huts that looked as inviting as a case of tetanus, we halted before one of them and stood in the cold biting wind while our guards handled our arrival. After being signed in, we were put in one of the huts until the next morning, with orders to stay inside during the night or risk being shot. There were a couple of tall cans at one end of the building which were to be used as toilets. As it was too late for a meal we went hungry again.

The following morning an American master sergeant got us outside, telling us we were at Stalag 12A, then detailing some men to bring the breakfast ration, two slices of black bread and *ersatz* coffee. There were no eating utensils, but most of us had acquired a spoon and a can for our mess gear. Other POWs came to see the new arrivals. Among them was George Miller from my company who had been captured the same day as me. He was a rifleman in the 2d Platoon, a replacement who had come in after Normandy. He advised me to give him any valuables as we were about to be questioned and the Germans would take anything they wanted. All I had was a fountain pen my wife had sent me and a pair of overshoes. I left them with him, hoping to get them back after the interrogation. I never saw them or him again.

After the interrogation, we were assigned to one of the buildings, forming outside in companies of 100 men, ten men in a rank, ten ranks deep, which supposedly made for easier counting. I was assigned as first sergeant of my company and chose Carl Robare as one of my platoon leaders. Then we were put in one of the overcrowded huts which had a dirt floor covered by filthy, lice-infested straw. Every man was given two heavy gray blankets.

An American staff ran the compound, which held British as well as Americans. The "British" were a mixed bag, including Indians and Canadians, as well as the British themselves, most with a complete kit including packs and overcoats. There was a lazarette and a medical staff but little in the way of medicine. There were other compounds nearby for other nationalities. Fences segregated us from one another. The building my company was assigned to was already occupied, so I went back to the master sergeant and told him there wasn't room for another hundred men. He glowered at me and snapped that I had to fit them in. I told the men to find places wherever they could.

The building was about 200 feet long with a row of straw along each outside wall and two in the center. There was a small washroom in the center with cold water and a vestibule at the end. During the day, men used an outside latrine, four holes in a concrete slab over a cesspool. There was no toilet tissue. During the night, three large cans were put in the vestibule. There were no lights after eight o'clock at night, so if anyone wanted to use the cans he had to feel his way in the dark, which wouldn't have been so bad had the aisles not been crowded with sleeping men.

A few days after our arrival Joe Damato's group, who had been separated from us during the march, got into Limburg. We had a reunion and they told us about their adventure at Siegburg and Bonn where they had been put in POW cages. The one in Bonn had been bombed at night and most of the huts destroyed with some casualties. As the buildings went up in flames, the Americans dashed in among them, grabbing the food from the Red Cross parcels that the Poles, French and Serbs had hoarded. However, the next morning the Americans were all lined up and all the stolen food taken from them and given back to the other nationalities who had lain shivering in slit trenches during the raid.

Stalag 12A was our first experience with prison camp routine. Everyone was roused at 05.00 by blasts from German whistles and shouts of "*Raus, Kommen sie hinaus! Macht Schnell! Macht Schnell!*" Laggards were hurried along by the kick of a hob-nailed boot or a swat with a rifle butt. Lining up outside in the mud and snow-covered street for roll call, the groups of 100 men were individually counted by the guards who usually lost count and would have to start all over. It was not unusual to spend more than an hour in such foolishness, which most of us believed to be deliberate, our teeth chattering, stomachs rumbling, and our bodies crawling with lice. After the count, names were called, men who would be shipped off to other camps. Men from my company were used to fill vacancies so eventually my company was broken up and I went to another one.

After roll call breakfast was served, coffee and a sixth of a loaf of black bread. Afterward, work details were drawn, to fill bomb damage in the town or work around the camp. At noon, the main meal was served, usually a thin bowl of soup, with a little more to those who were on a detail in rare cases. At supper another bowl of thin soup was served, but not always. It depended on the supply of rations getting into the camp. The soup was made from turnips, potatoes or other vegetables. Sometimes we were given small portions of cheese, jam or margarine, and, on several occasions a couple of cigarettes. The latter came from Red Cross parcels that got to the camp during February, before bomb damage stopped the train traffic.

During the day there was little for most of the men to do, so they rehashed old times or wandered around the yard. A lot of time was spent picking lice from our clothing. As there were no razors most of us never shaved. The British had cards and homemade chess sets and whiled away hours that way. There was sick call every morning and many men went on it for dysentery. They were given a handful of charcoal as medicine.

Night was the worst time. We were so crowded together that you could not turn over even if you wanted to. We slept in one position, flush against the next man like sardines in a can. The rampaging lice drove us crazy at night. The particularly unfortunate were those who were beside someone with dysentery who had to go to the cans several times each night—they didn't always make it—and were kept awake by the person's coming and going in the total darkness with only a match or a cigarette lighter to find his place in the mass of restless men. The cans in the alcove would be overflowing by morning, so many men had the bug, and we waded through the loose excrement on the way to and from roll call, tracking it everywhere. It was cleared up later in the day but one night was a repeat of another.

Most of us tried to wash in the four cold water taps. Unfortunately these taps had to serve several hundred men and that, combined with our lack of soap or towels, made it impossible to get really clean. Our hair grew long and our beards became matted. Our stomachs aching from hunger, most of us traded the last of our valuables for slices of bread. We had a slight reprieve several weeks after arriving when some British cigarettes came in. I swapped mine for bread, which I shared with Joe, who had smoked his cigarettes. I didn't mind, knowing he was hooked on nicotine. The staff tried to improve our living conditions without much success. There were just too many men in one place. A razor blade was eventually given to each man and by borrowing some of the few available razors, some of us shaved. Some men, however, had completely given up, refusing to bath or shave.

And once they gave up spiritually, they wasted away to nothing and often died in their sleep. It happened to the man next to me.

Some prisoners of war had been sent to nearby Gerolstein, a labor camp. Chester Sakwinski, Cecil Honea and Paul Trivey, from the tank destroyer at our roadblock, were among them. Their barracks at Gerolstein was an unheated abandoned warehouse. Each day they were made to work from dawn to dark repairing bomb-damaged roads and rail tracks or cleaning up rubble in bombed cities. They got no more rations than us even though they were expending more calories. As a result, when some of these men were moved to 12A I didn't recognize them, they had lost that much weight. Honea was especially thin, having lost nearly 100 pounds in two months after contracting a diarrhea bug. It was to trouble him the rest of his life. These men told us stories about Gerolstein, which bordered on being barbaric. A German sergeant at the camp named Eisenhower murdered a sick, weak POW who was unable to rise, shooting him with a pistol.

The prisoners from Gerolstein were in such wretched condition that some of them died during the following weeks. All had diarrhea, dysentery, pneumonia or diphtheria, 20 in all, I heard. Every day a grave-digging detail left for the cemetery and the corpses wrapped in sacking soon followed. There was always a brief funeral with a chaplain present.

A black market operation was in full swing and doing land office business. The labor gangs, mostly Russian, brought back staples traded from among the civilians, in turn swapping for jewelry or good clothing, like the new prisoners wore. The German guards were in on it also.

Given some raw horsemeat for one of our rations, we had no way to cook it without some pots or pans, so we traded it to the British who did, one cigarette for a bite-sized piece. On Sundays potatoes, and horsemeat, or cheese, hard cookies and tea were issued. However, we were only served one meal. We were always hungry. And the hunger had strange effects on the men aside from the debilitating ones. One man went around the hut collecting receipts for pancakes, another for something else. Several even laid out on pieces of discarded cardboard, the storefront of a restaurant they proposed to open after getting home, along with all the house specialties. One fellow from the Midwest collared men from different parts of the country, from different cities, taking down the names of local restaurants and their specialties, promising to visit every one if it took a lifetime. However, most of us simply promised ourselves that once we got home we would never go hungry again, no matter what the cost.

The air raids on Bonn, Koblenz and Cologne went on day and night. When they happened we weren't allowed out of the buildings. New prisoners arrived continually and we got the latest news of the war from them. We were allowed a helmet of hot water each week and even a few razors showed up. There was a barber now with scissors but nothing else. He cut hair free instead of charging three cigarettes as before.

However, there was no way to rid ourselves of the lice. They were in the straw and blankets as well as our clothing. We would pick hundreds a day from our uniforms, scraping away nests of eggs. Our bodies were covered by their bites, in some instances becoming a mass of infected sores. Nor had my wounded wrist healed completely; it still carried a scab and ached all the time. The Germans cut down the rations with only two slices of black bread and coffee in the morning and a cup of thin soup in the afternoon, nothing else. We all wondered where the promised Red Cross parcels were. Our deliverance seemed to come one morning when the first sergeant announced that a walking transport of men was being formed to march to another Stalag some 25 miles away. NCOs were excluded. A Red Cross parcel would be given to any man who volunteered for the trip. A mob crowded around the sergeant trying to sign up. Anything seemed better than starving or dying from disease in 12A. The first batch left a day later. Then a second and a third.

The men who made this trip, however, fared badly. They didn't get the Red Cross parcels, the walk was much longer than told, and the rest stops for the night were unfit and inadequate for the number of men involved. Many of the men were in too weakened a condition to make the hike and fell out. After a third shipment they were stopped.

What seemed to be my deliverance from 12A came at the beginning of March when rumors spread around the compound that many of the NCOs would be evacuated. A couple of days later about 400 or so names were called at the morning roll call and mine was included. I was jubilant, as were the others. Nothing could be worse, we thought. It had to be better.

We formed in front of our building with the few possessions we had acquired, a spoon and a can in my case, were checked and rechecked as the Germans were wont to do, and moved to another building for the night, being told that we would leave the following day. That night was one that I'll never forget. As cramped as we had been in the former building, we were doubly so in the new one. Men slept in a heap with arms and legs on someone else and with everyone digging at the lice bites. Sleep was impossible. In fact it's a wonder someone didn't smother because of the crush of bodies.

We flowed from the building the next morning, which was misty and gray as if it were about to snow. Two pieces of bread were doled to each man on the muddy street as well as a hot cup of powdered milk. Counted again and divided into groups of 100 men we were marched to the rail yard in Limburg, our elderly *Wehrmacht* guards augmented by *Volkssturm* men (home guardsmen), British Red Cross parcels were given out, one parcel to two men, so it was important to stay close to your partner if you wanted to eat on the trip. In our parcel was a small tin of powdered eggs, one of oatmeal, cocoa, oxtail soup, cottage pie, meat paste, some crackers, chocolate, soap and cigarettes. However, most of the content of the parcel was raw and had to be cooked. I don't remember my partner's name, I had never seen him before, but he seemed to be a nice fellow and as anxious to leave 12A as I was. As we marched along the string of waiting boxcars, 50 men at a time peeled off and were assigned to one of the cars. My trip through hell was about to begin.

CHAPTER 17

Hell Train

My partner and I settled on the rough floorboards of the boxcar, anxious to tackle our Red Cross parcel. We took some of the black bread we had been hoarding, smeared some of the meat paste on it and ate. With the cigarettes in the parcel we traded for some cocoa, mixing it with water given us to make a drink. We hadn't been in the car more than a few hours when men began pushing through the car to get to the latrine cans, the hot milk having given them diarrhea. Soon the noxious odor overcame that of unwashed bodies and filthy uniforms. I took it in my stride, burying it in my subconscious along with all the other adversities of the past year or so. While not being as catastrophic as combat, the past two months had been frightful in their own right. The degradation of living like an animal, the gut-wrenching uncertainty of each passing day, the lack of necessities, the fear and helplessness that tears one apart while on the receiving end of a bombing raid and the pain and anguish caused by my wounds were driving me deeper into a shell.

As close as Joe Damato and I were, having been good friends since the day I joined the airborne in June 1943, sharing food and confidences since being POWs, I could feel a chasm developing between us and I wondered why. Was each of us so engulfed in trying to survive that little else mattered? The thought was revolting to me.

Later in the day air raid sirens began to wail. The guards padlocked the car doors and we were like ducks in a shooting gallery while our captors ran for shelters. I sat breathless listening to the deep rumble of plane engines in the distance. Then, like hawks swooping down on prey, they hit the rail yard. I could hear the screaming dives, the rattle of flak and cannon fire, and the sharp explosion of bombs. The wooden sides of the car rattled from the concussion, then rang from the sharp crack of striking bits of debris and shrapnel. It was terrifying, especially after some of the uninitiated in the car began to holler and scream. Other cursed the guards, calling them names even the most vulgar rarely used. We didn't know it but some of the other cars had been badly damaged and the train couldn't leave until they were taken away. At any rate, the raid didn't last very long, even though it seemed like an eternity, and it left me trembling all over.

Night came and the train still sat on the siding. It was pitch black. As there wasn't enough room for everyone to lie down, some of us stood while others sat, leaning against a neighbor or the side of the car. Around midnight I could hear the Germans outside, their hobnails crunching the ballast, their voices loud and abusive. The door was unlocked and opened and the Germans began to shout angry phrases at us. Finally, it dawned on us that they wanted us out of the cars. We poured out, helped along by booted feet and rifle butts. Someone said the Krauts wanted us to find places in other cars. My partner and I stayed together like baby possums hanging onto teats, knowing that to be separated meant going hungry. We came to an open car door and were booted in by the guards despite the protestations of those already inside telling us that there was no room. We were pushed into the mass of bodies and the car door slammed shut and locked. Now the car held more than 70 men stacked like cigarettes in a pack.

The train started with a jerk, sending us sprawling, and our nightmare began. We were a leaderless mob without discipline or direction. Tempers flared when men jostled or trampled on one another. Harsh words were exchanged and punches were even thrown. We were cold from the wind leaking through the wide cracks between the siding, sick and despondent. The swaying, the rapid stopping or accelerations as we ran over uneven rails tended to make matters worse. Long hours were spent at sidings. Daylight came as a blessing. Elbowing a spot on the floor, my partner and I sampled some of our parcel. Although some of the food should have been heated, we wolfed it down cold.

The train made erratic progress through pine forests and hills covered with snow. It would have been a typical winter pastoral scene off a Christmas card under any other circumstance. While passing through towns, we could frequently hear air raid sirens wailing. The train was like a gopher trying to evade a predator with guards posted on top of the cars as lookouts. The swaying had spilled refuse from the latrine cans and it was soon spreading throughout the car. Some men worked on a loose floorboard, finally raising it enough to pour the waste on the tracks. Late in the afternoon the train stopped in a siding, the door was slid open and the guards allowed several men out to empty the cans. When this was done a bucket of water with some small pieces of salty fish was put into the car. That was the day's rations.

Another night fell with most of us totally exhausted. Because we were such a diversified group of men representing so many different units with all the rivalry that goes with it, it seemed that we no longer shared a common bond. We were degenerating into a mob, which I think the Germans wanted. Finally, after another shouting match that almost got out of control, cooler heads prevailed and it was agreed that half the men would stand for two hours while the other half sat. No one could lie down, there wasn't room. Even so we were so mashed against one another that a stranger's arms or legs might be draped over you as tired bodies fell into exhausted sleep.

Morning finally came with the same erratic progress as before. We searched through the parcels for the last scraps of food. At one of the siding stops the guards put in a bucket of water with some horsemeat scraps. Those near the meat gobbled the pieces as if they were hamburgers. Later the train stopped in a small town to take on coal and water and villagers came to the station when word spread that American prisoners were aboard the train. They stared at us as if we were beasts in a cage. However, when they were offered cigarettes they brought buckets of water. The guards, either too young or too old for combat duty, looked on in amusement. I hated them for their behavior, knowing from accounts in hometown newspapers how well we were treating German POWs in America.

Night brought with it chaos but to a lesser degree. Man can adapt to most anything to a point if he has the proper foundation through training. It was that way in the boxcar. An older man in his mid-30s had been having a more difficult time than the rest, however, cursing and babbling incoherently and lashing out with his fists at those near him. Finally, he became so abusive that he had to be forcibly restrained. His shouting and screaming continued and cut right to one's soul.

When daylight finally came and it was my turn to stand I could hardly rise because of a severe pain in my right leg. I thought at first it was because the man on one side of me had slept across me for the last two hours. It wasn't, but fortunately the man on the other side of me was a medic from the 35th Infantry Division and he and I had been having friendly chats about home, the army and our campaigns in Europe. He was especially interested in airborne operations. He had recently been captured and still wore a fairly clean uniform. More importantly, he still had his aid pack with him. When he saw my discomfort he had me pull down my pants and long johns. My leg was terribly swollen below the knee. He gave me one of his few remaining sulfa tablets and said I had an infection of some kind. He had no idea of the cause, but my body was covered with sores from the lice bites and my wrist still hadn't properly healed.

The train still kept heading north, but no one knew our destination. It was getting colder and the snow on the fields looked deeper. But the sky was clear and the guards more alert with eyes glued to the skies. We stopped at a small town and the latrines were emptied and we were given some water. There would be no food that day. I had developed a fever and couldn't eat the few scraps of cookie which were my share of the remaining parcel contents which we had hoarded as if it were gold. I gave them to my partner. Each time it was my turn to stand I could barely get up. I knew something was radically wrong with my leg and it was getting worse.

That day was a blurry nightmare, the laborious pace, frequent stops and no food or water. Those who spoke German screamed abusively at the guards, making all sort of threats for the inhumane treatment. However, the guards claimed that they, too, were short of food and that the trip was taking longer than planned because of air raids which were not their fault. None of the men believed their excuses.

The older man was becoming hysterical at times and it was more difficult to keep him in place. That evening just after dark he went berserk, pulling a sliver of butcher's knife from the cuff of his combat boot and flailing away at those around him. He was finally subdued and tied up with a belt and a woolen scarf. He lay sobbing and begging for water. Even though it was as precious as blood, one of the men with a canteen moistened his lips and gave him a few swallows. During the night he had a last bout of hysteria and slowly succumbed. He was dead by daybreak.

At one of the stops the next day, the guards were asked to remove the dead man's body. They refused. We learned from the other cars that others had died or gone over the edge. I could no longer stand. The swelling had taken over my entire leg and a hard red streak ran along the inner side of it from calf to groin. The medic said it was a cellulite infection. He convinced the others to let me sit for the rest of the trip, but when others lay across me, the pain nearly drove me wild. We were not given any food or water that day, but at one of the stops beside a station, rail workers looked in the cars and saw our condition. Some went to a nearby field of sugar beets and brought some back, tossing them through the tiny ventilator openings in the upper side of the cars. I was too ill to eat any when they were cut and passed around. Our guards didn't object, feeling, I believe, that what they were involved in would have repercussions later.

Another night passed like a bad dream. More men were sick and unable to get up. The cans still overflowed and the stench was worse even though every effort was made to dump the feces through the floor. There were just too many men with dysentery. Most of them wore wet pants stained with the stuff, unable any longer to get to the cans. Some were hysterical, begging for food and water, which hadn't been given out despite the fact that several times the train stopped to take on water. Most of the chaos in the car had subsided. Men were just too hungry and exhausted to be belligerent. But the nightmare was about to end. The following morning the train pulled into the station on the outskirts of Bremervörde, a small town between Hamburg and Bremen.

CHAPTER 18

Bremervörde: Stalag 10B

The car doors were noisily slid open and the guards began their usual haranguing, *"Raus! Kommen sie hinaus! Mach schnell! Mach schnell!"* This time, however, some of their usual hostility seemed to be lacking. The filthy, sick prisoners poured from the cars, blinking against the sunlight. With great difficulty the guards formed the 400 or so POWs into ranks, only to have some pass out as soon as they were lined up. I, along with other sick or dead, had to be carried. The sick were placed on the station platform, our backs against the building.

Just then a limousine drove up. Out stepped two German officers and an American master sergeant, a big, rough-looking Ranger. When they saw the condition of the prisoners the officers' faces blanched. The Ranger's got so red it threatened to explode. He began berating the officers in such an abusive way that I thought one of them was going to pull a pistol from his holster and shoot. But the Germans said little, walking along the ragged ranks with grim faces.

The Ranger told us that we were going to Stalag 10B and that there would be a short walk to camp, a kilometer or so. He went on to say that anyone who thought he couldn't make it was to fall out; he would be transported. A few men did drop out, but I think pride drove most to finish the trip. They marched off leaving the dead on the platform. I had seen Joe Damato, Chester Sakwinski, Cecil Honea, Carl Robare and Lewandowski pass. The look on their faces told me that they thought I was finished. Nevertheless, they waved encouragingly.

As the column straggled up the road, I felt a sense of pride in being an American soldier. Despite what we had undergone, the privation, starvation, and brutal treatment, we had adjusted to it, helping those less fortunate. One comrade had saved my life, though I didn't know it at that moment, and others had done what they could for the unfortunate soldier who had gone insane. I'm certain it was the same in other cars.

Eventually a large flat-bed truck loaded with white firebricks came along. The German NCO in charge of us waved it down and commandeered it. The dead as well as the sick were loaded aboard and we took off down the dirt road. We had left Limburg about March 6th for a rail trip of about 250 miles, passing through Marburg on the west, Paderborn, Herford, Hannover, Nienburg, Rotenburg and Bremen. Bremervörde lies about 30 miles west of Hamburg, which is on the Elbe River. It was about March 13th when we finally reached the Stalag.

On the way to the camp our truck passed the dirty ragged marching column from the train. Some had dropped out beside the road and they were loaded aboard our big truck. A short while later we passed through the main gate of 10B and stopped before the administrative building, being helped off the truck by waiting GIs who brought us water and said we would be fed shortly. Prisoners from within the compound came to the wire fence to get a glimpse of us, shouting encouraging words and tossing us some treasured cigarettes.

The big Ranger brought the German camp commandant, a thin wiry colonel with a chest full of campaign ribbons, to get a look at the results of the manner in which his Army treated its POWs. The colonel walked along our rank of sitting or lying men, grim lipped and asking questions in English. When the men told him their ages—most were in their early 20s—his mouth curled in disbelief. All looked much older because of their sallow thin faces and long dirty beards and hair. I'm sure most of us looked nearly as bad as the Jews in concentration camps.

After being registered, it was close to dark by that time, we saw the main body of our convoy coming through the main gate. We waved but had no chance to talk to them, being taken right to the clinic where we were told to strip. A couple of Russians with scissors and razors shaved all the hair off our bodies and helped us to a steaming hot shower. It was only the second proper wash I'd had in nearly three months. We scrubbed with brushes until our bodies turned red, trying to rid ourselves of the hordes of lice. Under the light I could clearly see the red streak running nearly the length of my leg. It felt as hard as concrete and I thought it was blood poisoning. After the bath we were taken back to the dispensary to wait for our clothing, which had been taken away to be washed.

The dispensary consisted of a series of small rooms in a big wooden hut. There were straw pallets on the floor, little other furniture aside from an egg stove, and American and British orderlies to care for the sick. Most of the sick were Americans from the train but there was a sprinkling of British who had just completed a grueling 450-mile hike from Poland in the worst kind of freezing snowy weather. Most had frozen toes or fingers. The British were generally much older than us. Many had been captured in the debacle at Dunkirk in 1940 and for almost the past five years had been working on Polish farms. The Russian advance had caused them to be moved west. These men said many of their number had died during the march, being buried in places where their bodies would probably never be recovered.

Just before we turned in for the night an orderly brought us tea, black bread and a square of corned beef. The British had some cocoa, mixing it with water and heating it on the stove. The meat was fabulous, like a Thanksgiving feast.

The medical officer, an Australian captain, made the rounds the next morning, gingerly examining my leg and leaving instructions with one of the orderlies. The orderly later rubbed black salve on it and bandaged it with a paper dressing. At noon a large bowl of turnip soup was served. With some of the beef we had kept from the night before, we had a good filling meal, so much so that our stomachs ached.

I never learned or have since forgotten the full names of the men with me at this time or through my final weeks in captivity, but I remember many of them well. An Englishman had the pallet on my left, I only knew him as Charley, a tall, well-built fellow with skin like a baby, and a Scot we called Jock the one on my right. He was from Aberdeen, about 35, not very big but strong as a horse. Because of my high fever I couldn't eat much and gave my soup to either Charley or Chester, who had just been brought into the dispensary. Jock always refused, telling me those in worse shape should have it. Extra rations were issued the week I was in the place, food that should've been given to us on the train ride. My dislike for the callous guards on that trip turned to hatred. How could they have done such a thing with men dying. German people aren't any more inhuman than any other nationality. Was it because of what our bombs did to their towns? I think it was.

Men from the train ride died every day. One came to our ward seemingly better off than the rest of us, but the following morning he was cold and stiff. The doctor made the rounds every day, checking on our problems. There wasn't much in the way of medicine but at least we were free of the lice.

The salve treatment didn't do me any good. I was able to get up and go to the latrine but when I did it was like my leg was on fire.

Finally, after the sixth day, the doctor said he was transferring me to a hospital. A German doctor also examined me to make sure the diagnosis was competent. The morning I was moved Red Cross parcels were given to us, two men to a parcel. Rumors had been circulating that the parcels were in the camp, but, like most rumors, we didn't believe them. So I had my portion on my litter as four POWs carried me from the clinic. The distance was close to a half-mile and the litter bearers had to stop twice to rest because of their weakened condition. However, when we got there I offered them the cigarettes I had just gotten and they refused, another example of American generosity.

I was taken right to the hospital and examined by a kindly Serbian doctor, also a POW. Then I was put in the surgical ward. It was a compressed grass one-story hut with too many double deck bunks with the usual straw ticks without any linens. Corporal "Pep" Peploski, a paratrooper from the 82d Airborne who had been captured in Sicily, ran the ward. Bert Hanna, a corporal from the Canadian Army was in charge of the rations. Both men were dedicated to their jobs, doing everything in their power to insure that their charges were well taken care of. Later we learned that Hanna wasn't an NCO at all but had assumed the rank for the privileges it might bring—which really weren't many as the war wound down.

I learned right off that the contents of my parcel weren't mine. The British, who made up the majority of the ward, did what was called "mucking in." It meant that all the canned goods in the parcels were put in a common pool. Each day a large pot of stew was made from the cans, augmented by potatoes and whatever was furnished by the Germans. The British, having been prisoners for so long, knew the ropes about such things and ran the ward with the efficiency of a business. None of the Americans objected after one pot of the stew.

The contents of the Red Cross parcels varied, I was told, according to where they were from, America, Canada, or England. As far as I can recall they contained cans or packets of: raisins or prunes, soluble coffee (Nescafé), powdered milk (called Klim), salmon, liver paté or chicken, cheese, jam, margarine, sugar, corned beef, cookies, chocolate bars, cigarettes and soap. Other parcels substituted certain items with cocoa, sardines, powdered orange juice, dehydrated soup, and smoking tobacco. In the British parcels would be condensed milk, meat roll, herring, pudding, oatmeal and Spam. Prisoners rarely got an entire parcel of their own. As long as I was in the surgical ward we mucked in with the British and I never had a complaint.

The ward had a regular hospital routine with a German sergeant, whom we called "Blue Eyes," in charge. He was a handsome, easygoing medic who had been a POW himself, captured in North Africa and repatriated. Probably because he had been treated so well as a POW, he did his best to look out for us. He could barely speak a word of English, however, and everything had to be said in German. For his kindness and thoughtfulness we POWs contributed coffee, chocolate and cigarettes, which he used for his own welfare. The British used to kid him unmercifully about being a ladies man who drove the local girls mad. He took it in good grace, though a little leery because he had a wife nearby who was seemingly insanely jealous.

Karl, a German Army *Oberschütze*, was a frequent visitor to our ward. The only English he could speak were vulgarities the British had taught him. Once encouraged to speak English, he would rattle the words off in almost endless dialog, never having the slightest notion of what they meant.

Jack "Jock" Robertson, did a lot of work around the ward in the absence of any German help, this despite having lost four fingers on his right hand due to frostbite. His wounds were only partially healed but he still helped bath the bedridden, empty urinals, and swept the place. He used to regale me with tales about his once having been a poacher, how he would relieve trout, pheasant and deer from the estates of wealthy landowners around Aberdeen.

Percy was about 25, big and husky, a farmer from the English Midlands. Although his feet had been badly frostbitten, amputation had been unnecessary. He also helped around the ward. An excellent checker player, he also played the harmonica like a professional. In the evenings he would play tunes popular in England before the war with most of us chiming in on choruses.

Ralph Meyers was an 82d Airborne trooper captured in Holland less than a half hour after hitting the ground. A German had shot him through the knee while he was getting out of his 'chute. The knee had healed but still leaked pus. He was an articulate talker with strong opinions, having friendly arguments with the British, which never got nasty.

I remember a couple other Englishmen very well, like Toddy who was almost like a mother to the sick and disabled. Despite having had three fingers amputated from one hand and two from the other, he was a workhorse in the ward. He was assisted in his efforts by his good pal, Tabby, who had lost four toes on one foot. These two men would help with bathing, shaving, changing bandages and any other light duty, refusing remuneration in the form of cigarettes or candy.

Pop Jones was the oldest POW, close to 50. He had been captured at Dunkirk in 1940. He seemed completely out of place in uniform, more like an English shopkeeper on a holiday. He made coffee and tea, toasted bread and helped cooking. A very nervous sort, he became more so as the fighting got closer. He could neither eat nor sleep for days on end.

Stapleton was probably the best educated among the British, a patrician sort of person one might associate with the arts. Young and handsome, he lay on a bunk with both feet amputated at the ankles, trying mightily to stifle his moans at night but failing. No one minded, knowing his condition.

There were a number of Americans in the ward beside Ches Sakwinski and I. He had been brought in a week after me with a bad ankle infection and put in the bunk over mine. Frank Perenski had been captured in the Bulge and was probably the healthiest person in the ward with an abscess on either side of his neck. A deadly serious person with little sense of humor, he was the butt of much kidding. He took it to heart, not accepting it for what it was, and even called in the priest for last rites on several occasions when he was sure he was dying. Tony, big, dark and pugilistic, had stepped on a landmine and lost a leg. The Germans had treated him pretty badly when he was captured for which he never forgave them. He and Barroni would argue and talk in Italian much to our consternation as most of us wanted to be part of most everything that went on.

There were even a couple of airmen in the ward, not normal because they usually went right to a Stalag run by the *Luftwaffe*. Lieutenant Nash was a B-17 pilot who had been shot down over Hamburg and brought to the ward with a broken spine. He had little control over his bowels or bladder. Lieutenant Hilderbrand was another B-17 crewman, a navigator, I believe, who had broken his leg on the jump from his flaming plane. He was in a cast up to his waist. Flight Lieutenant Wilson was from the RAF, also shot down over Hamburg, but at night. He had both legs in a waist-high cast. Mike was in the RAF too, shot down on the last mission he was to fly before being assigned to a ground job. All the airmen were good sports and went along with our kidding about their having nine to five jobs with evenings free to chase British girls around pubs.

There were two other fliers in the ward; both had been shot down over Bremen. One had a broken jaw and his mouth was wired shut, the other a broken leg. And we had a professional musician, a violinist from London who had lost three fingers from one hand and two from the other. What sort of future was in store for him?

Each morning the Serbian doctor made the rounds with Corporal Peploski. After he examined the patients and gave instructions, wounds were dressed and bandages changed. The odor coming from the wounds permeated the room, making one sick to the stomach. The doctor spoke few English words, things like, "How are you feeling, Mister Bowen?" or, "It looks very good Mister Bowen." Every day he wrote our progress on our individual chart. He was a gentleman whom all of us adored.

My leg was getting no better, in fact, it was worse. I knew it would have to be operated on. On Good Friday, 1945, I was placed on a litter and carried to the operating room. It was almost completely bare of anything that would identify it as an operating room. All it was equipped with was a small steel table, a sterilizer and a cabinet. A couple of windows were missing and there was no heat in the place. I nearly froze by the time the doctor got there.

Pep and Bert Hanna were standing at the head of the table, the two litter bearers at the foot, as the doctor came in and donned rubber gloves. He picked up a shiny scalpel leaned over me and said, "A little pain, Sergeant Bowen." Pep sprayed a liquid, a local anesthetic, I assume, on the groin area. The scalpel cut into the outer skin and I didn't feel a thing, not until it went deeper. I wanted to jump off the table but didn't, and couldn't even if I tried to, because the four who brought me had a firm grip on my body. The knife went deep and a surge of stinking pus gushed out. Bert's face turned white. I thought he was going to faint. The doctor told him to go to the window and get a breath of fresh air, finished the five-inch incision, then pressed all the corruption out of the wound. He worked fast but the pain was nearly unbearable. He put in a short rubber drain, packed the wound with gauze and wrapped it with a paper bandage.

I thought the ordeal was over as I lay in a pool of my own sweat despite the freezing room. But it wasn't. Pep sprayed the calf area and the doctor cut once more, this time more painful than the first. I fought to lay still and cursed like a stevedore on a bad day. Once more he cleaned the wound, put in a drain and wrapped the leg. Then it was immobilized in an open metal leg cast. I was hustled off the table and taken back to the ward on the verge of blacking out.

Holy Saturday and Easter Sunday were nothing but a hazy memory as I lay there wracked with a fever and my leg a throbbing mass of pain. There were no sedatives, sulfas, penicillin, or pain relievers. After surgery you simply sweated until the healing process ended.

The following week was nearly as bad. If I hadn't been so rundown and under-weight with my stomach in such an upheaval, I could've handled it better, but I wasn't alone. All the other surgery cases went through the same thing, some much worse.

Every day Peploski would irrigate the two five-inch incisions, flush out the pus, replace the drains and wrap the leg again. When I tried to crush the wooden supports of the bunk with my grip, he would try to make it easier by talking like a mother to a child. Al Pinski, in a bunk nearby, would actually cry when the rubber tubes in his forearm were cleaned with pus running out like water. The smell gagged those around us.

The Polish nurses would visit the barracks every day, helping Pep if they could. In fact, Pep became very friendly with one, a beautiful brunette in her early 20s. The friendship eventually turned into love.

Red Cross parcels now began arriving on a regular basis. If it hadn't been for them, I as well as others wouldn't have survived. My stomach was in such bad shape that I could no longer eat the black bread and coarse vegetables furnished by the Germans. The oatmeal in the morning and the stew later brought me through those rough days after the operation. And the cigarettes, chocolate and coffee in the parcels began bringing what we though of as luxuries into the ward, traded to the German guards for eggs, vegetables and other staples. They also paid for a Russian POW to clean the ward, empty the urinals and bed pans, and do other odd jobs. One Russian was no more than 20, a handsome kid who had a gaping open wound in his chest. When he breathed you could hear the air whistling through it. I think our cigarettes saved him from starving, as so many of his comrades had. Another was an artist and would do charcoal portraits for a couple of cigarettes. God only knows where he got the art materials. Others would make cigarette cases and other trinkets out of aluminum mess gear, another slippers or clothing from uniforms. A Frenchman gave haircuts and shaves for cigarettes and even a victrola was purchased with German and Italian records.

The parcels alone provided all this and more, all because of the donations made at home by righteous people and the work of many volunteers who packed and delivered the parcels to the national organization. Detractors be damned, the Red Cross did a fine job during the war.

I don't mean to intimate that we lived like kings, we didn't. There was still little in the way of medication; there was only two bed pans for the whole ward and the urinals were Klim cans; amputations were still done under local anesthetics; we still depended on ambulatory patients for our daily needs; and, as the weeks dragged by, a new problem was added. Bremen and Hamburg, the large cities nearby, were under increasingly heavy bombardment. When the raids occurred during the day, water and electricity were turned off, so no coffee or tea could be made. Later a few pots were obtained and water collected so that at least we could drink. Coal was strictly rationed, meaning many extremely cold nights in the ward until the guards were bribed with cigarettes and chocolate to furnish more. A newly arrived airman still wore his electrically heated flying suit and he somehow used the wiring in it to make a small heater, which was used to boil water when the coal was scarce.

More prisoners came into the ward, most badly injured fliers. One was an Aussie who had escaped three times only to be recaptured. He told a chilling tale of these escapes. When his crew bailed out of a Wellington bomber and got rounded up by some SS men, they were placed up against a barn and machine-gunned. The Aussie made a break for it in the dark even though wounded in the hip. Recaptured he was put in a cold cellar with 15 other POWs, and transferred to a barge some days later. As the barge was being towed across a river, it began filling with water and sank. The prisoners clambered onto the deck only to be fired on by the guards in a nearby boat. The Aussie was the only one to escape alive. He swam away in the darkness, wounded again. Recaptured the next morning, he was locked in a barn for several days, escaping a third time. Again he was wounded after being fired on by guards. Finally, he was brought to our ward, bandaged from head to foot.

Living under such primitive medical conditions meant that wounds did not heal naturally and, when they did, often left one with after affects. With me it was to be phlebitis. I was bedridden for over a month, and when I did get up my leg would swell as if the outer skin was going to pop open. But I spent a lot of time sitting by a window watching the snow gradually leave the hills and woods around the camp and the inmates of the main compound wandering listlessly around the yard. The Germans relaxed restrictions and visitors from other compounds passed freely in and out of ours. Russians came in like carpet-baggers, trying to peddle all sorts of black market wares, their lives depending on the sales because the Germans gave them next to nothing in the form of rations.

The Germans released a news bulletin saying President Roosevelt had died. None of us believed it because most of their news was propaganda. However, when Red Cross representatives from Switzerland inspected our ward, one whispered to me that it was true. Most of us were deeply shocked because we had liked the president, though, perhaps surprisingly, the British were more concerned than the Americans. Roosevelt was their savior, sending Lend-Lease material and eventually bringing America into the war on their side.

New prisoners were brought in, this time from the British Army instead of the RAF or USAAF. We knew the Allies had crossed the Rhine and that the British had broken out of their bridgehead and were advancing toward Bremen with the Canadians. Two young Canadian men from a reconnaissance unit of the Guards Division, the same outfit we had fought with in Holland, were brought slightly wounded to the ward. They confirmed the news of the Allied advances.

Rumors flew that the Germans were going to evacuate the Stalag. Each camp had a "man of confidence" on the Allied side, one who looked after the affairs of POWs, and ours was an excellent one. I don't remember his name but will never forget his face. He stood firmly for the POWs, doing everything in his power for us. When the rumors of evacuation began to circulate, he protested strongly that none of the sick and wounded even be considered. Several thousand men from the main compound were sent away, but none of us.

News from the radio in the commandant's office told of fighting south of Bremen and we began to feel for the first time that it would soon be over. The British, naturally, were exultant; after nearly five long years as POWs the end was near. To be truthful, the first four years or so were less harrowing than the last six months had been. When the war had been going well for the Germans they had worked on farms and gotten decent food. However, when their death march began in late fall 1944, so did their troubles. Many died on the march and many of those who survived came out of it with frozen or frost-bitten limbs. At least they had been able to send cards and letters home while in Poland, letting families know that they were prisoners of war. We Americans were simply listed on Army records as missing in action. Our families never knew whether we were dead or alive.

However, we weren't liberated yet. The Germans rushed some of their best remaining troops to hold the line south of Bremen. Panzergrenadiers and Waffen SS troops moved up as reinforcements and the British Second and Canadian First Armies ran headlong into them south of the Weser River. For more than a week the battle lines were static and rumors that the Germans were using some sort of secret weapon were rampant. We feared the Germans would fight to the death because of the unconditional surrender ultimatum Roosevelt had given them. We could see the fanaticism around us. A Panzer battalion moved into our area, digging defensive positions just outside the wire fences of the stockade and in a copse nearby. We could see them working feverishly. Most of their unit moved into Bremervörde, only a few miles away.

Days passed and our hopes of liberation seemed to hang by a thread. All sorts of rumors now circulated through the wards: the Germans were going to execute all POWs; the entire camp would be evacuated; the POWs would be held as bargaining chips. Then we heard the British were bypassing Bremen, had crossed the Weser on either side and were going to isolate it.

Finally we knew something big had happened when the troops guarding the Stalag pulled out, leaving only a contingent of medics behind. The higher-ranking Allied officers in the camp now took over, appointing committees and units to run the place. Our man of confidence left with several other emissaries to contact the British.

Days went by with everyone's nerves on edge. We could hear the roar of artillery and mortars in the distance, the sharp crack of tank guns and the rattle of small arms. That evening some wounded British soldiers were brought in to the camp, their tank having been knocked out by the Germans. They said their outfit wasn't too far away and they were part of a reconnaissance force.

At last the British advanced to Bremervörde. We went outside and saw the brown-clad figures of British soldiers and their vehicles moving into the town. German artillery located somewhere behind our camp responded, sending shells whistling right over our hut. Once again I heard the German six-barreled mortars, the screaming meanies, as they howled through the air. The battle raged all day. Time seemed to stand still. Why were the Germans fighting so stubbornly? For God's sake, the Russians were in the suburbs of Berlin, the Americans at the Elbe. No one in the camp could understand it.

We slept little that night and were awakened near dawn by the rattle of small arms fire. Several shells had dropped into our compound during the night and most POWs went into slit trenches, which had been dug as air raid shelters. However, we in the surgical ward who were ambulatory went outside to see what was happening.

It was like viewing a movie. Artillery and mortars boomed and the British moved out of woods and started to cross a rolling stretch of ground behind supporting fire. The Germans fired back. Shells dropped in and around our compound and, as the British got closer, small arms and mortar fire aimed at the Germans outside the wire began dropping around our hut, some of the bullets going through it. Most of the British POWs dove in the shelter pits, but foolishly most of the Americans just stood and watched from outside the building or inside from windows. We had canned goods on shelves, which were pierced by bullets passing through the walls of the clinic. That sent most of us to the floor but we were soon up again and watching. It was all too good to be true.

Finally we saw the Germans beginning to pull out, leaving dead and wounded behind. Their tanks backed away to somewhere in the east, the infantry following. Then we saw the Tommies streaming over the hill and into the camp. Everyone was rejoicing. Wild jubilation reigned throughout the camp and lazarette. British soldiers were being borne about on the shoulders of half-starved POWs. The British POWs were especially happy, not only because of their liberation but because it had been done by their own countrymen. We were free at last, at 15.30, Friday April 29th, 1945. I had been a POW less than six months but it seemed like six years. Now weighing just over 100 pounds, I had lost about 50, with my right leg looking like it belonged to a 300-pound man, a right wrist which wouldn't bend, constant pains which shot up through my left lung, and skin which was covered by scabs from lice bites. I was nothing like the person who went up to Bastogne to stop the Germans, but I was as happy as anyone else and eagerly awaited evacuation.

The POWs made hot coffee and pots of stew from the Red Cross rations, which they handed out to the Tommies. Their tanks surrounded the stockade and infantrymen dug defensive positions for the night just outside the wire. They also cleaned up after the Germans, bringing in wounded and seeing that German prisoners were put to work. There weren't that many, but they removed the German dead and brought in the wounded. British casualties were surprisingly light, one officer killed and four enlisted men wounded. It seemed like a miracle to us, but that's how the British operated, infantry and tank attacks behind massive heavy weapons support. The Tommies brought us some white bread, the first I had seen since being captured. We covered it with margarine and Spam and made sandwiches.

Being liberated and out of harm's way were two different things. In the distance to the east we could hear German guns booming, then the shells screaming toward us. They broke around the compound in thunderous blasts. Huts were hit and men killed and wounded. The shelling kept up all night at intervals. No one slept much, especially the British POWs who had been away from home for so long. They huddled around the egg stove flinching every time a batch of shells came screaming at us. Nerves were at a breaking point. More prayers were said in those couple of days than at any time in captivity.

The following morning British medical teams invaded the camp, registering the POWs and taking medical histories. We were given brown postcards saying we had been liberated. We signed them with the date and the British sent them along. The entire day was spent in registration, with the Germans still continuing the sporadic shelling.

One of the British prisoners died, an RAF officer who had suffered for a long time. The men in the ward were as depressed by his death as if he'd been a relative, almost as sad as when Stapleton died a week earlier. He had a hard death, moaning and groaning for days followed by delirium and then his last choking gasp. It was heart-breaking.

The following morning accompanied by German shellfire, the ward was evacuated. The patients had been classified as either being litter cases or ambulatory. I was in the latter category. Collecting our few belongings, we were loaded aboard big canvas-topped trucks and slipped out of the camp, past huts where political prisoners had been kept. We had heard the sound of machine guns firing for several nights before the British arrived. Now we saw why. Naked bodies were stacked around the huts like piles of wood. Senseless, barbaric, illogical! What sort of animal would give an order like that? What kind of halfwit would obey such an order? Were the Germans so indoctrinated by hate that religion, upbringing, and morals meant nothing any more? Or was it just a by-product of the past five years?

With this gut-wrenching scene in our minds we left 10B, happy to have survived but saddened by the brutality of it all. For me it further numbed my senses. I had seen men die in every conceivable way, shot, blown apart, drowned, dying slowly from wounds, starved and from infection. As I looked at those piles of white bodies a pain shot through my stomach, a pain which bothered me for many years whenever I thought about or saw something which reminded me of 10B.

Staff Sergeant Ken Ripple was on the truck also, having been a patient in the medical ward, which was the hut next to ours. He was from Baltimore, the intrepid bugler of our casual company at Fort

Bragg. He had made life a living hell for our martinet of a company commander, a captain who thought glidermen were the scum of the earth, much to the delight of the rest of us. Rip had gone to the 327th, served in Normandy, Holland and Belgium, where he was wounded and captured. His battalion held the southern sector of the defensive perimeter and had been badly mauled near Marve. Now Rip was thin and drawn, his face as yellow as a Chinaman's from jaundice. However, still a raconteur, he visited me most every day in the surgical ward, regaling all of us with his stories. Often he brought the "Chief", a South Dakota Indian who was manic-depressive, another victim of the train ride from Limburg. Mostly calm and agreeable when he came to see us, at night the Chief became a roaring tiger, having to be tied to his bunk. However, on the ride to freedom he was happy.

The trucks took a roundabout route to avoid the German artillery, which fired at anything moving. The convoy followed the winding hilly road southward through villages and towns, eventually reaching, I believe, Verden where an RAF field was located. We were loaded aboard C-47s with British insignia painted on them, crowded on the metal bucket seats. Most in my plane were British who had been captured at Dunkirk, men who were older and had never been in a plane before. They were as nervous as young gazelle in a field of lions. The plane took off, heading right into a distant thunderhead. The sky got blacker, the plane began to tremble because of the wind shear and the lightning came out of the heavens as if God was angry with us. The British were terrified, and naturally those of us who had had many flights under our belts not that far behind. But the storm was short-lived even though the rain and wind nearly tore the plane out of the sky. We flew out of it and into a beautiful, sunny spring day.

In a following plane were Corporal Peploski and his Polish nurse, she disguised as a G.I., completely dressed from head to toe in an American uniform. He hoped to smuggle her to American control and marry her. I heard later that they were married by a British chaplain, but I can't say for sure if this is true.

I was reminded, as I looked into the beautiful sky, of a documentary of World War I, which ran in Baltimore movie houses in the early 30s. The movie was full of hundreds of feet of film illustrating the terrible nature of trench warfare. Music accompanied the narration. It was a piece, I believe, called, *The World Is Waiting for the Sunrise.* For us the sunrise represented our deliverance to freedom. For Pep it was even more, if his plan worked, it meant the beginning of a new life in more ways than just liberation.

AFTERWORD:

And Yet So Far

Our plane landed on an airfield near Liège, Belgium, where ambulances were waiting to take us to a British military hospital. We swooned at the luxury of cleanliness, beds with linen, wholesome food, a dedicated staff of physicians and aids, female nurses, called sisters, who treated us royally. We bathed in wonderfully warm water, changed into hospital gowns while our clothing was being fumigated and washed, English battle dress was given out to all those whose uniforms were worn out and finally we were classified after being examined. I was made a litter patient because of the phlebitis in my right leg and put into bed.

We were asked to fill out another postcard which was sent home. In my case, and I'm sure in many others, all my wife and family knew of my disappearance was that I was "missing." Unfortunately my cousin, who was in the 463d PFA and had been assigned to my company as a forward artillery observer the day after my capture, had written home to my wife and mother telling them that my company commander believed I had been killed in action on December 23d. Because of the confused nature of the withdrawal of that night and conflicting eyewitness reports, it was a natural mistake to make. However, as long as I was with the company, a man wasn't listed as dead until his body was recovered.

The British and American POWs were separated, each going their own way. We said our goodbyes and were put on a train for Brussels to another British hospital. Ches Sakwinski and I were still in the same group and in fact remained so until we hit New York. After another week in Brussels we were fattened up and went through more examinations before being sent by train to the first Air Evacuation Hospital in Paris. I was put in the orthopedic ward with mostly amputees. The young man in the bed next to mine, no more than 18, had lost both legs and part of one arm when a bazooka exploded in his hands. He was still somewhat shocked, naturally, and I spent long hours talking consolingly to him. I don't know if he believed me but at least he seemed happy to have someone to talk to.

I was bedridden for the week I was in the hospital, seeing nothing of Paris except from a window. I did meet an old acquaintance from my hometown—we played on rival football teams and had never got along too well—and, foolishly, I gave him eight cartons of cigarettes the Red Cross had given me during my travels. I never saw him again but heard he had taken the cigarettes to town and sold them for $35 a carton, then went out and got roaring drunk.

We left Paris in ambulances, to be taken to an airfield where we were loaded onto a C-54 transport plane with beautiful nurses attending us. The first stop was the Azores for refueling. Shortly after takeoff, one of the engines began throwing oil and the plane turned back. We sat on the ground for hours while a new engine was installed, then flew to Newfoundland. After a short lay over, we flew on to Mitchell Field in New York, where ambulances took us to Walter Reed Medical Center in Silver Spring. After a month of travel by truck, ambulance, train and plane, I was finally near home, just 35 miles east, eagerly awaiting the chance to see my wife and family and not worried about the rest of the war still raging in the Pacific.

Walter Reed Medical Center seemed like a dream hospital, at first a fantasy, and then becoming a nightmare. Put in a ward with mostly orthopedic cases, I went through all sorts of exams and tests. And while I was running this gamut I called my wife and her visits began. Toward the end, they were wearing her down. She was the secretary to the head of the claims division of the Legal Department of the City of Baltimore, and, after working all day, she would get a train into the city, ride to Washington, then get a bus to Silver Spring. She always stayed until visiting hours had ended, going back to Arbutus where we lived and getting home at one or two in the morning. Despite my objections, she did this every day of my confinement: nine long months, aside from a convalescent furlough.

The nightmare began a month after reaching the hospital. The ward physician truthfully seemed more interested in when he would be discharged and back in practice than in caring for some of the patients. Despite my leg, which had swollen like a balloon, he sent me out to Forest Glen to be discharged. I had complained the night before about severe pain in my lung, and, without even checking it out, he gave me a couple of pills and left me to my fate. When I got to Forest Glen, I went right to the head physician. He immediately put me on a litter, called an ambulance, and within half an hour I was back in bed at the hospital. The following day I was practically paralyzed; the clots in my leg had broken loose and gone to my left lung. I had a massive pulmonary embolism.

Most of June, July and August I was bedridden in a private room, being given huge doses of cummadin to thin my blood. Major Stanley, the pulmonary specialist, told me later it was the largest embolism he had ever seen. On VJ-Day the hospital went wild. I remember that night, lying in bed with the only visitor allowed being my wife, listening to the mêlée in the lab across from my room. Glass beakers breaking, wild jubilation, more like a fun house at a circus than a hospital. After my wife left I wondered if I would be like the RAF officer who had died at 10B after our liberation.

My recovery was slow but sure. Six months after the initial attack, I was sent to Forest Glen again, this time to be discharged as 100 percent disabled. I returned to civilian life in mid-February 1946, going back to my former company, Progressive Brass Die Company Inc., as an embossing die engraver. Because my work was mostly sedentary I was able to function. During the course of my 58 years of service to the company I became a shop superintendent and, eventually, Vice President. While working I began night school, taking the fourth year of high school again and graduating from Baltimore Polytechnic, attending the Maryland Institute of Fine Arts for several years as well as McCoy College. I was encouraged in all of my educational pursuits by my wife.

My wife became ill with dementia in January 1993. Within six months she could not walk, talk, recognize anyone or care for herself. Unable to care for her at home, I had her placed in a nearby nursing facility. Aside from two days per week, I spent nine hours a day by her side for the remaining four and a half years of her life. This was the worst time of my life, much more difficult than anything I had endured during the war.

Now, aside from taking care of our home, I spend my time reading, painting, playing golf and writing fiction. I have also helped numerous students and scholars who are researching the wartime accomplishments of the 101st Airborne Division.

I was once asked if it was all worth it. In addition to my other medical difficulties I also suffered from Post Traumatic Stress Disorder (PSTD) for many years after the war. I was troubled by nightmares, feelings of guilt and sleeplessness that turned me into almost a recluse. My wounds also continued to bother me. The wrist that had been wounded at Bastogne refused to return to a normal range of motion, the ankle injured in Normandy was so weak that I had to wear a steel brace, and the right leg, where the Serbian doctor operated on my groin and calf, developed phlebitis which meant it became very swollen if I spent time on my feet. In addition, my rapid weight loss while in the camps seemed to have messed up my immune system because I was in the hospital numerous times afterward. I had to have a Venus ligation, tying off veins in my legs because of pain after my feet were frosted in Belgium, six sinus operations, and an appendicectomy, all in civilian hospitals because the Veterans Administration hospitals didn't want to link any of these physical problems to my wartime experiences. In addition, my pension was cut to 60 percent because I was able to work.

Throughout their campaign in Europe, Hitler's minions had killed over thirteen million people. In the Pacific, the Japanese killed over twenty million, mostly innocent civilians. As badly as the Germans treated POWs toward the end of the war, the Japanese were much worse. They had no regard for human rights, the Geneva Convention regarding POWs or the fact that they would later be brought to account for all they had done. And, had not the atom bomb been used against them, no one knows what the toll in American lives might have been.

War did leave me with a bitter taste in my mouth, and the conviction that it should only happen as a last resort. When everything else fails.

Bibliography

COMPILED BY CHRISTOPHER J. ANDERSON

Although there have been literally thousands of pages written on the exploits of the 101st Airborne Division during World War II, relatively few of them have been devoted to the contributions of the 1st Battalion, 401st Glider Infantry Regiment and their fellow glidermen in the 327th Glider Infantry Regiment. There have, however, been several books that, at least in part, consider this overlooked part of the Screaming Eagles' story. This brief bibliography provides an overview of those books that can provide additional information on Sergeant Robert Bowen's unit.

The *Epic of the 101st Airborne*. The "Epic," as it is commonly known among students of the 101st, is the first history of the division. Published in 1945 by the 101st's Public Relations Office in Auxerre, France, while the division was waiting to be returned home, the *Epic* is primarily a photographic history of the division but it does provide additional information about the campaigns of the 101st. Long out of print, copies of the *Epic* are becoming increasingly scarce and valuable.

Rendezvous With Destiny: A History of the 101st Airborne Division, by Leonard Rappoport and Arthur Northwood, Jr. (101st Airborne Division Association, 1948). The granddaddy of all 101st histories, *Rendezvous With Destiny* provides the most comprehensive study of the division's service during World War II. Although much of the discussion is about the three paratrooper regiments, there is still a thorough discussion of the 401st's activities during some of the war's bloodiest encounters. The book has been updated and reprinted several times and is essential for any student of the 101st Airborne Division.

Sky Riders: History of the 327/401 Glider Infantry (Battery Press, 1980). *Sky Riders* is the only complete history of Bowen's unit ever written. Authors James Lee McDonough and Richard Gardner filled a void in the historiography of the 101st with this volume. The book itself provides a thorough overview of the regiment's operations interspersed with accounts of the men. *Sky Riders* also includes a great many interesting illustrations of the unit.

D-Day With the Screaming Eagles (101st Airborne Association, 1970). George Koskimaki, General Maxwell Taylor's radio operator for much of the war, has compiled a history of the division's activities during the Normandy Campaign from hundreds of interviews and surveys conducted by division members. While much of this volume, understandably, concerns itself with the division's paratrooper regiments, there are still some accounts of glider activities.

Hells Highway (101st Airborne Association, 1989). Written in the same format as his D-Day book, Koskimaki's *Hell's Highway* provides a detailed look at the division's service during the operations in Holland. Much more information is provided in this book on the activities of the glidermen than in the D-Day volume. Particularly valuable are the accounts of the fighting around Opheusden where Bowen's platoon suffered so terribly.

The Battered Bastards of Bastogne (101st Airborne Division Association, 1994). The final volume in Koskimaki's trilogy of the 101st's activities, *Battered Bastards* provides a wealth of personal stories of the men of the 101st during, perhaps, their greatest battle. There are numerous accounts of the fighting provided by the men of the 401st; including an account of the fighting on December 23d when Bowen was captured.

Bastogne the First Eight Days (Infantry Journal Press, 1946). Written primarily using interviews collected immediately after the battle, S.L.A. Marshall's account of the 101st's defense of Bastogne is a classic. Particularly interesting is Marshall's description of how General Anthony McAuliffe's refusal of the German surrender ultimatum was delivered by the colonel of the 327th/401st.

The Men of Bastogne (David McKay Company, Inc., 1968). Like Koskimaki's works, Fred McKenzie's story of the fighting around Bastogne relies heavily on first person accounts of the battle. The author provides a good description of the 401st's defense of the western part of the Bastogne perimeter.

The editor is working on a new history of the 327th/401st and is anxious to hear from veterans, families or students with any information, photographs, artefacts or other material on the regiment that they would be willing to share. He can be reached at: Chris Anderson, Editor, World War II Magazine, 741 Miller Drive, SE, Suite D-2, Leesburg, VA 20175; or via email at chrisa@cowles.com.

Roll of Honor

Company C, 401st Glider Infantry Regiment

This list was compiled with reference to an official Army roster dated 1945, an unofficial roster compiled by the veterans of Company C after the war, and the recollections of Sergeant Robert Bowen. While every effort has been made to compile a complete and accurate listing of the members of Company C, the very nature of such an undertaking lends itself to error. Any mistakes in the finished product are entirely unintentional. Asterisks * indicate those men who gave their lives in action.

Pvt Earl Adams
Sgt Willis E. Adams*
Pfc Floyd "Red" Adkins
Pvt James R. Albert
Pfc Lester Allred
Pvt William L. Andrews
Pfc Ebon Angel
Pvt Lyle L. Appel
Pvt Conrado
  Armendarez
1 Lt Quentin Armstrong
Pvt Allen E. Arnold
2 Lt John E. Aspinwall*
Pfc Earl Bacus*
Pvt Peter Bachna
Pfc Bernard B. Baker
1 Lt S.S. Baker
Pfc Forrest H. Bates*
Sgt Allen B. Barlow
Pfc Arnold Barnett
Pvt Henry S. Baum
Pfc Kenneth W. Baum
Pfc Leroy Beezley
Sgt Ramon Bomgardner
Pfc Frank S. Bobko
Pfc Robert C. Booth

Pfc Herman Boswell
TSgt Robert M. Bowen
SSgt Loman Bowers
Capt Howard G. Bowles
Sgt Ray Braunschiedel
Cpl. Charles Bray
2 Lt Claude Breeding
SSgt Louis A. Butts
Pfc William C. Budds
Pfc Willard D.
  Burgmeier
Pvt Charles R. Buhl
Cpl Joseph J. Caban, Jr.
Pfc Joseph Cammarata*
TSgt Cecil C. Caraker
Pvt John O. Cartwright*
Sgt Glen Cassidy
Pfc Millard H. Castle
Pvt Harold L. Chalfin
Pvt Lloyd Cheney
Pvt John A Christnagel
T/5 Floyd C. Chrysler
Pvt Amelito Ciucci
Pvt James A. Clark
Sgt Stanley V. Clark*
Pvt John E. Clayton

Pfc Walter Click
Pfc Armand R. Cloutier
Pfc Jesse L. Collier
Pfc Henry Condor
Pvt Albert S. Coughlin
Pvt Elton Crump
Pvt Stanley W. Curr
Pvt Raymond J. Daigle
Sgt Joseph D. Damato
Pfc George Damato*
Pvt Amos Damron*
SSgt Amos Datwyler*
SSgt Grayson A. Davis
Pvt James C. Davis
Pfc Paul Deliberto
Pvt Sylvester Delorenso
SSgt Frank DeMarco*
Pvt Charles J. Denney
Pvt Harry D. Dickoff
Pvt Johnnie Diggs
Pvt Herbert G. Dingler
Pfc Louis Dokupil
TSgt Larry M. Donoho*
Pfc Virgil L. Dousette
Pvt Charles F. Dorton
Pvt Joe A. Doychak

Sgt Jack Q. Emler*
Pfc Pat Enright
Pfc William J. Epson*
Pfc Antonio Esparza*
Pfc Felipe Esquivel*
Pfc William S. Farrell
Pfc Thomas W. Feeney
SSgt Ted Feldman
SSgt Elmer Felker
SSgt John S. Ferko
Sgt Robert M. Fleming
Pfc August L. Fortuna
Sgt Walter W.
 Fragnoski
Pfc Carlton W. Frost
SSgt Charles F. Fulton
Pfc John B. Gardner
SSgt John M. Garrett
Pfc John Gaydas
Pfc Earl J. Gerard
Pfc James O. Gilstrap
Med. Edward
 Grapentine*
Pvt Jack Greon
Pvt John H. Gresh, Jr.*
Sgt Fred W. Grethel*
Sgt Tony Guiterriz
Pfc Byron L. Gunderson
Pfc Harry A. Haas, Jr.
Pfc Edward L. Halstead
SSgt Verland Harrell
Sgt Jerry Hanss
Pfc Sion G. Harrington
Pfc Ray E. Harris
T/5 Burt R. Hart
Pfc Leonard W. Hart
Pfc Donald Harwig
Pvt Gerald Helton
Pvt William A. Higgins
Pfc Glenn Hodge
Sgt James J. Hodge
Cpl Milton B. Honaker

Pfc Demetri M.
 Honcharik
Pvt Ray A. Honeycutt*
Pfc Stephen Horkey
Pfc Ernest P. Howard*
Pvt Claude R.
 Humphreys
TSgt Richard E. Irvin
Pfc Donald J. Jenkins
T/4 Howard W. Johns
Pfc Homer R. Johnson*
SSgt John H. Johnson
Pvt Lamon O. Johnson
Pvt Edward K. Jones
Pfc George B. Kalb
Pvt David Kalbert
2 Lt Ray A. Karcy*
T/4 Charles S. Katkie
Capt. John A. Kindig
Pfc Terry G. Kirby
Sgt Joseph A.
 Kloczkowski
TSgt Oakley G. Knapp
Pfc Howard Koester
1 Lt Howard F. Kohl*
Pvt Wilbur A.
 Koklaoner
Pvt Norman Labbe
Pfc Arthur W. Lamb
T/5 Lawrence LaMire
Sgt James M. Lavelette*
Tomas F. Lavin
Pfc Herbert Lawhorn
SSgt Thomas Leamon
Pvt Clarence C.
 Leverich
Paul J. Liliberto
Pfc James F. Liming
Sgt Roy Liston
Pfc George Lolley
Pfc Frank V.
 Lombardino*
1 Sgt James V. Long

Pfc Robert D. Lott
Pvt Charles E. Lowe
Pfc William R. Lyons
Pvt Forrest Manning
1 Lt Richard P. Marcy*
Pfc Frank A. Marine*
Pfc Chester N. Mazur*
1 Lt Martinson
Sgt Leo McBride
Pfc Thomas A. McDyer
Pfc Frank McFadden
Pvt James E. McGill
Pfc Clayton McGinnis
Pvt Marvin N. McGraw
Pfc Argyle B. McKeown
1 Lt William A.
 McLelland, Jr.
Pfc Harold M. McNeil*
Pfc John Meadows*
Pfc James Meade
Pfc Fred L. Meinhardt*
Pfc Stanley Mihaelick
T/4 Frank Miller
Pfc George A Miller
SSgt Andrew E.
 Mitchell
Pfc James C. Mitchell
Sgt Frank Mocik
Pfc Ben Molinaro
Pfc Daniel W. Morgan
Pfc Darsel M. Morgan
Pfc Thomas L. Morrow
Sgt Robert A. Mullins
Sgt George Naegle
Sgt John T. Neisch
Pvt John J. Neiser
2 Lt Amos Norman
TSgt Yeiser O'Guin
Pvt Robert O. Olsen*
Pfc Robert O'Mara
Pfc James L. O'Melia*
Pfc John J. Orf
Cpl Douglas F. Osborne

Cpl Cleon Overbay
Pfc Ray L. Pacheco
Pvt Everett G. Padgett*
Pfc Ordway H. Padgett*
Pvt Edwin F. Paradise
1 Sgt Matt Pas
Pfc Eli Pauley
Pvt Paul E. Percival
Pvt Mario Perfetto
2 Lt R.T. Peterson
Pfc Tony P. Petracarro
Pfc William W. Phillips
Pvt John E. Pirie
Pfc Ignacious Plantago
Pfc Frank Plesec
Cpl Lloyd B. Platt
1 Lt Harold Plyler
Pfc Frank S. Pokigo
Sgt Fred D. Poling*
T/5 John D. Porter
Sgt Ralph A. Porter
Pfc William Preslar
Pvt Bruno Primas
SSgt Gerald Rafferty
1 Sgt Joseph Ratynski
Pfc Louis Rausch
Pfc Donald J. Reed
Pfc Harold Reeser
Sgt Robert W. Rehler*
Pfc Lawrence A. Reid
Pvt J. Robertaccio
SSgt Bruce S. Roberts*
Pfc Joseph B. Roberts*
Sgt Edward A. Ruder
Pvt Stephen J. Santola
Pfc Cletus L. Schaffer
Pfc Theodore Schlitz
Pvt Sidney
  Schneiderman
Pfc Kenneth Schnese
Sgt Robert Schrandt
Pfc William Schremp
Pvt James H. Sealy

Pvt Cecil S. Seibert
1 Lt Michael A. Settani
Pfc Ressie P. Shannon
Pfc Harold H. Shaver
Pvt Michael J. Shea, Jr.
Pvt Francis J. Sheehan
Pvt Charles R.
  Shepperd
Pvt James E. Shoemaker
Pvt Robert R. Shreve
Pvt Richard J. Sigler
Pvt Harold Silverman*
Pfc Rankin Simpson
Pvt Russell W. Skell
Pfc Joseph Slachta
Pfc Jack Sloan
Pfc Theodore Sliz
Pvt Albert V. Slonaker
Pfc Albert Smith
Pfc William W. Smith
Pfc Abe Spector
Pfc Howard Spivey
SSgt Billy Standley*
Pfc Chester
  Stempkowski
Pfc Willard J. Sturm
SSgt Clience Sutherland
Pvt Robert O. Tabor
Pfc Cecil Taylor
Pfc Edward J. Taylor
Pvt Harry N. Teachout
Pfc William L. Temples
Pfc Harry R. Thompson
Pfc Howard Thornton
Pvt Floyd J. Tishaw*
Pvt Lorne J. Torrence*
Pfc Ernest Toth
Capt Preston E. Towns*
Cpl Cecil P. Trent
SSgt Frank V. Trudeau*
Pfc George D. Tunder
Pfc James R. Turner
Pvt Irvin Turvey, Jr.

Pvt Edward S. Urbaniak
Pfc Thomas C.
  Vanderberg
Pfc Roy F. Vance
Pvt Clarence Vander
  Sander
Pfc Francis Van
  Drunen, Jr.
Pfc Ray Vigus
Pvt Edgar W.
  Vollbrecht
Pfc Leonard
  Waddlington
1 Lt Robert A. Wagner
Pvt Joy Waldrop
SSgt Wayne Walker
Pvt Eugene L. Wall
Pfc Orr H. Wallace
Pvt John E. Walshe
T/4 Carl W. Warner
Pvt Frey E. Westover
Pfc Arvin White
Pfc Walter Wicks
Pvt John A. Widner
Pvt Harmon C. Wilson*
Pfc Verland E. Wilson
Pfc Harold W. Winchell
Pfc George F. Wolffer
Pvt Louis O. Wollford*
Pfc Gustaf T. Wolski
Pvt George F. Worman
Sgt Wayne W. Woody
Pfc William C. Wright
Pfc Harold Zimburg
Pfc Morris Zion*
Pfc John C. Zukosky*